AF566832

GTO

A SOURCE BOOK

EDITED AND ANNOTATED BY

Thomas E. Bonsall

Bookman Dan!

Printed in the U.S.A.
Copyright 1980 in U.S.A. By Bookman Dan!

ISBN 0-934780-03-X

First Edition
First Printing

All rights reserved. No part of this publication may be reproduced or transmitted in any form or by any means, electronic or mechanical, including photography, recording, or any information storage or retrieval system, without permission in writing from the publisher.

Inquiries may be directed to: Bookman Dan!
P.O. Box 13492, Baltimore, Maryland 21203

Printed in Chester, Virginia, by
First Impressions

Preface

When Semon Knudsen assumed his post as general manager of Pontiac Motor Division in the summer of 1956, he inherited a car that was clearly not living up to its potential. Pontiacs in that era had a reputation for being solid but deadly, deadly dull. They were the sort of cars that elderly school teachers bought. Knudsen had different ideas. "You can sell a young man's car to old people," he observed, "but you can't sell an old car to young people." He understood that if Pontiac's sales were to grow, its appeal would have to be widened to include the enthusiasts as well as the older people interested in transportation only. He therefore set about making Pontiac the youngest car in the industry.

With the help of a dynamic engineering team headed by Elliott M. Estes as chief engineer and John Z. DeLorean as director of advanced engineering, Knudsen launched Pontiac on the road that was to lead it to undisputed supremacy in the medium price field by the mid-Sixties. One of Knudsen's first acts was mostly symbolic: he ordered the twin hood stripes removed from the near-production 1957 models. His own father, the legendary William S. "Big Bill" Knudsen, had seen the Silver Streak styling theme started in the mid-Thirties, but twenty years later they were no longer fresh. Knudsen thought they looked like suspenders. He was right about a couple of things: removing them made the Pontiac look much younger than before and also sent a signal to people inside and outside the division that Pontiac was finally on the move. By the middle of 1957, the fuel injected Bonneville series was launched and Pontiac was hip deep into stock car racing. By 1959, and for four breathtaking years thereafter, Pontiacs were next to unbeatable on the stock car circuit. It took an order from the highest levels in General Motors Corporation to put an end to the Pontiac racing program, but by then the division had reaped fabulous amounts of free publicity and established a solid position at the top of its field in both excitement and sales.

Pontiac seemed to know no way but up during most of the 1960s. The revolutionary Tempest was produced in 1961, and this same year saw the division capture the coveted third position in national sales, a position it was to maintain for the rest of the decade. The ongoing Pontiac engineering revolution was followed by the Pontiac styling revolution in 1963 with the stunningly beautiful Grand Prix. This car was so beautiful that some people still think it was the first Grand Prix. Pretty soon, the entire industry seemed to be diligently cranking out ersatz Pontiacs complete with wider treads, split grilles, stacked headlights, hidden tail lights, concave rear windows, unadorned sides with the Coke bottle effect, etc., etc. Pontiac hadn't actually invented all of these styling themes, but Pontiacs displayed them with such flair that most people thought they had.

Knudsen left Pontiac in 1961 to assume similar duties at Chevrolet. His position at Pontiac was filled by Estes, and when Estes went to Chevy, DeLorean took over. In the early months of 1963, the Pontiac team was wondering what to do next. What worlds were left to conquer? They were already kings of all they surveyed. The GM racing ban had been a disappointment, but like the weather, there wasn't much to be done about it. Or was there? One of the provisions of the corporate high peformance ban had been that no intermediate sized car could come standard with an engine of more than 350 cubic inches displacement. At some point, someone noticed the loophole. The ban did not appear to apply to options. Why not try to get a big engine OPTION through? Thus the GTO was born.

It is hard to remember how dramatic the GTO was when it was introduced. This was the first time anyone had taken a huge American V-8 and stuffed it into a (relatively) small car. The resulting performance was little short of fantastic. Here was a rather inexpensive car that could challenge the fabled Chevrolet Corvette in straight line acceleration! It wasn't a sports car, to be sure, but it was clearly something very special and almost single-handedly launched the great American high performance car boom of the 1960s.

More than 32,000 "Goats" were built that first model year. By 1966, the car had become a series in its own right—not just a performance option on the LeMans—and reached to within an eyelash of the century mark in production. By this time, of course, nearly every make in the industry had a high performance contender. GTO sales would no doubt have suffered a bit even without skyrocketing insurance rates, a result of the insurance people's observation that these new performance machines seemed to be involved in a disproportionate number of serious accidents. What the competition and the insurance companies didn't do to the GTO the 1970 recession did. By 1971, the GTO was dead in the water. It continued on until 1973 and then returned in 1974 in an ill-starred compact version before succumbing to the inevitable. It was, as they say, fun while it lasted.

Interest in the GTO has remained high despite the cessation of production at the end of the 1974 model run. A lot of this interest is no doubt due to the nature of the industry today. Times have changed, to say the least. The sanitized, safety-ized, economized cars of our own era form a rather stark contrast to the early GTOs, and it is highly unlikely that they will be equalled anytime soon for sheer, brute excitement. Even the earliest GTOs are still modern cars in most respects. They are also dependable, tremendous fun, and except for the gasoline it takes to feed them, relatively affordable. It is a potent combination.

Preface

While interest in the GTO remains at high levels and even increases as the years go by, the supply of original manufacturer's literature is actually decreasing. It is getting harder and harder to find GTO related catalogues and brochures and, indeed, some important GTO items were almost impossible to locate even when the cars were new. Assuming it can be found, the original literature is becoming more and more expensive to the point that many enthusiasts already feel priced out of the market. The obvious solution is for someone to gather together all of the important GTO and GTO related items, especially including the rare and expensive ones, and reprint them in an organized, inexpensive format. That is, in fact, precisely what this book seeks to do.

This book reproduces all of the essential GTO customer sales literature from 1964 through 1974. Included are all major items exclusively pertaining to the GTO as well as the GTO sections from other important full-line Pontiac brochures. The wealth of information available here is enormous. All models are covered as well as options, accessories, colors and trims. The short preface at the beginning of each yearly section also lists price and production figures as well as important historical information about that particular model run. This is truly a source book of essential GTO information. It does not seek to be a repair manual or a parts guide—those are readily available from other sources, anyway—but everything else the GTO enthusiast is likely to want to know is here. Incidentally, for those seeking the original catalogues, the front covers of the items used in each section are reproduced in a montage on the first page of each section. The items are not reproduced in this book at the actual, original size (necessarily) but have been reduced, or, in a few cases, expanded to fit the available space. Readibility has been the utmost concern. The information is carefully and consistently organized with the basic models information presented first and then the accessories presented in the back of the book in a special accessories section.

The major GTO related literature for each model year generally consisted of a spread in the main, full-line Pontiac catalogue, a spread in the special Pontiac high performance cars catalogue, plus scattered coverage in the color and trim and accessories literature. From time to time there was also special GTO literature, and most of this has been included here as well. A couple of these exclusive GTO pieces are exceptionally scarce and even the high performance catalogues are becoming harder and harder to find and more and more expensive when they are found.

It would probably cost several hundred dollars to purchase all of the literature contained in this book if the items were purchased individually. This, of course, assumes that the items could be found. My experience has demonstrated that this is neither easily accomplished nor financially feasible for most enthusiasts. This book, then, should fill a definite need.

Every attempt has been made to insure the absolute accuracy of the information contained here. I will be anxious to hear of any discrepancies so that future editions may be corrected. For those wishing more historical information about the GTO or the Pontiac in general, I would modestly suggest my book, "PONTIAC, The Complete History 1926-1979", which has also been published by *Bookman Dan!* and is, as the saying goes, available through better booksellers everywhere, and especially through *Bookman Dan!* at the address listed elsewhere in the front of this book.

Washington, D.C.
August, 1980

Contents

1964

1964

The 1964 model year was the most successful in Pontiac history up to that time. Production rose 20% above the 1963 level, and the all-new intermediate size Tempests were up an astonishing 80%. The new Tempests were so well received by the public that it was easy to overlook that fact that virtually all of the remarkable engineering features that had made the 1961-1963 models so special were dropped. The 1964 Tempests were, in fact, entirely conventional except for one accessory group added at the last minute to the LeMans series—the GTO option.

The GTO option was available on any LeMans and consisted of a fire-breathing Pontiac 389 V-8 rated at 325 horsepower and mated to a floor mounted, heavy duty 3-speed manual transmission, plus non-functional hood scoops and a few identification plates denoting the car as a GTO. The heart of the package was, of course, the 389 V-8 engine and the effect was fantastic, especially by 1964 standards. No car at the price (a mere $3,400 or so, fully equipped) had ever delivered this sort of performance. Indeed, the GTO threatened the fabled Corvette for sheer acceleration and speed and cost a lot less.

The GTO option, code #382, was listed at $295.90. It was available on the LeMans Sports Coupe ($2,491), Hardtop Coupe ($2,556) and Convertible ($2,796). A full range of options and accessories was available including a 348 horsepower version of the 389 V-8 engine.

A grand total of 32,450 GTOs were built during the 1964 model run. This included 7,384 Sports Coupes, 18,422 Hardtop Coupes and 6,644 Convertibles.

GTO literature is pretty slim for this first model. The GTO option was not developed in time to make the regular 1964 Pontiac and Tempest literature, so an attractive GTO color catalogue was issue instead. this is the catalogue that is reproduced in this chapter, along with relevant sections of the 1964 Pontiac color and trim brochure.

To be perfectly honest, the GTO is not everyone's cup of tea. Designed as a piece of performance machinery, its purpose in life is to permit you to make the most of your driving skill. Its suspension is firm, tuned more to the open road than to wafting gently over bumpy city streets. Its dual

exhausts won't win any prizes for whispering. And, unless you order it with our lazy 3.08 low-ratio rear axle, its gas economy won't be anything to write home about. If all this dismays you, then you're almost certainly a candidate for one of our 27 other Pontiac Pontiacs and Pontiac

Tempests. (Most people are.) But if you're tuned in to our particular wave length, if you start vibrating when you're at the controls of a sudden automobile, if you've driven enough different kinds of performance to know what it's all about, then you've got GTO written right across your forehead.

OPTIONS & ACCESSORIES

Comfort & Convenience: Power steering, power brakes, power tilt driver's seat, power windows. Custom air conditioner, tinted glass all around or just in the windshield, rear-window defogger (except Convert.). Washers, two-speed wipers. Seven-position tilting steering wheel, padded dash, console. Radios, electric antenna, regular or reverberating rear seat speakers (except Convert.). Luggage compartment light, ski racks, removable luggage carrier. Deluxe wheel discs, wire wheel discs, custom wheel discs. Black or white fabric top. Rayon cord whitewalls optional at no extra cost.

Performance: 4-speed all-synchro transmission with Hurst shifter, 2-speed automatic. Metallic brake linings, heavy-duty radiator, Safe-T-Track limited-slip differential. Custom sports steering wheel, handling kit (extra-stiff shocks and 20:1 quick steering) or extra-stiff shocks alone. Tachometer or rally clock, vacuum gauge. Exhaust splitters, mechanical 3-2BBL carburetor linkage (dealer installed). High-performance full transistor (breakerless) ignition.

ENGINES	Standard	Optional
Type	ohv V-8	ohv V-8
Bore and Stroke	4.06 x 3.75	4.06 x 3.75
Displacement, cu. in.	389	389
Compression ratio	10.75:1	10.75:1
Minimum allowable combustion chamber volume, cc	66.0	66.0
Carburetion	1-4BBL	3-2BBL
Total throttle bore area, sq. in.	7.62	12.19
Bhp @ rpm	325 @ 4800	348 @ 4900
Torque, lb-ft	428 @ 3200	428 @ 3600

Alloy cast iron block, five main bearings. High-compression flat-top pistons with valve indents. High-lift camshaft, high-performance hydraulic valve lifters. Large-diameter valves—1.92" intake, 1.66" exhaust. Dual exhausts. Clutch is 10.4" bent-finger Belleville with 2300-lb. minimum load. Seven-blade, 18" fan, with declutching unit. Low-restriction air cleaners on 3-2BBL engine.

Dimensions & Capacities: Wheelbase is 115 inches. Overall length is 203 inches. Tread is 58 inches, front and rear. Overall width is 73.3 inches. Height is 53.5 inches for the Sports Coupe and Hardtop, 53.6 inches for the Convertible. Total trunk capacity is 32.1 cubic feet. The gas tank holds 21.5 gallons. Shipping weights: Coupe—3272; Hardtop—3292; Convertible—3422.

Transmissions: A 3-speed manual transmission is standard, with Hurst shifter curving up into your hand from between the seats. Ratios are 2.58:1, 1.48:1, 1.00:1, and 2.58:1 reverse.

Then there are two versions of the optional floor-mounted, aluminum case, fully synchronized 4-speed: Wide-ratio—2.56:1, 1.91:1, 1.48:1, and 1.00:1; Close-ratio (available only with 3-2BBL carburetor engine and axle ratio of 3.90:1)—2.20:1, 1.64:1, 1.31:1, and 1.00:1.

And, of course, there's a 2-speed torque converter automatic, its lever mounted on the steering column. Ratios are 1.76:1, 1.00:1, and 1.76:1 reverse, with a total torque multiplication off the line of 3.87:1. The governor is set for a maximum automatic upshift at 5200 rpm. The optional console accommodates the shift lever for all three transmissions.

AXLE RATIOS

Engine	Transmission	Standard axle		Special Order axle ratios		
325 bhp	3- or 4-speed	3.23#	3.08	3.36* **	3.55* **	3.90*‡§**
	automatic	3.23	3.08#	3.36*†**	3.55*†**	3.90*†‡§**
348 bhp	3- or 4-speed	3.23#	3.08	3.36**	3.55*†**	3.90‡§**
	automatic	3.23	3.08#	3.36	3.55*†**	3.90†‡§**

Axle ratio	Mph per 1000 rpm in high gear
3.08	25.2
3.23	24.0
3.36	23.1
3.55	21.9
3.90	19.9

*Special radiator required at extra cost.
†Speedo adapter required at extra cost.
‡Heavy duty fan required at extra cost.
§Metallic brake linings and Safe-T-Track required at extra cost.
#Standard axle with air conditioning.
**Air conditioning not available.

Special-purpose axle ratios of 4.11:1 and 4.33:1 are also available, dealer installed—only with close-ratio 4-speed.

Steering: Recirculating ball bearing steering gear. Standard ratio is 24:1. Optional quick steering is 20:1. Power steering is 17.5:1.

Suspension: Ball joint independent front, four-link rear. Shocks are valved specifically for firm ride and control. Heavy-duty coil springs have wheel rates of 90 and 110 pounds per inch, front and rear. Diameter of stabilizer bar is 0.938".

We'd suggest you try this already heavy-duty standard suspension before you make up your mind about the stiffer suspension components we have available.

Brakes: Hydraulic, duo-servo, self-adjusting. Diameter of finned drums is 9.5", with a swept area of 269.8 sq. in. Metallic brake linings are available as a separate option with all axle ratios except 3.08:1, but are recommended only for extreme duty service since they have the usual metallic brake ailments of squeaks, grunts, and high pedal pressure when cold.

NOTICE: All the options noted herein, including vinyl top, radio, wheel discs, custom sports steering wheel, and backup lights illustrated on some models, are extra-cost equipment unless otherwise specified. Ask your dealer for all price information on any model or special equipment you desire. Pontiac Motor Division of General Motors Corporation reserves the right to make changes at any time. Pontiac Motor Division, General Motors Corporation, 196 Oakland Avenue, Pontiac, Michigan.

You'll find one of these on each side. If you don't think this is enough warning, you could always fly the skull and crossbones.

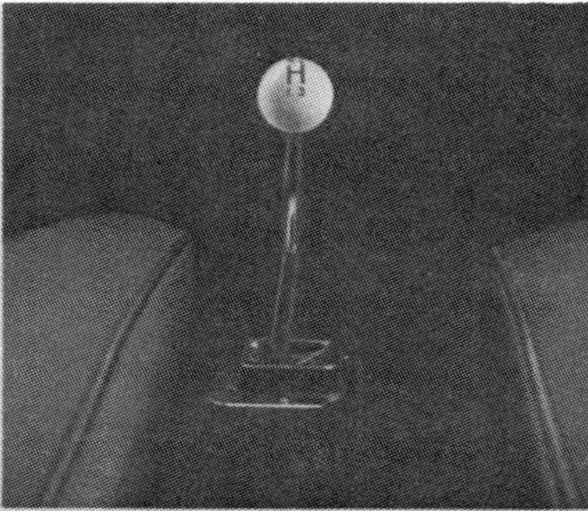
A 3-speed manual transmission with Hurst shifter is standard, located between the seats. Ratios are 2.58:1 first, 1.48:1 second, and 1.00:1 third.

With 325-plus horsepower on tap, traction can be a sometime thing. We strongly recommend Safe-T-Track, our optional limited-slip differential. See?

High speed 7.50 x 14 nylon tires were designed specially for the GTO, mounted on 14 x 6JK wide rims. This is the optional deluxe wheel cover.

The standard suspension is made up of heavy-duty springs, shocks, and stabilizer bar. If a GTO clung to the road any closer, it'd be a white line.

And, to contain your change of gear—3-speed, 4-speed, or automatic transmission—the optional console with lockable glove box.

This is the standard engine. Horsepower—325. Carburetion—1-4BBL. Fan—declutching. Air cleaner, rocker covers, oil filler cap—chrome. Very strong.

This is the standard interior. Black, red, saddle, aqua, dark blue, or parchment. Morrokide with nylon blend carpeting. Everything's color-coordinated.

That high speed red-line tire again, this time with our optional custom wheel disc, complete with spinner and brake cooling slots.

This is the optional engine. Horsepower—348. Carburetion—3-2BBL. Fan—declutching. Chrome. Very, very strong.

The custom sports wheel. Looks like wood but isn't. Stainless steel spokes. Optional. Four round, easy-to-read dials, optional tachometer on right.

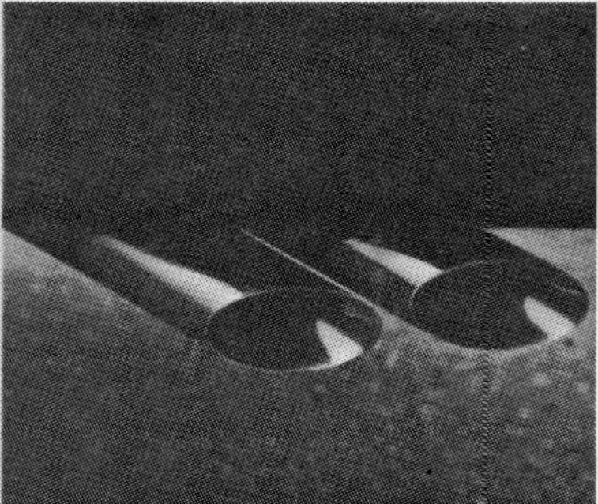
We call these exhaust splitters. A pair apiece for the dual exhausts, lurking just behind the rear wheels on each side of the car. A factory- or dealer-installed option.

PONTIAC EXTERIOR TWO-TONE COMBINATIONS *(ALL MODELS)*

LOWER AREA		UPPER AREA A	C	D	F	H	J	L	N	P	Q	R	S	T	V	W
STARLIGHT BLACK	A		X	X												
CAMEO IVORY	C	X		X	X	X	X	X	X	X	X	X	X	X	X	X
SILVERMIST GRAY (Med.)	D	X	X													X
YORKTOWN BLUE (Med.)	F		X	X		X										X
SKYLINE BLUE (Lt.)	H		X	X	X											X
PINEHURST GREEN (Med.)	J		X													
MARIMBA RED (Med.)	L		X													
SUNFIRE RED (Med.)	N		X													
AQUAMARINE (Med.)	P		X								X					
GULFSTREAM AQUA (Dark)	Q		X							X						
ALAMO BEIGE (Lt.)	R		X										X	X		
SADDLE BRONZE (Med.)	S		X									X				
SINGAPORE GOLD (Med.)	T		X									X				
GRENADIER RED (Lt.)	V		X													
NOCTURNE BLUE (Dark)	W		X	X	X	X										

LITHO IN U.S.A. 8-63 SP 1548

LE MANS *Sports Coupe (2227) Convertible (2267)*

Expanded Morrokide.

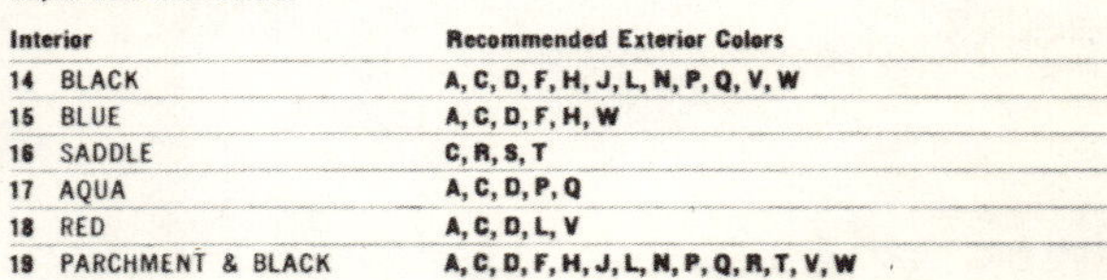

Interior	Recommended Exterior Colors
14 BLACK	A, C, D, F, H, J, L, N, P, Q, V, W
15 BLUE	A, C, D, F, H, W
16 SADDLE	C, R, S, T
17 AQUA	A, C, D, P, Q
18 RED	A, C, D, L, V
19 PARCHMENT & BLACK	A, C, D, F, H, J, L, N, P, Q, R, T, V, W

1964 CONVERTIBLE TOP USAGE CHART

Coded To Exterior Color & Interior Trim

Top Colors:

#1 Ivory	#2 Black
#4 Blue	#5 Aqua
#6 Beige	#7 Saddle

Cordova Top Option—vinyl coated fabric roof covering in Ivory or Black for Sports Coupe body styles (2127, 2227).

LE MANS CONVERTIBLE

INT. 14 BLACK	A-1,2 C-1,2 D-1,2 F-1,2,4 H-1,2,4 J-1,2 L-1,2 N-1,2 P-1,2,5 Q-1,2,5 V-1,2 W-1,2,4
INT. 15 BLUE	A-1,2,4 C-1,2,4 D-1,2,4 F-1,2,4 H-1,2,4 W-1,2,4
INT. 16 SADDLE	C-1,2,6,7 R-1,2,6,7 S-1,2,6,7 T-1,2,6,7
INT. 17 AQUA	A-1,2,5 C-1,2,5 D-1,2,5 P-1,2,5 Q-1,2,5
INT. 18 RED	A-1,2 C-1,2 D-1,2 L-1,2 V-1,2
INT. 19 PARCHMENT	A-1,2 C-1,2 D-1,2 F-1,2,4 H-1,2,4 J-1,2 L-1,2 N-1,2 P-1,2,5 Q-1,2,5 R-1,2,6,7 S-1,2,6,7 T-1,2,6,7 V-1,2 W-1,2,4

GTO
1965

1965

The 1965 GTOs were not greatly altered from the highly successful 1964 models. The front and rear styling was revised and horsepower was slightly increased, but that was about the extent of it.

The headlights on the 1965 GTO were set vertically, one on top of the other, in the new Pontiac fashion. The grille was also recessed, but otherwise similar to the 1964 example. Around back, the tail lights were also similar, but wrapped around the sides of the rear fenders.

The 389 V-8 was continued over from the previous season. It was, however, upped in power. The standard engine was now rated at 335 horsepower and the optional version was rated at 360 horsepower.

Prices actually declined slightly in 1965. The LeMans Sports Coupe listed at $2,727, the Hardtop Coupe at $2,791 and the Convertible at $3,026.

Production on all Pontiac lines was up substantially in 1965, and the GTO led the way. A total of 75,352 GTOs were built—a 132% increase over 1964! Of this number, 8,319 were Sports Coupes, 55,722 were Hardtop Coupes and 11,311 were Convertibles.

Three major pieces of literature were issued covering the 1965 GTO. These are reproduced on the following pages and include the GTO sections of the full-line Pontiac catalogue (pages 17-18), the Pontiac high performance cars catalogue (pages 14-16) and an odd little GTO folder. This latter item doubled as a 45 rpm record jacket and remains one of the rarest of all GTO items. It is reproduced on pages 12-13. The relevant sections of the 1965 Pontiac color and trim brochure are shown on page 19.

A musical tribute to America's most popular performance car... the GTO!

What does GTO really mean? Briefly, GTO stands for Gran Turismo Omologato—or Homologated Grand Touring. That's a mouthful in any language, but it means that any car bearing this name must have certain combinations of features and be an able performing, high-speed road car. In addition, at least 100 of these cars must be produced. Then—and only then—will the car be recognized as a legal and true GTO by the FIA (Federation Internationale Automobile) a world governing body of motor sports events. To meet the rugged specifications for a GTO, Pontiac mated its torrid 389-cubic inch engine with a Tempest-sized body that features special suspension, braking and drive line. The result? America's most popular performance car . . . the GTO by the Wide-Track Tigermakers (who else?).

"She's got a Hurst floor shifter and the wildest screamin' mill around!"

"Transistorized ignition and a power pack o' three-deuce carbs!"

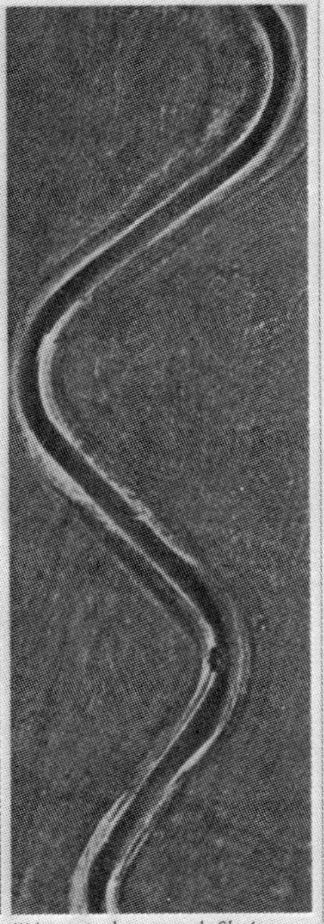

"Listen to her growl. She's always on the prowl! GeeTO Tiger, Go!"

"She's got a Wide-Track action on a groovy set o' red-line tires!"

"I mean a three eighty-nine, all super-tuned to really shut 'em down!"

"You gotta fasten your seat belts and we'll make it to the drags on time!"

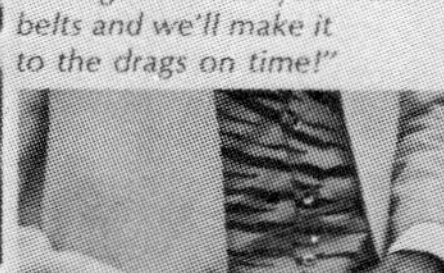

Swing out with the Tigers!

The newest swinging teen sensation.

Barry Hockenberger, *Organ (top)*
Neal Moser, *Lead Guitar*
Jerry Cervenka, *Drums*
Enzo Piazza, *Bass Guitar*
John Anderson, *Rhythm Guitar*

GeeTO Tiger!

There's a Tiger on the market and I got the ve-ry first in town!
She's got a Hurst floor shift-er and the wild-est screamin' mill a-round!
I mean a three eight-y nine, all sup-er tuned to real-ly shut 'em down!

Drag Strip, She don't bluff! On the street, She looks tough!
G - T - O, that's e-nough! List-en to her growl!
She's al-ways on the prowl! Gee-TO Tig-er, Go!

She's got a Wide-Track action on a groovy set o' red-line tires!
Trans-ist-or-ized ig-nit-ion--and a power pack o' three deuce carbs!
And she chews up oth-er cars--yeah! 426 MoPars!

(Chorus)

You gotta fasten your seat belts and we'll make it to the drags on time!
We're go-in' huntin' for a Mustang or a dual quad four-oh-nine!
We're gon-na shoot 'em all down 'fore they ev-en get off the line!

(Chorus)

Listen to her growl! She's always on the prowl! Gee-TO Tiger, Go!

Big sounds of the GeeTO Tiger

At the General Motors Proving Grounds.

You've heard the GeeTO swing. Now listen to it scream--as it runs through the gears--with all three deuces feeding 389 cubes--through the 75 miles of roads at the GM Proving Grounds. Here's your chance to ride shotgun with a top Pontiac test driver as he puts the GTO through its paces. It's a thrill-packed ride through the GM Proving Grounds. So, fasten your seat belt for real true excitement. Man, like listen to this Tiger roar.

Printed in U.S.A. by Tiger lovers

The GTO

If you're looking for a mobile living room in these pages, forget it.

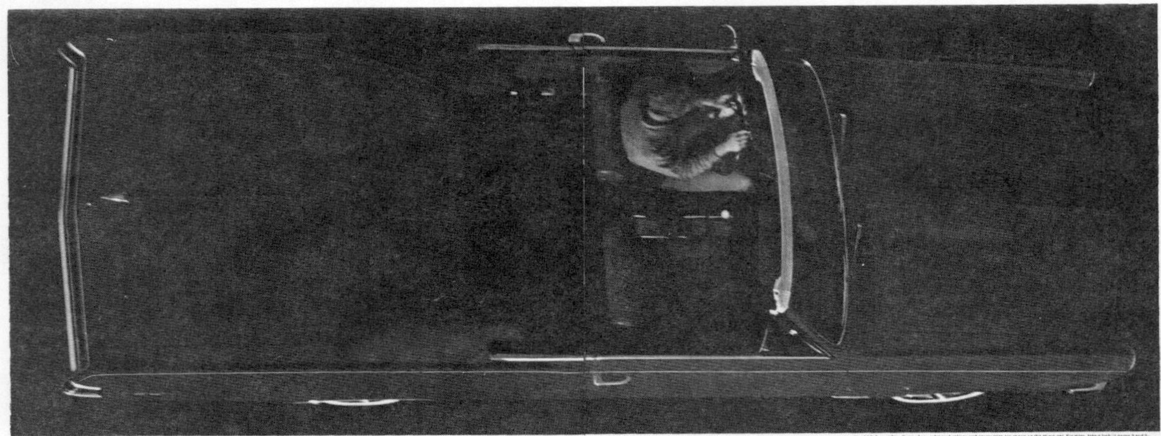

Okay, so the GTO isn't exactly underprivileged in the comfort department, what with its great big bucket seats and floorful of carpeting and soft stuff like that. But that's just a cover for the real operation: Performance.

Think of the GTO as 389 cubic inches of big-voiced engine, surrounded by a pretty good-looking pinstriped body and resting on heavy-duty springs and shocks with you cradled in there aiming it. Yeah!

GTO

Performance Options: 360-bhp, 3-2BBL engine. 3- and 4-speed all-synchro transmissions. 2-speed automatic. Safe-T-Track limited-slip differential. Metallic brake linings. Extra-stiff shocks. 20:1 quick steering, 17.5:1 power steering. Competition-type steel wheels. Tachometer, oil pressure and water temperature gauges. Exhaust splitters. High-performance transistorized ignition. Heavy-duty radiator. Rally clock.

Comfort & Convenience Options: Custom sports steering wheel. Seven-position tilting wheel. Washers, 2-speed wipers. Radios, electric antenna, regular or reverberating rear seat speakers (except Convert.). Console. Padded dash. Power brakes, power windows, power seat (driver only). Air conditioner, tinted glass all around or just windshield. Rear window defogger (except Convert.). Floor mats. Ski racks. Tonneau cover. Wheel discs—deluxe, custom spinner, and wire wheel. Rayon cord whitewalls optional at no extra cost. Black or beige coated fabric top. Trailer hauling equipment (see salesman).

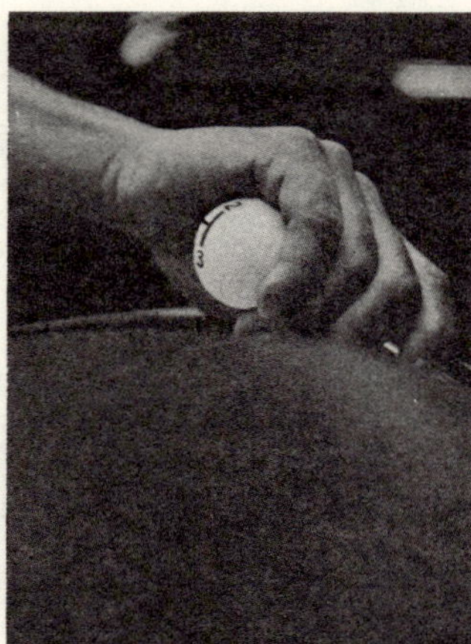

A 3-speed is standard equipment. A fully-synchro 3-speed will be available approximately March 1, 1965, at extra cost. Both rate Hurst shifters.

You want an extra-cost 4-speed for maximum acceleration? With either wide- or close-ratio gear sets? And a Hurst shifter? What a coincidence!

The automatic route, via the GTO's 2-speed torque convertor unit. Extra cost, as is the console.

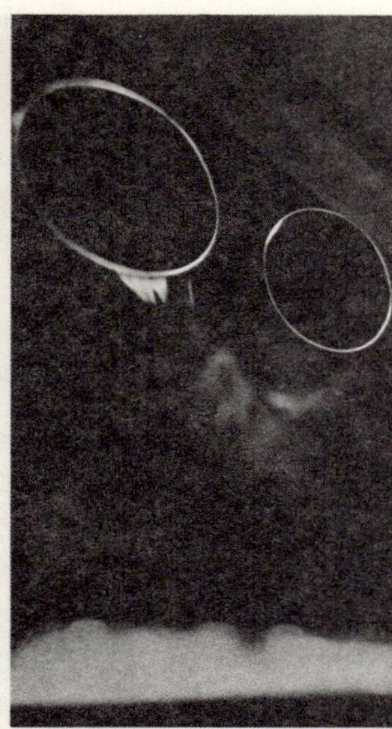

Exhaust splitters. They poke out from each side of the GTO, just behind the rear wheels. Extra cost.

Don't just sit there. With 335-plus horsepower to slap down on the pavement, you'll need a limited-slip differential for maximum traction. Safe-T-Track. Extra cost.

We've got our own competition-type steel wheels, with brake cooling slots. Extra cost.

The deluxe wheel cover. Extra cost. Rayon cord whitewalls are optional at no extra cost.

Red-circle 7.75 x 14 premium-cord tires are standard. Custom spinner cover is extra cost.

Engines:

	Standard	Optional
Bhp @ rpm	335 @ 5000	360 @ 5200
Torque, lb-ft.	431 @ 3200	424 @ 3600
Type	ohv V-8	ohv V-8
Bore and stroke	4.06 x 3.75	4.06 x 3.75
Displacement, cu. in.	389	389
Compression ratio	10.75:1	10.75:1
Minimum allowable combustion chamber volume, cc.	65.0	65.0
Carburetion	4BBL	3-2BBL
Total throttle bore area, sq. in.	7.72	12.19
Camshaft duration, deg.—intake	273	288
exhaust	289	302
overlap	54	63
Jetting, primary	0.091	0.063 (w/stick) 0.060 (w/auto.)
secondary	0.0785	0.068 (w/stick or auto.)

Short-stroke 90° V-8, alloy cast iron block, five main bearings, heavy-duty Moraine-400 aluminum-on-steel main and rod bearings. High-compression flat-top pistons with valve indents. High-lift camshaft, high-performance hydraulic valve lifters and springs. Large diameter valves—1.92″ intake, 1.66″ exhaust. Dual exhausts, low-restriction mufflers, lightweight resonators. Seven-blade, 18″ declutching fan. Low-restriction air cleaners.

Dimensions & Capacities: Wheelbase is 115 inches. Overall length is 206.1 inches. Tread is 58 inches, front and rear. Overall width is 73.4 inches. Height is 53.5 inches for the Coupe and Hardtop, 53.6 inches for the Convertible. Total trunk capacity is 32.1 cubic feet. The gas tank holds 21.5 gallons.

		Shipping Weight and lbs/HP			
Model	Engine	Stick—lbs/HP		Auto.—lbs/HP	
Coupe	335 bhp	3444	10.28	3454	10.31
	360 bhp	3459	9.61	3469	9.64
Hardtop	335 bhp	3462	10.33	3472	10.36
	360 bhp	3478	9.66	3488	9.69
Convertible	335 bhp	3555	10.61	3565	10.64
	360 bhp	3571	9.92	3581	9.95

Transmissions: A 3-speed manual transmission with Hurst floor shifter is standard. Ratios are 2.58:1, 1.48:1, and 1.00:1.

Or you can order a fully-synchro 3-speed with Hurst floor shifter, available March 1, 1965. Ratios are 2.42:1, 1.61:1, and 1.00:1.

Next come two versions of the fully-synchronized, aluminum-case 4-speed with Hurst floor shifter: Wide-ratio—2.56:1, 1.91:1, 1.48:1, and 1.00:1; Close-ratio (available only with 3.90:1 axle ratio for special driving)—2.20:1, 1.64:1, 1.28:1, and 1.00:1.

Then there's our 2-speed torque converter automatic, its lever mounted on the steering column. Ratios are 1.76:1 and 1.00:1, with a total torque multiplication off the line of 3.87:1. The governor is set for a maximum automatic upshift at 5200 rpm.

The standard engine. Horsepower—335. Cubic inches—389. Carburetion—4BBL. Declutching fan. Chromed air cleaner, rocker covers, oil filler cap.

The extra-cost engine. Horsepower—360. Cubic inches—389. Carburetion—3-2BBL, with mechanical linkage on stick shift jobs. Declutching fan. Chrome.

The custom sports steering wheel. Looks like wood. Feels like wood. Isn't. So it won't splinter like wood. Extra cost.

New instrumentation. Fuel and ammeter; 250° tach where it should be—beside speedo; water temp, oil pressure gauges. Extra cost.

Delco transistorized ignition. No points, no condenser. The next best thing to a magneto. Extra cost.

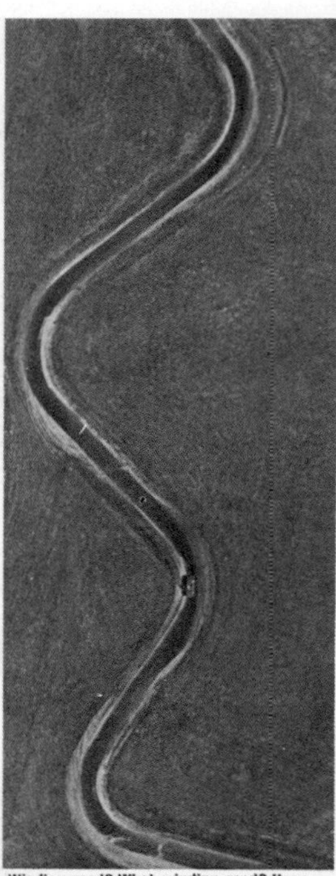

Winding road? What winding road? Heavy-duty springs, shocks, and stabilizer bar are standard equipment on the GTO.

Metallic linings. The most. They work even better coupled with power brakes. Aluminum front drums also available. Extra cost.

The optional console accommodates the shift lever for all transmissions.

Axle Ratios:

Engine	Transmission	Standard axle ratio	Special order axle ratios
335 bhp	3- or 4-speed	3.23†	3.08 3.36* 3.55* 3.90*
	automatic	3.23	3.08† 3.36* 3.55* 3.90*
360 bhp	3- or 4-speed	3.55	3.08 3.23† 3.36* 3.90*
	automatic	3.55	3.08† 3.23* 3.36* 3.90*

†Standard axle ratio with air conditioning
*Air conditioning not available

Special axle ratios of 4.11:1 and 4.33:1 are also available, dealer installed, but make sure you order the car originally with the close-ratio 4-speed and 3.90:1 axle ratio.

Axle ratio	No. of teeth—pinion/ring gear	Mph per 1000 rpm in high gear
3.08	13/40	25.2
3.23	13/42	24.3
3.36	11/37	23.1
3.55	11/39	21.8
3.90	10/39	19.9
4.11	9/37	18.9
4.33	9/39	17.9

Steering: Recirculating ball bearing steering gear. Standard ratio is 24:1. Optional quick steering is 20:1. Power steering is 17.5:1.

Suspension: Ball joint independent front, four-link rear. Shocks are valved for a firm, controlled ride. Heavy-duty coil springs have wheel rates of 89 and 110 pounds per inch, front and rear. Diameter of stabilizer bar is 0.938".

We'd suggest you try this already heavy-duty standard suspension before you make up your mind about the stiffer shock absorbers we have available.

Brakes: Hydraulic, internal expanding, two-shoe self-adjusting. Diameter of finned drum is 9.5", with a swept area of 269.8 sq. in. Aluminum front drums available. Metallic brake linings are also available as a separate option with all axle ratios. Because they require a high pedal pressure, consider ordering them in conjunction with power brakes.

GTO

Ever wondered what it feels like to be shot from a cannon? The GTO comes in three models — the Hardtop, the Sports Coupe, and the Convertible. Both engines for it are 389-cubic inchers, the standard one putting out 335 hp and high-performance one 360 hp. And both engines have chromed rocker covers, air cleaners and oil filler caps. The suspension is firmed up with heavy-duty springs, shocks and stabilizer bar. Bucket seats with belts are standard, as are a 3-speed floor shift, dual exhausts, custom pinstriping and performance 7.75 x 14 red-circle tires (the ones they call tiger paws). Care to know more? Ask the salesman for the special combined GTO/2+2 performance catalog, why don't you?

GTO HARDTOP COUPE

Left is the standard 2 + 2 interior. All-Morrokide seats and door panels, with a thick slather of carpeting in a matching color. Pretty plush, wouldn't you say? This one's done in a straight black. The other colors are red, parchment, and blue charcoal. Below is the standard GTO interior. Besides parchment, you can have it in blue, black, turquoise, gold, and red. The seats and door panels are expanded vinyl, while the cushy carpeting all over the place is a nylon blend. They help make a GTO the kind of car you hate to have to get out of.

1965 PONTIAC EXTERIOR TWO-TONE COMBINATIONS *(All models except 25237, 26237)*

Lower/Upper Area		Upper/Lower Area A	B	C	D	E	H	K	L	N	P	R	T	V	W	Y
STARLIGHT BLACK	A			X											X	
BLUE CHARCOAL	B			X											X	
CAMEO IVORY	C	X	X		X	X	X	X	X	X	X	X	X	X	X	X
FONTAINE BLUE	D			X		X									X	
NIGHTWATCH BLUE	E			X	X										X	
PALMETTO GREEN	H			X												
REEF TURQUOISE	K			X					X							
TEAL TURQUOISE	L			X				X								
BURGUNDY	N	X		X												
IRIS MIST	P	X		X												
MONTERO RED	R	X		X												
CAPRI GOLD	T	X		X										X		
MISSION BEIGE	V			X									X			
BLUEMIST SLATE	W	X	X	X	X	X										
MAYFAIR MAIZE	Y	X		X												

LITHO IN U.S.A. 6-64 SP 1830

1965 CONVERTIBLE TOP USAGE CHART *(TEMPEST CUSTOM & LE MANS)*

Coded to Exterior Color & Interior Trim

Exterior Colors:

A Starlight Black
B Blue Charcoal
C Cameo Ivory
D Fontaine Blue
E Nightwatch Blue
H Palmetto Green
K Reef Turquoise
L Teal Turquoise
N Burgundy
P Iris Mist
R Montero Red
T Capri Gold
V Mission Beige
W Bluemist Slate
Y Mayfair Maize

Top Color Code Numbers:

#1 White
#2 Black
#4 Blue
#5 Turquoise
#6 Beige

Cordova Top Option—vinyl-coated fabric roof covering in "Levant" grain in either Black (#2), or Beige (#6), for Sports Coupes (23327—23527—23727), Hardtop Coupes (23537—23737) and Le Mans Sedan (23769).

TEMPEST CUSTOM Convertible *(23567)*

INT. 93 BLUE	**A-1, 2, 4 B-1, 2, 4 C-1, 2, 4 D-1, 2, 4 E-1, 2, 4 W-1, 2**
INT. 94 GOLD	**A-1, 2 C-1, 2, 6 T-1, 2, 6 V-1, 2, 6 Y-1, 2, 6**
INT. 95 RED	**A-1, 2 C-1, 2 N-1, 2 R-1, 2**

LE MANS Convertible *(23767)*

INT. 30 BLACK	**A-1, 2 B-1, 2 C-1, 2 D-1, 2, 4 E-1, 2, 4 H-1, 2 K-1, 2, 5 L-1, 2, 5 N-1, 2 P-1, 2 R-1, 2 T-1, 2, 6 V-1, 2, 6 W-1, 2 Y-1, 2, 6**
INT. 36 TURQUOISE	**A-1, 2, 5 C-1, 2, 5 K-1, 2, 5 L-1, 2, 5**
INT. 34 GOLD	**A-1, 2 C-1, 2, 6 T-1, 2, 6 V-1, 2, 6 Y-1, 2, 6**
INT. 35 RED	**A-1, 2 C-1, 2 N-1, 2 R-1, 2**
INT. 33 BLUE	**A-1, 2, 4 B-1, 2, 4 C-1, 2, 4 D-1, 2, 4 E-1, 2, 4 W-1, 2**
INT. 3E PARCHMENT & BLACK	**A-1, 2 B-1, 2 C-1, 2 D-1, 2, 4 E-1, 2, 4 H-1, 2 K-1, 2, 5 L-1, 2, 5 N-1, 2 P-1, 2 R-1, 2 T-1, 2, 6 V-1, 2, 6 W-1, 2 Y-1, 2, 6**

Pontiac Motor Division of General Motors Corporation reserves the right to make changes at any time, without notice, in prices, colors, materials, equipment, specifications, and models, and also to discontinue models.

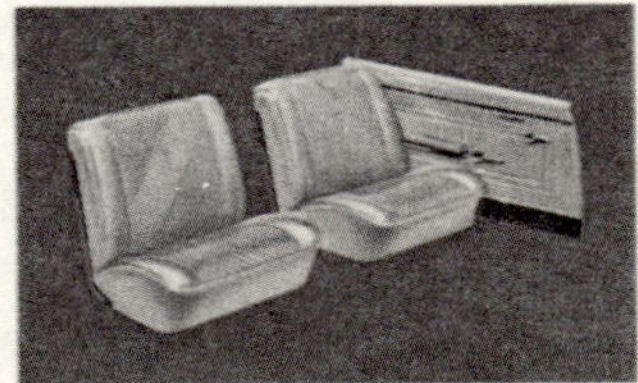

LE MANS Sports Coupe *(23727)*
Hardtop Coupe *(23737)*
Convertible *(23767)*
G.T.O. (Code 382) available on these models.
Expanded Morrokide

Interior	Recommended Exterior Colors
30 BLACK	**A, B, C, D, E, H, K, L, N, P, R, T, V, W, Y**
36 TURQUOISE	**A, C, K, L**
34 GOLD	**A, C, T, V, Y**
35 RED	**A, C, N, R**
33 BLUE	**A, B, C, D, E, W**
3E PARCHMENT & BLACK	**A, B, C, D, E, H, K, L, N, P, R, T, V, W, Y**

1966

1966

Pontiac's 1966 slogan was, "The Tiger Scores Again!" While it was true of the entire Pontiac line, it was, if anything, even truer for the GTO. The GTO ceased to be an accessorized LeMans and became a series in its own right. As if in approval of this decision, the public bought enough series 66-42 GTOs to increase final production totals by better than 28% over 1965's highly successful achievement.

The intermediate Pontiacs were completely reskinned for 1966, and the GTO was a prime beneficiary. Basic styling themes remained, but the whole package was much more rounded than before. The Coke bottle, or venturi, effect on the sides had by this time become something of a minor Pontiac trademark to go with the wide-track stance, the split grille and the vertically stacked headlights. A new "hidden" tail light treatment was also inaugurated on the GTO. The mechanicals were much the same as in 1965.

Base prices rose a bit with the new models. The Sports Coupe listed at $2,783, the Hardtop Coupe listed at $2,847 and the Convertible came in at $3,082.

Production, which seemed to know no way but up at Pontiac in this era, hit what was to be the all-time GTO high: 96,946 units. Of this number, 73,785 were Hardtop Coupes, 12,798 were Convertibles, and, bringing up the rear, 10,363 were Sports Coupes.

The literature issued was essentially a repeat of that offered in 1965, except that there was no exclusive GTO piece, even of a novelty nature, unless post cards are considered. The GTO section of the main Pontiac catalogue is reproduced on pages 22-24. The GTO section of the Pontiac high performance cars catalogue is reproduced on pages 25-28. Finally, the relevant sections of the color and trim brochure are found on page 28.

GTO SPORTS COUPE

GTO HARDTOP COUPE

The integral wheels shown on the GTO Hardtop Coupe are not available at start of production. Check with your dealer for availability.

GTO is a very special road machine. So special, in fact, we call it the ultimate tiger. (And that's noteworthy considering all Pontiacs are tigers.) It packs a 335-hp, 389-cu. in. V-8 up front, and harnesses the energy with a column-mounted, all-synchro 3-speed transmission, heavy-duty clutch, heavy-duty shocks, springs and stabilizer bar. The engine doesn't really have to attract any more attention than it already does, but our enthusiastic engineering department insisted on dressing it up with chromed rocker covers, low restriction air cleaner, and oil-filler cap. Naturally, Strato bucket seats and carpeting are standard. And so is the sleek pinstriping on the outside. We've even trimmed the beautiful new instrument panel in genuine wood and given you a choice of red-line or whitewall tires at no extra cost. (There's also a 360-hp V-8 available with 3 2-barrel carburetors, plus a whole lot of stuff on the next page.) And there's more in the special GTO/2 + 2 catalog. Ask your dealer for it. (Just be sure you're slightly whacky about cars!)

GTO CONVERTIBLE

(Shown on the cars in this catalog are some items from the many options and custom features offered by Pontiac on the back cover. They're available at extra cost and well worth it in driving comfort and convenience.)

GTO, too, has a list of options that'll make you wish you had two cars to put them on. For instance, you can get the sports rally wheels, or wire wheel covers with spinners, or even the all-new, integral wheel and brake drum assembly* that's got to be the best-looking wheel since wheels were invented. You can get the instrument cluster that features a tachometer and gauges for water temperature and oil pressure. And you can select from the optional transmissions (four on the floor or automatic) with or without a console. Aluminum front brake drums, transistorized ignition and a whole slew of other goodies might be what you want for your personal requirements. But there are many other accessories and optional equipment available for the GTO, and they're all listed in the special GTO/2+2 catalog. Get one.

*Not available at start of production. Check with your dealer for availability.

Wire Wheel Discs

Custom Wheel Discs

Rally Wheels

Standard 335-hp GTO V-8

Precisioned Tachometer

New Bucket Seats available in six beautiful colors

The tiger scores again!

There is only one GTO. Never forget that. There are a lot of pretenders around. There always are in the wake of a winner. But it takes more than a big bore V-8 on a little chassis to make a GTO. The genius of the GTO is that it's the world's greatest compromise. In its proletarian version, it's a very manageable machine to drive. With its 4-barrel, standard cam, and firm but civilized suspension, your grandmother can even pick up her sauerkraut juice with it. But if you want to start grubbing around in the parts bin, you can turn your GTO into the famous GeeTO Tiger in nothing flat. The parts bin is down a few pages. Go get 'em, tiger.

GTO Sports Coupe

GTO Convertible

The posh standard interior. Blue, turquoise, bronze, red, black, or parchment.

Standard engine: 335-hp 4-barrel 389. Chromed air cleaner, rocker covers.

Our famous 360-hp Tri-Power. Mechanical throttle linkage with stick. Extra cost.

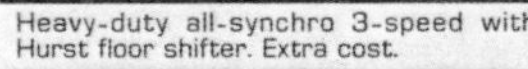

Heavy-duty all-synchro 3-speed with Hurst floor shifter. Extra cost.

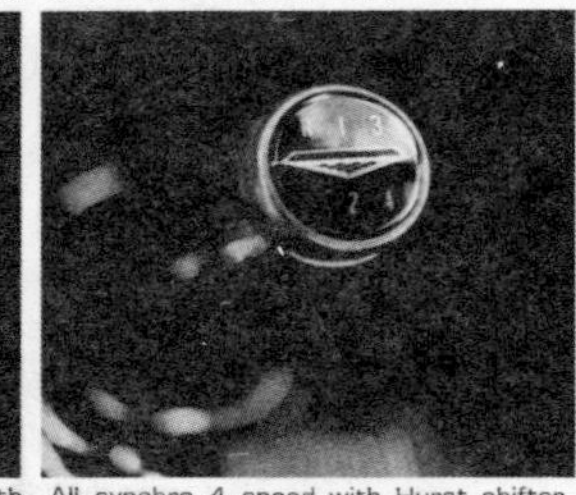

All-synchro 4-speed with Hurst shifter. Extra cost. So is the special shift knob.

The custom sports wheel. Only a hungry termite will know it's not wood. Extra cost.

What the 2-speed automatic looks like with console. Both extra cost.

Full instrumentation. Fuel, ammeter, tach, water temp, oil pressure. Extra cost.

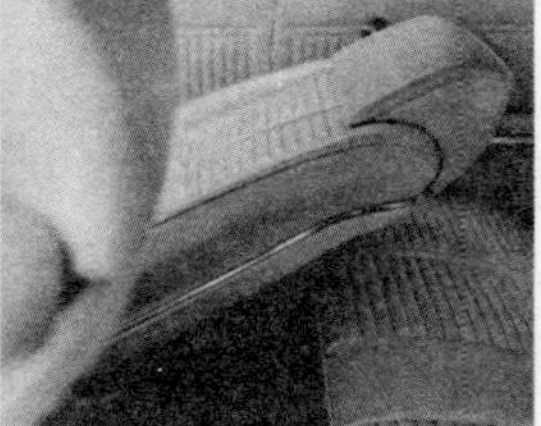

Reclining passenger seat. Headrests. Extra cost. But worth it on long hauls.

GTO Hardtop Coupe

Rally wheels with cooling slots. Extra cost, but you also get red brake drums.

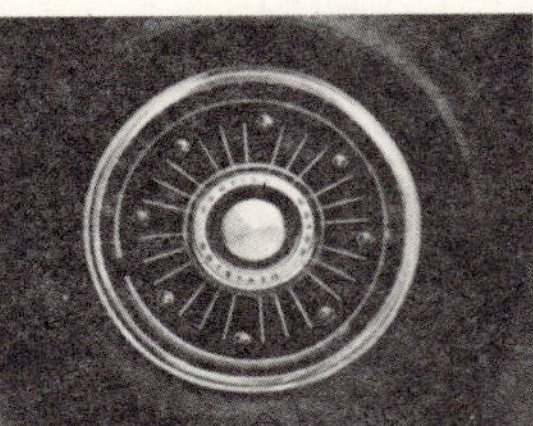
Cast-iron brake drum with integral hub.* Extra cost. Red-line nylon tires standard.

Custom wheel disc. Extra cost. Special brake cooling slots are functional.

Extra cost plastic wheelhouse inserts* never discolor or fade. They're washable.

Heavy-duty shocks, springs, stabilizer bar standard. Stiffer shocks are extra cost.

Deluxe wheel disc. Extra cost. Rayon cord whitewalls are optional at no extra cost.

Safe-T-Track limited-slip differential. A must for maximum traction. Extra cost.

Delco transistorized ignition. It's the next best thing to a magneto. Extra cost.

Finned aluminum brake drum for front wheels, seen from inside. Extra cost.

*Not available at start of production—See dealer for availability.

GTO

Engines:	Standard	Optional
Bhp @ rpm	335 @ 5000	360 @ 5200
Torque, lb.-ft.	431 @ 3200	424 @ 3600
Type	ohv V-8	ohv V-8
Bore and stroke	4.06 x 3.75	4.06 x 3.75
Displacement, cu. in.	389	389
Compression ratio	10.75:1	10.75:1
Minimum allowable combustion chamber volume, cc.	65.0	65.0
Carburetion	4-BBL	3/2-BBL
Total throttle bore area sq. in.	7.72	13.43
Camshaft duration, deg.—intake	273	288
exhaust	289	302
overlap	54	63
Camshaft Lift @ Zero Lash (Intake)	.406 ± .011	.409 ± .011
(Exhaust)	.408 ± .011	.409 ± .011
Jetting, primary	.0935	.062 (w/stick)
	.0935	.060 (w/auto)
secondary	.0785	.068 (w/stick or auto)

Heavy-duty Moraine-400 main and rod bearings. Flat-top pistons with valve indents. High-lift camshaft, high-performance hydraulic valve lifters and springs. Large diameter valves—1.92" intake, 1.66" exhaust. Dual exhausts, low-restriction mufflers, lightweight resonators. Seven-blade, 18" declutching fan. Low-restriction air cleaners.

Capacities: The gas tank holds 21.5 gallons. Oil capacity is 6 quarts, 7 with filter. Radiator holds 20 quarts.

Model	Engine	Shipping Weight, lbs. Stick	lbs./hp	Auto.	lbs./hp
Coupe	335 bhp	3445	10.28	3450	10.29
	360 bhp	3462	9.62	3467	9.64
Hardtop	335 bhp	3465	10.34	3470	10.35
	360 bhp	3482	9.67	3487	10.40
Convertible	335 bhp	3555	10.61	3560	10.62
	360 bhp	3572	9.92	3577	9.68

Transmissions: A 3-speed all-synchro manual transmission with column mounted lever is standard. Ratios are 2.54:1, 1.50:1, and 1.00:1.

Or you can order a fully-synchro heavy duty 3-speed with Hurst floor shifter. Ratios are 2.42:1, 1.61:1, and 1.00:1.

Next come two versions of the fully-synchronized, aluminum-case 4-speed with Hurst floor shifter: Wide-ratio—2.52:1, 1.88:1, 1.46:1, and 1.00:1; Close-ratio (available only with 3.90:1 axle ratio for special driving)—2.20:1, 1.64:1, 1.28:1, and 1.00:1.

Then there's our 2-speed torque converter automatic, its lever mounted on the steering column. Ratios are 1.76:1 and 1.00:1, with a total torque multiplication at the start of 4.23:1. The governor is set for a maximum automatic upshift at 5200 rpm.

The console accommodates the shift lever for all floor-shift transmissions.

Axle Ratios:

Engine	Transmission	Standard axle ratio	Special order axle ratios					
335 bhp	3- or 4-speed	3.55	3.08	3.23†	3.36*	3.90*	4.33*	
	automatic	3.23	3.08†	3.36*	3.55*	3.90*	4.33*	
360 bhp	3- or 4-speed	3.55	3.08	3.23†	3.36*	3.90*	4.33*	
	automatic	3.55	3.08†	3.23*	3.36*	3.90*	4.33*	

†Standard axle ratio with air conditioning
*Air conditioning not available

Special 4.11:1 axle ratio is available, dealer installed, but make sure you order the car with the heavy-duty 3-speed or close-ratio 4-speed and 3.90:1 axle ratio. Certain special order combinations require extra cost items such as a heavy-duty radiator, limited slip differential, special brakes and speedometer gear adapters. Be sure to see your dealer's detailed power train specifications for this information.

Total Final Drive Ratios

Axle Ratios	Wide-ratio 4-speed 1 2.52	2 1.88	3 1.46	4 1.00	Close-ratio 4-speed 1 2.20	2 1.64	3 1.28	4 1.00	MPH per 1000 rpm in high gear
3.08	7.76	5.79	4.50	3.08	N.A.	N.A.	N.A.	N.A.	25.1
3.23	8.14	6.07	4.72	3.23	N.A.	N.A.	N.A.	N.A.	23.9
3.36	8.47	6.32	4.90	3.36	N.A.	N.A.	N.A.	N.A.	23.0
3.55	8.95	6.67	5.18	3.55	N.A.	N.A.	N.A.	N.A.	21.8
3.90	9.83	7.33	5.69	3.90	8.58	6.40	4.99	3.90	19.8
4.11	10.36	7.73	6.00	4.11	9.04	6.74	5.26	4.11	18.8
4.33	10.91	8.14	6.32	4.33	9.53	7.10	5.54	4.33	17.8

Steering: Recirculating ball bearing steering gear. Standard ratio is 24:1. Quick steering is 20:1. Power steering is 17.5:1.

Suspension: Heavy-duty coil springs have wheel rates of 89.5 and 110 pounds per inch, front and rear. Diameter of stabilizer bar is 0.938".

We'd suggest you try this already heavy-duty standard suspension before you make up your mind about the stiffer shock absorbers we have available.

Brakes: Diameter of finned drum is 9.5", with a swept area of 269.2 sq. in. Aluminum front drums available. Metallic brake linings are also available as a separate option with all axle ratios. Because they require a high pedal pressure, consider ordering them in conjunction with power brakes.

1966 CONVERTIBLE TOP USAGE CHART

TEMPEST CUSTOM (23567), LEMANS (23767), GTO (24267), CATALINA (25267), VENTURA (25267), 2+2 (25467), BONNEVILLE (26267) AND BROUGHAM (26267)

TOP COLOR CODE NUMBER:
#1 WHITE, #2 BLACK, #4 BLUE, #5 TURQUOISE, #6 BEIGE

BLACK INTERIOR TRIM NUMBERS 223, 520, 521, 567, 572, 597:
A—1, 2 B—1, 2, 4 C—1, 2 D—1, 2, 4 E—1, 2, 4
H—1, 2 K—1, 2, 5 L—1, 2, 5 N—1, 2 P—1, 2, 4
R—1, 2 T—1, 2, 6 V—1, 2, 6 W—1, 2 Y—1, 2, 6

PARCHMENT INTERIOR TRIM NUMBERS 224, 524, 568, 573:
A—1, 2 B—1, 2, 4 C—1, 2 D—1, 2, 4 E—1, 2, 4
H—1, 2 K—1, 2, 5 L—1, 2, 5 N—1, 2 P—1, 2, 4
R—1, 2 T—1, 2, 6 V—1, 2, 6 W—1, 2 Y—1, 2, 6

RED INTERIOR TRIM NUMBERS 216, 222, 519, 522, 566, 571:
A—1, 2 C—1, 2 N—1, 2 R—1, 2

TURQUOISE INTERIOR TRIM NUMBERS 220, 517, 564:
A—1, 2, 5 C—1, 2, 5 K—1, 2, 5 L—1, 2, 5

BRONZE INTERIOR TRIM NUMBERS 215, 221, 518, 565, 596:
A—1, 2 C—1, 2, 6 T—1, 2, 6 V—1, 2, 6 Y—1, 2, 6

BLUE INTERIOR TRIM NUMBERS 213, 219, 516, 523, 563, 570:
A—1, 2, 4 B—1, 2, 4 C—1, 2, 4 D—1, 2, 4
E—1, 2, 4 P—1, 2, 4 W—1, 2

CORDOVA TOP OPTION—Vinyl-coated fabric roof covering in a "grain" texture in Ivory (#1), Black (#2) and Beige (#6) available with all models except 2- and 4-door post sedans and Tempest and Tempest Custom Station Wagons. Decor option required on Tempest, Tempest Custom and Catalina Series with Cordova Top Option.

New 1966 Pontiac Exterior Finishes

A Starlight Black Two-Tone Combinations—**C, P, W**

B Blue Charcoal Two-Tone Combinations—**C, W**

C Cameo Ivory Two-Tone Combinations—**A, B, D, E, H, K, L, N, P, R, T, V, W, Y**

D Fontaine Blue Two-Tone Combinations—**C, E, W**

E Nightwatch Blue Two-Tone Combinations—**C, D, P, W**

H Palmetto Green Two-Tone Combinations—**C**

K Reef Turquoise Two-Tone Combinations—**C, L**

L Marina Turquoise Two-Tone Combinations—**C, K**

N Burgundy Two-Tone Combinations—**A*, C** (*Upper Only)

P Barrier Blue Two-Tone Combinations—**A, C, E**

R Montero Red Two-Tone Combinations—**A*, C** (*Upper Only)

T Martinique Bronze Two-Tone Combinations—**A*, C, V** (*Upper Only)

V Mission Beige Two-Tone Combinations—**C, T**

W Platinum Two-Tone Combinations—**A, B, C, D, E**

Y Candlelite Cream Two-Tone Combinations—**A*, C** (*Upper Only)

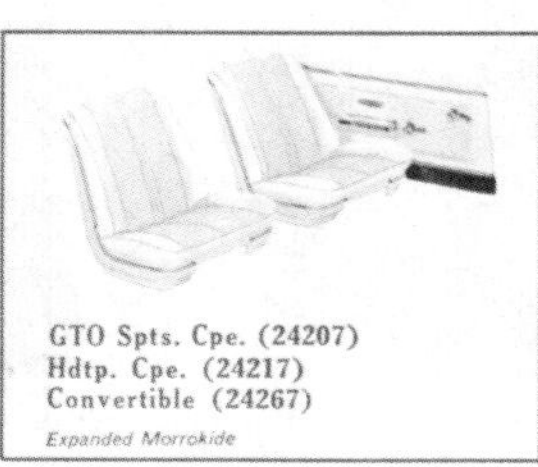

GTO Spts. Cpe. (24207)
Hdtp. Cpe. (24217)
Convertible (24267)
Expanded Morrokide

Interior	Recommended Exterior Colors
219 BLUE	A, B, C, D, E, P, W
220 TURQUOISE	A, C, K, L
221 BRONZE	A, C, T, V, Y
222 RED	A, C, N, R
223 BLACK	A, B, C, D, E, H, K, L, N, P, R, T, V, W, Y
224 PARCHMENT	A, B, C, D, E, H, K, L, N, P, R, T, V, W, Y

1967

Pontiac, taken as a whole, attained the greatest success in its history in 1967 as sales penetration hit 9.98% of the industry. No medium priced car had ever reached that level of acceptance, and it was the last time that Pontiac would do so. The bloom was already off the GTO rose. The car was just as good, but the competition, which hadn't existed at all in 1964, was suddenly scrambling for every sale. Even American Motors was after a piece of the market, and it was probably a notable achievement that GTO production was only off by about 15%. A lesser product would have been hurt much worse.

The 1967 body was little altered from the previous season. Most of the attention was paid to the rear end treatment, but even then it was only changed in detail. The models too remained the same. There was, however, some important mechanical news. The 389 V-8 was bored out to 400 cubic inches in displacement. Quoted horsepower was unchanged, but a new engine option was added to the list. Ram Air could be specified on the high performance 360 horsepower engine. At the other end of the scale, the Pontiac two-barrel, 255 horsepower economy engine could also be ordered, but only with the automatic transmission. Incidentally, this was the first year for the Turbo-Hydramatic option for the GTO. Previously, the only automatice available was the anemic Tempest two-speed unit. A new hood-mounted tachometer was also optional.

Three GTO models were listed for 1967, as in the past. Prices were up slightly, once again, and now the Sports Coupe cost $2,871, the Hardtop Coupe cost $2,935 and the Convertible cost $3,165.

Production for the 1967 run slipped to 81,722 units. Of this number, 65,176 were Hardtop Coupes, 9,517 were Convertibles and 7,029 were Sports Coupes.

The 1966 literature program was repeated once more in 1967. The main Pontiac catalogue GTO section is reproduced on pages 30-32. The GTO section from the Pontiac high performance cars catalogue is reproduced on pages 33-35. And, lastly, the GTO parts of the color and trim brochure appear on page 36.

GTO

This is The Great One. The ultimate driving machine. If you don't know what that means, you may be excused from this section of Wide-Track country. But if suddenly you're aware of an almost uncontrollable urge to plant yourself behind the wheel of one of these automotive masterpieces, you have found yourself a home. Turn to page 32 and then ask your Pontiac dealer for the special GTO/Sprint/2+2 performance catalog and learn how beautiful life can really be.

GTO SPORTS COUPE

GTO HARDTOP COUPE

28

GTO

GTO

GTO is an idea on wheels—the idea that there's more to driving than moving from place to place in isolated indifference. Nevertheless, enough of the essence may be captured in words to create within the heart of the initiated an undying devotion to the Great One. The Great One is 400 cubic inches of chromed V-8, in 335- and 360-hp designations, an all-synchro three-speed, bucket seats, carpeting, paint striping, simulated walnut-grain instrument panel, dual exhausts, heavy-duty shocks, springs and stabilizer bar, red-line or whitewall tires, and an option list as long as your arm and twice as hairy—four-speed stick, 3-speed Turbo Hydra-Matic, 255-hp 2-bbl (with Turbo Hydra-Matic only), disc brakes, instrument package, special wheels—get the idea? Of course you do.

This all-expanded Morrokide interior is standard in blue, turquoise, gold, black, parchment or red. Or you can specify bench seats.

Wide-oval tires are standard. Take your choice of redlines or whitewalls.

Wood-grain instrument panel is standard. You can order the Rally cluster gauge option.

You can even order a special Ram-Air engine option that draws air through the scoop.

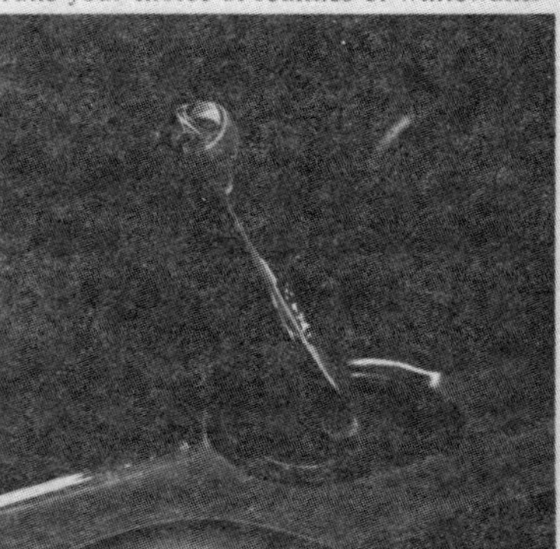

Our floor-mounted stick shift option with extra-cost console and wood shift knob.

The Rally I wheel. An extra-cost option.

The Le Mans interior with extra-cost stereo, floor-mounted stick shift, and console.

The hood-mounted tach option. Where else?

What makes them run.

GTO

Engines:

	Standard	Optional 2-bbl	Quadra-Power 400	Ram Air
Bhp @ rpm	335 @ 5000	255 @ 4400	360 @ 5100	360 @ 5400
Torque, lb.-ft.	441 @ 3400	397 @ 2400	438 @ 3600	438 @ 3800
Type	ohv V-8	ohv V-8	ohv V-8	ohv V-8
Bore and stroke	4.12 x 3.75	4.12 x 3.75	4.12 x 3.75	4.12 x 3.75
Displacement, cu. in.	400	400	400	400
Compression ratio	10.75:1	8.6:1	10.75:1	10.75:1
Minimum allowable combustion chamber volume, cc.	65.0	90.0	65.0	65.0
Carburetion	4-BBL	2-BBL	4-BBL	4-BBL
Camshaft duration, deg. — intake	273	269	288	301
exhaust	289	277	302	313
overlap	54	47	63	76
Camshaft Lift @ Zero Lash (intake)	.410 ± .011	.375 ± .011	.414 ± .011	.413 ± .011
(exhaust)	.413 ± .011	.410 ± .011	.413 ± .011	.413 ± .011
Jetting, primary (w/stick)	.070 (rod) .039		.070 (rod) .039	.070 (rod) .039
(w/auto)	.070 (rod) .041	.060	.070 (rod) .041	.070 (rod) .041
secondary (w/stick)	.1365 tapered rod "BE"		.1365 tapered rod "BE"	.1365 tapered rod "BE"
(w/auto)	.1365 tapered rod "BE"		.1365 tapered rod "BE"	.1365 tapered rod "BE"

Heavy-duty Moraine-400 main and rod bearings. Flat-top pistons with valve indents. High-performance hydraulic valve lifters and springs. Large diameter valves—2.11" intake, 1.77" exhaust (1.92" and 1.64" on 2-bbl). Dual exhausts, low-restriction mufflers. Seven-blade, 18" declutching fan. Low-restriction air cleaner on 335 and 360. Functional hood scoop option on Ram Air; high-output cam and springs.

Capacities: The gas tank holds 21.5 gallons. Oil capacity is 6 quarts, 7 with filter. Radiator holds 17.8 quarts.

Model	Engine	Shipping Weight, lbs. Stick	lbs./hp	Auto.	lbs./hp
Hardtop	255 bhp	N.A.	N.A.	3486	13.67
	335 bhp	3426	10.22	3486	10.40
	360 bhp & Ram Air	3426	9.51	3486	9.68
Coupe	255 bhp	N.A.	N.A.	3483	13.65
	335 bhp	3423	10.21	3483	10.39
	360 bhp & Ram Air	3423	9.50	3483	9.67
Convertible	255 bhp	N.A.	N.A.	3582	14.04
	335 bhp	3522	10.51	3582	10.69
	360 bhp & Ram Air	3522	9.78	3582	9.95

Transmissions: A 3-speed all-synchro manual transmission with column-mounted lever is standard. Ratios are 2.54:1, 1.50:1 and 1.00:1.

Or you can order a fully synchro heavy-duty 3-speed with Hurst floor shifter. Ratios are 2.42:1, 1.61:1, and 1.00:1.

Next come two versions of the fully synchronized, aluminum-case 4-speed with Hurst floor shifter: Wide ratio—2.52:1, 1.88:1, 1.46:1 and 1.00:1. Close ratio (available only with 3.90:1 and 4.33:1 axle ratio for special driving)—2.20:1, 1.64:1, 1.28:1 and 1.00:1.

Then there's our new heavy-duty 3-speed torque converter Turbo Hydra-Matic, its lever mounted on the steering column. No lag, no lurching, no surprise shifts. Ratios are 2.48:1, 1.48:1 and 1.00:1, with a total torque multiplication at the start of 5.70:1 (5.09:1 with 2-bbl). The governor is set for a maximum automatic upshift of 5000 rpm.

The console accommodates the shift lever for all floor-shift transmissions.

The GTO sports coupe. Seen departing with extra-cost cordova top and Rally I wheels.

The pinstripes along each flank are standard. Backup lights, side-view mirror, aforementioned wide-oval redline tires are also standard.

Axle Ratios:

Engine	Transmission	Standard axle ratio	Special order axle ratios					
255 bhp	automatic only	2.93*	2.56*	2.78†	3.23			
335 bhp	3- or 4-speed	3.55	3.08	3.23†	3.36*	3.90*	4.33*	
	automatic	3.36*	2.93†	3.23*	3.55*	3.90*	4.33*	
360 bhp	3- or 4-speed	3.55	3.08	3.23†	3.36*	3.90*	4.33*	
	automatic	3.55		3.23†	3.36*	3.90*	4.33*	
360 bhp Ram Air	4-speed only	4.33*		N.A.				
	automatic	4.33*		N.A.				

†Standard axle ratio with air conditioning
**Air conditioning not available*

Special 4.11:1 axle ratio is available, dealer installed, but make sure you order the car with the heavy-duty 3-speed or close ratio 4-speed and 3.90:1 axle ratio. Certain special order combinations require extra-cost items such as a heavy-duty radiator, limited slip differential, special brakes and speedometer gear adapters. Be sure to see your dealer's detailed power train specifications for this information.

Total Final Drive Ratios:

	Wide ratio 4-speed				Close ratio 4-speed				MPH
Axle Ratios	1 2.52	2 1.88	3 1.46	4 1.00	1 2.20	2 1.64	3 1.28	4 1.00	per 1000 rpm in high gear
3.08	7.76	5.79	4.50	3.08	N.A.	N.A.	N.A.	N.A.	24.5
3.23	8.14	6.07	4.72	3.23	N.A.	N.A.	N.A.	N.A.	23.4
3.36	8.47	6.32	4.90	3.36	N.A.	N.A.	N.A.	N.A.	22.5
3.55	8.95	6.67	5.18	3.55	N.A.	N.A.	N.A.	N.A.	21.3
3.90	9.83	7.33	5.69	3.90	8.58	6.40	4.99	3.90	19.4
4.11	10.36	7.73	6.00	4.11	9.04	6.74	5.26	4.11	18.4
4.33	10.91	8.14	6.32	4.33	9.53	7.10	5.54	4.33	17.4

Steering: Recirculating ball bearing steering gear. Standard ratio is 24:1. Quick steering is 20:1. Power steering is 17.5:1.

Suspension: Heavy-duty coil springs have wheel rates of 89.5 and 110 pounds per inch, front and rear. Diameter of stabilizer bar is 0.938".

We'd suggest you try this already heavy-duty standard suspension before you make up your mind about the stiffer shock absorbers we have available.

Brakes: Diameter of finned drum is 9.5", with a swept area of 269.2 sq. in. Front disc brakes are optional at extra cost. Diameter: 11.1"; swept area: 323.6 sq. in.

1967 CONVERTIBLE TOP USAGE CHART

Tempest Custom (23567), Le Mans (23767), GTO (24267), Catalina (25267), Ventura (25267), 2+2 (25267), Bonneville (26267), and Grand Prix (26667)

TOP COLOR CODE NUMBER: 1 Ivory-White 2 Black 4 Blue 5 Turquoise 7 Cream

Black Interior Trim Numbers 217, 223, 520, 521, 567, 572, 583

A—1, 2, 7 L—1, 2, 5
C—1, 2, 7 M—1, 2
D—1, 2, 4 N—1, 2
E—1, 2, 4 P—1, 2, 7
F—1, 2 R—1, 2
G—1, 2, 7 S—1, 2, 7
H—1, 2 T—1, 2, 7
K—1, 2, 5

Parchment Interior Trim Numbers 224, 524, 568, 573, 585

A—1, 2, 7 L—1, 2, 5
C—1, 2, 7 M—1, 2
D—1, 2, 4 N—1, 2
E—1, 2, 4 P—1, 2, 7
F—1, 2 R—1, 2
G—1, 2, 7 S—1, 2, 7
H—1, 2 T—1, 2, 7
K—1, 2, 5

Gold Interior Trim Numbers 221, 518

A—1, 2, 7 S—1, 2, 7
C—1, 2, 7 T—1, 2, 7
G—1, 2, 7

Red Interior Trim Numbers 218, 225, 519, 522, 566, 594

A—1, 2 P—1, 2
C—1, 2 R—1, 2
N—1, 2

Blue Interior Trim Numbers 213, 219, 516, 523, 563, 580

A—1, 2, 4 E—1, 2, 4
C—1, 2, 4 P—1, 2, 4
D—1, 2, 4

Turquoise Interior Trim Numbers 220, 564

A—1, 2, 5 L—1, 2, 5
C—1, 2, 5 P—1, 2, 5
K—1, 2, 5

Cordova Top Option. Vinyl-coated fabric roof covering in a "grain" texture in Ivory (#1), Black (#2) and Cream (#7) available with all models except 2- and 4-door post sedans and Tempest, Tempest Custom and Tempest Safari Station Wagons. Decor option required on Tempest, Tempest Custom and Catalina Series with Cordova Top Option.

NEW 1967 PONTIAC EXTERIOR FINISHES

A Starlight Black
Two-tone Combinations
C, P, T

C Cameo Ivory
Two-tone Combinations
A, D, E, G, K, L, P

D Montreux Blue
Two-tone Combinations
C, E

E Fathom Blue
Two-tone Combinations
C, D

F Tyrol Blue
Two-tone Combinations
A*, C*
(*upper only)

G Signet Gold
Two-tone Combinations
A*, C, S*, T
(*upper only)

H Linden Green
Two-tone Combinations
A*, C*
(*upper only)

K Gulf Turquoise
Two-tone Combinations
C, L

L Mariner Turquoise
Two-tone Combinations
C, K

M Plum Mist
Two-tone Combinations
C*
(*upper only)

N Burgundy
Two-tone Combinations
A*, C*
(*upper only)

P Silverglaze
Two-tone Combinations
A, C

R Regimental Red
Two-tone Combinations
A*, C*
(*upper only)

S Champagne
Two-tone Combinations
A*, C*, T
(*upper only)

T Montego Cream
Two-tone Combinations
A, C*, G, S*
(*upper only)

GTO

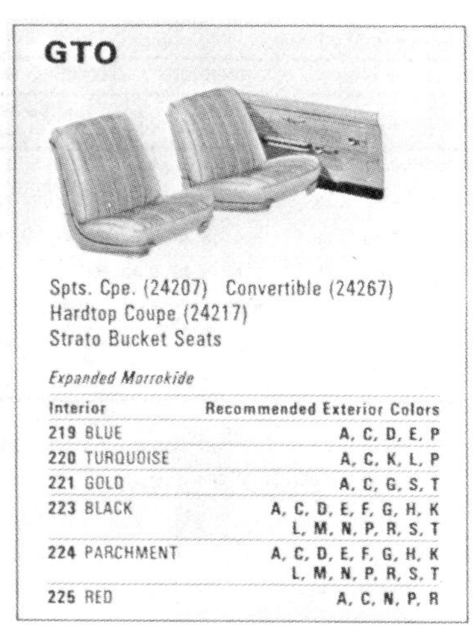

Spts. Cpe. (24207) Convertible (24267)
Hardtop Coupe (24217)
Strato Bucket Seats

Expanded Morrokide

Interior	Recommended Exterior Colors
219 BLUE	A, C, D, E, P
220 TURQUOISE	A, C, K, L, P
221 GOLD	A, C, G, S, T
223 BLACK	A, C, D, E, F, G, H, K L, M, N, P, R, S, T
224 PARCHMENT	A, C, D, E, F, G, H, K L, M, N, P, R, S, T
225 RED	A, C, N, P, R

1968

This was an important sales year for Pontiac. While market penetration was down slightly, total production surpassed the 900,000 mark for the first time in Pontiac history. The GTO was up, too, and managed to recoup about half of the 1967 production loss thanks to a remarkable new model that boasted a host of interesting new features.

All intermediate Pontiacs were new in 1968. They not only sported new sheet metal, but a new chassis as well. The GTO was on a new 112 inch wheelbase, while the four-door Tempest and LeMans models used a 116 inch wheelbase. All intermediates featured styling that was even more rounded than before, and all had, in addition, the novel disappearing windshield wipers that Pontiac had pioneered the year before. The GTO's major styling achievement, however, was the dramatic Endura rubber front bumper. This was not only the first impact absorbing safety bumper, it was also a styling revolution. Since it was painted body color, stylists were able for the first time to make the bumper an integral part of the front end styling—not something hung onto the design after the fact. Another styling innovation was represented by the concealed headlights. The Endura bumper, incidentally, was a delete option. A GTO could have been specified without it, although few were.

The engine story was much the same as in 1967, with the exception of a couple of horsepower ratings. The economy engine was listed at 265 horsepower and the standard engine was now rated at 350 horsepower.

Only two models were available in 1968, and prices rose substantially to $3,103 for the Hardtop Coupe and to $3,327 for the Convertible.

Total production climbed to 87,684. A total of 77,704 of these were Hardtop Coupes, while 9,980 were Convertibles.

The basic GTO literature remained much as before. There was a section in the main catalogue (pages 38-40) and in the high performance cars catalogue (pages 41-43). The color and trim section relating to the GTO is shown on page 44.

In '68, the Great One again is GTO.

Have no doubts. The GTO is first and foremost, a driver's car. One that has spawned many pretenders. The beauty that generates a false placidness is a pleasing coincidence. It begins up front with the most fantastic bumper since the invention of the bumper. It's the same color as the car, but won't chip, fade or corrode. The Great One's equally impressive credentials in the world of concrete and asphalt are easily discovered. Just climb behind the wheel, negotiate a few turns, try a few hills and presto! You'll never want to go back to plain ordinary driving. Of course, those are just two of the reasons why we call the GTO The Great One. There are others, like our famous disappearing windshield wipers that come as standard equipment. Or you can order disappearing headlights and a 4-speed stick shift—floor-mounted, of course. They cost extra, but are worth every penny. Want to know more about The Great One? Be patient—we divulge more on the next page.

GTO CONVERTIBLE

GTO HARDTOP COUPE

Can we reconstruct on paper those things that make The Great One great? Hardly. But if you're searching for a machine that's been created with enough foresight to include more than just a beautiful body, we can promise you Euphoria. For the GTO is 400 cubic inches of V-8 with 350 hp (available in a regular-gas, 265-hp version), an all-synchro 3-speed with Hurst shifter, dual exhausts, sports-type springs and shocks, new Fastrak (improves traction and handling) redline tires, buckets or notch-back bench seat, with center armrest—just to name part of its standard makeup. The option list includes goodies like a 4-speed stick, 360-hp Ram Air engine (that includes functional hood scoops), hood-mounted tach, special wheels, 3-speed Turbo Hydra-Matic and rally gauge cluster. The GTO great? Yes, until someone comes up with a better word.

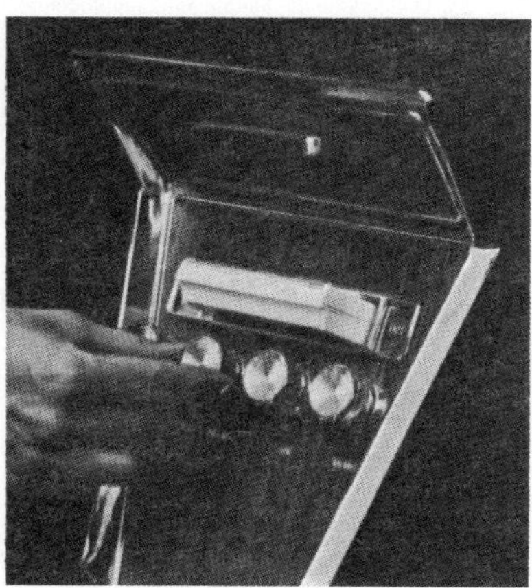

Engines:

	Standard	Optional 2-BBL	400 H.O.	400 Ram Air
Bhp @ rpm	350 @ 5000	265 @ 4600	360 @ 5100	360 @ 5400
Torque (lb.-ft.)	445 @ 3000	397 @ 2400	445 @ 3600	445 @ 3800
Type	OHV V-8	OHV V-8	OHV V-8	OHV V-8
Bore and Stroke	4.12 x 3.75	4.12 x 3.75	4.12 x 3.75	4.12 x 3.75
Displacement (cu. in.)	400	400	400	400
Compression Ratio	10.75:1	8.6:1	10.75:1	10.75:1
Minimum Allowable Combustion Chamber Volume (cc.)	65.0	90.0	65.0	65.0
Carburetion	4-BBL	2-BBL	4-BBL	4-BBL
Camshaft Duration (deg.)	Manual			
intake	273	269	288	301
exhaust	289	277	302	313
overlap	54	47	63	76
Camshaft Lift @ Zero Lash—intake	.410 ± .011	.376 ± .011	.414 ± .011	.413 ± .011
exhaust	.413 ± .011	.412 ± .011	.413 ± .011	.413 ± .011

Heavy-duty Moraine-400 main and rod bearings. Flat-top pistons with valve indents. High-performance hydraulic valve lifters and springs. Large diameter valves—2.11″ intake, 1.77″ exhaust (1.96″ and 1.66″ on 2-bbl). Dual exhausts, low-restriction mufflers, Power-Flex fan. Low-restriction air cleaner on 350 and 360. Functional hood scoop and air trap option on Ram Air; high-output cam and springs, 4-bolt main-bearing caps.

Capacities: The gas tank holds 21.5 gallons. Oil capacity is 5 quarts, 6 with filter. Radiator holds 17.8 quarts.

Estimated Shipping Weight, lbs.

Model	Engine	Stick	lbs./hp	Auto.	lbs./hp
Hardtop	265 bhp	N.A.	N.A.	3516	13.26
	350 bhp	3506	10.01	3538	10.10
	360 bhp & Ram Air	3506	9.73	3538	9.82
Convertible	265 bhp	N.A.	N.A.	3599	13.58
	350 bhp	3589	10.25	3621	10.34
	360 bhp & Ram Air	3589	9.96	3621	10.05

You can rally to your heart's desire when you order this Rally cluster. Includes special fuel gauge, battery light, speedo, oil-pressure and water-temp gauges. That sporty, wood-like steering wheel is also available as an option.

Buckets are standard. You can add the head restraints and reclining passenger seat. Worth every cent.

When you choose to go the automatic route in a GTO, it means floor-mounted, 3-speed, Turbo Hydra-Matic, Hurst shifter (naturally) and console. "Dual-Gate" shift quadrant lets you shift manually when the whim strikes.

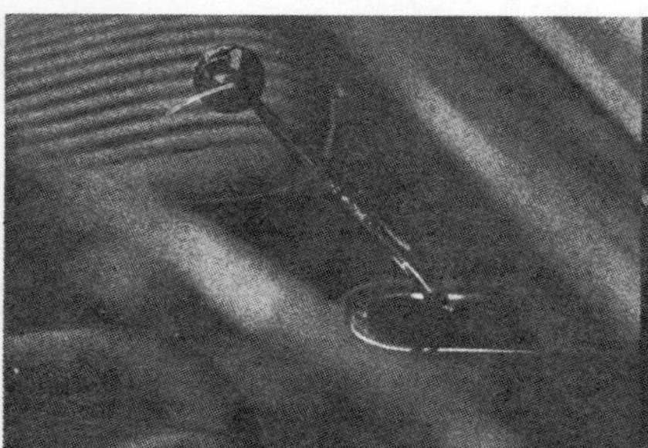

If you've got the gift of grab, order this 4-speed with Hurst shifter. Or specify an all-synchro, heavy-duty 3-speed.

Dress up your GTO with Rally II wheels. The redline wide-ovals or Fastraks are on us—your choice.

Whitewalls are standard. The Rally I steel wheels would make a shrewd investment.

Transmissions: A fully synchro, heavy-duty, 3-speed with Hurst floor shifter is standard. Ratios are 2.42 :1, 1.61 :1, and 1.00 :1.

Next come two versions of the fully synchronized, aluminum-case 4-speed with Hurst floor shifter: Wide-ratio—2.52 :1, 1.88 :1, 1.46 :1 and 1.00 :1. Close-ratio (available only with 3.90 :1 and 4.33 :1 axle ratio for special driving)—2.20 :1, 1.64 :1, 1.28 :1 and 1.00 :1.

Then there's our new heavy-duty, 3-speed torque converter Turbo Hydra-Matic, its lever mounted on the steering column. No lag, no lurching, no surprise shifts. Ratios are 2.48 :1, 1.48 :1 and 1.00 :1, with a total torque multiplication at the start of 5.70 :1 (5.09 :1 with 2-bbl). The governor is set for a maximum automatic upshift at 5000 rpm

When you order the console, it will accommodate the shift lever for all floor-shift transmissions.

Axle Ratios:

Engine	Transmission	Standard Axle Ratio	Special-order Axle Ratios				
265 bhp	automatic only	2.93	2.56	2.78†	3.23		
350 bhp	3- or 4-speed	3.55	3.08	3.23†	3.36*	3.90*	4.33*
	automatic	3.36	2.93†	3.23*	3.55*	3.90*	4.33*
360 bhp	3- or 4-speed	3.55	3.08	3.23†	3.36*	3.90*	4.33*
	automatic	3.55		3.23†	3.36*	3.90*	4.33*
360 bhp Ram Air	4-speed only	4.33*		N.A.			
	automatic	4.33*		N.A.			

†Standard axle ratio with air conditioning
*Air conditioning not available

Special 4.11 :1 axle ratio is available, dealer-installed, but make sure you order the car with the heavy-duty 3-speed or close-ratio 4-speed and 3.90 :1 axle ratio. Certain special-order combinations require extra-cost items such as a heavy-duty radiator, limited slip differential, special brakes and speedometer gear adapters. Be sure to see your dealer's detailed power train specifications for this information.

Total Final Drive Ratios:

	Wide-ratio 4-speed				Close-ratio 4-speed				MPH
Axle Ratios	1 2.52	2 1.88	3 1.46	4 1.00	1 2.20	2 1.64	3 1.28	4 1.00	per 1000 rpm in high gear
3.08	7.76	5.79	4.50	3.08	N.A.	N.A.	N.A.	N.A.	24.5
3.23	8.14	6.07	4.72	3.23	N.A.	N.A.	N.A.	N.A.	23.4
3.36	8.47	6.32	4.90	3.36	N.A.	N.A.	N.A.	N.A.	22.5
3.55	8.95	6.67	5.18	3.55	N.A.	N.A.	N.A.	N.A.	21.3
3.90	9.83	7.33	5.69	3.90	8.58	6.40	4.99	3.90	19.4
4.11	10.36	7.73	6.00	4.11	9.04	6.74	5.26	4.11	18.4
4.33	10.91	8.14	6.32	4.33	9.53	7.10	5.54	4.33	17.4

Steering: Recirculating ball bearing steering gear. Standard ratio is 24 :1. Power steering is 17.5 :1.

Suspension: Heavy-duty coil springs have wheel rates of 91.0 and 110 pounds per inch, front and rear. Diameter of stabilizer bar is 1″.

We'd suggest you try this already heavy-duty standard suspension before you make up your mind about the stiffer shock absorbers we have available.

Brakes: Diameter of finned drum is 9.5″, with a swept area of 269.2 sq. in. Front disc brakes are optional at extra cost. Diameter: 11.1″; swept area: 323.6 sq. in.

If you order dual exhaust splitters, here's how they'll look to a groundhog.
You do use a tach to shift, don't you? Order a hood-mounted tach.

Our Ram Air engine includes functional hood scoops, high-output cam and valve springs. You can guess what that will do for top-end breathing.

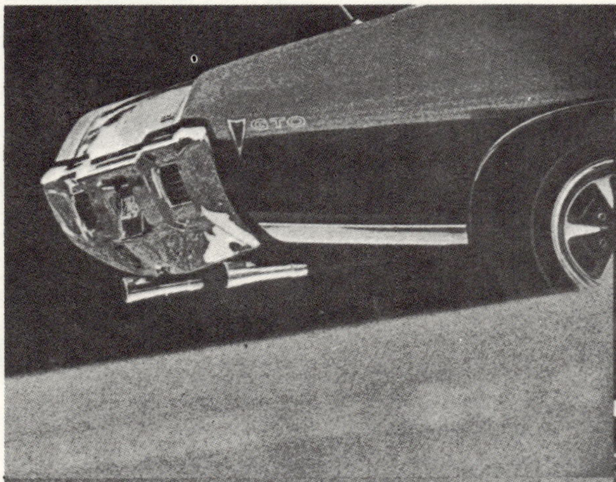

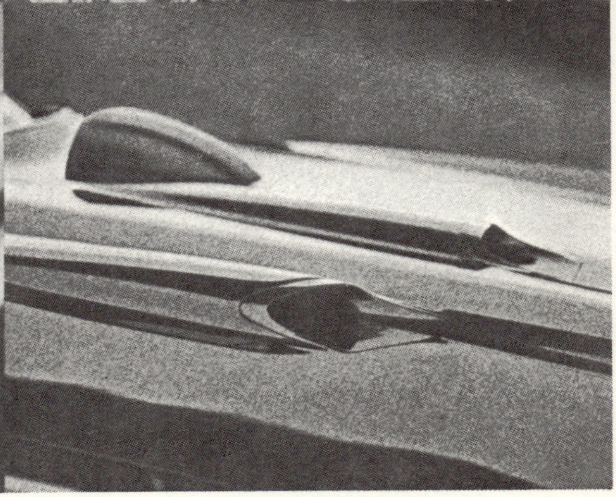

GTO

Hardtop Coupe (24237)
Convertible (24267)

Expanded Morrokide

Interior	Recommended Exterior Colors
219 TEAL	A, C, D, E, F, L
220 TURQUOISE	A, C, K
221 GOLD	A, C, G, Q, T
223 BLACK	A, C, D, E, F, G, K, L N, P, Q, R, T, V, Y
224 PARCHMENT	A, C, D, E, F, G, K, L N, P, Q, R, T, V, Y
225 RED	A, C, N, R

Hardtop Coupe (24237)
Convertible (24267)
Notch Back Front Seat with Center Armrest

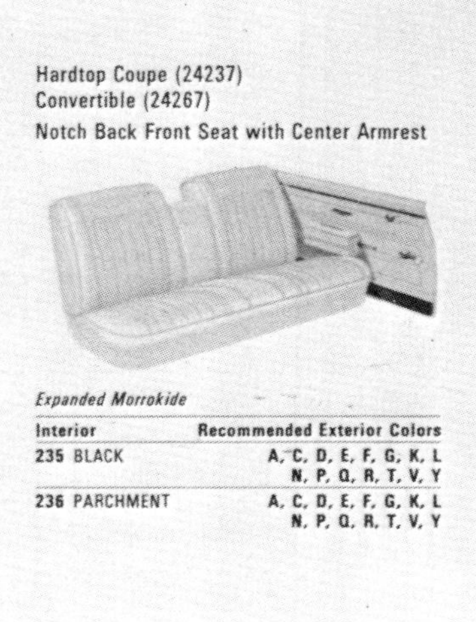

Expanded Morrokide

Interior	Recommended Exterior Colors
235 BLACK	A, C, D, E, F, G, K, L N, P, Q, R, T, V, Y
236 PARCHMENT	A, C, D, E, F, G, K, L N, P, Q, R, T, V, Y

New 1968 Pontiac Exterior Finishes

Color	Two-tone Combinations
A Starlight Black	C, F, P
C Cameo Ivory	A, D, E, G, K, L
D Alpine Blue	A*, C, E (*upper only)
E Aegena Blue	C, D
F Nordic Blue	A, C*, L (*upper only)
G April Gold	A*, C, (*upper only)
K Meridian Turquoise	A*, C (*upper only)
L Aleutian Blue	A*, C, F (*upper only)
N Flambeau Burgundy	A*, C* (*upper only)
P Springmist Green	A, C*, V (*upper only)
Q Verdoro Green	A*, C* (*upper only)
R Solar Red	A*, C* (*upper only)
T Primavera Beige	A*, C* (*upper only)
V Nightshade Green	A*, C*, P (*upper only)
Y Mayfair Maize	A*, C* (*upper only)

1968 Convertible Top Usage Chart

Firebird (22367), Tempest Custom (23567), Le Mans (23767), GTO (24267), Catalina (25267) and Bonneville (26267).

Top Color Code Number: 1 Ivory-White 2 Black 5 Teal 8 Gold

Black Interior Trim Numbers 217, 223, 235, 253, 259, 520, 521, 567, 570, 572

A—1,2	N—1,2
C—1,2	P—1,2
D—1,2	Q—1,2
E—1,2	R—1,2
F—1,2,5	T—1,2,8
G—1,2,8	V—1,2
K—1,2	Y—1,2
L—1,2,5	

Parchment Interior Trim Numbers 224, 236, 260, 262, 524, 568, 573

A—1,2	N—1,2
C—1,2,5	P—1,2
D—1,2	Q—1,2
E—1,2	R—1,2
F—1,2,5	T—1,2,8
G—1,2,8	V—1,2
K—1,2	Y—1,2
L—1,2,5	

Gold Interior Trim Numbers 221, 251, 257, 518

A—1,2,8	Q—1,2
C—1,2,8	T—1,2,8
G—1,2,8	

Red Interior Trim Numbers 218, 225, 252, 258, 519, 566

A—1,2	N—1,2
C—1,2	R—1,2

Turquoise Interior Trim Numbers 220, 256, 261, 563

A—1,2	K—1,2
C—1,2	

Teal Interior Trim Numbers 219, 250, 255, 564

A—1,2,5	E—1,2
C—1,2,5	F—1,2,5
D—1,2	L—1,2,5

Blue Interior Trim Numbers 213, 516

A—1,2,5	E—1,2
C—1,2,5	F—1,2,5
D—1,2	L—1,2,5

Cordova Top Option. Vinyl-coated, fabric roof covering in a "grain" texture in (#1) Ivory-white, (#2) Black, (#5) Teal and (#8) Gold, available on all models except Catalina 2-door Sedan and Tempest Custom and Tempest Safari Station Wagons. Decor option required on Tempest, Tempest Custom and Catalina Series.

1969

The 1969 model run was an interesting one for GTO enthusiasts even though the performance car boom was clearly nearing the end of its line. Despite a dramatic new model, the GTO experienced a production drop of 17%, and that was just a taste of things to come. In fact, by the end of the 1969 model run, over 86% of all the GTOs that would ever be built had been built. There were five model years left to the marque but they were not destined to be happy ones.

The 1969 Pontiac intermediates were very close to the all-new 1968s. Grilles were now of a honeycomb texture and the tail lights sat on the rear bumpers instead of in them, but that was the extent of the important visual developments. Presaging a disturbing trend, however, the vent windows were deleted on all two-door intermediate models, which, of course, included all GTOs. The big news in the beginning of the year was the two Ram Air options. The H.O. engine was dropped and a 366 horsepower Ram Air unit was offered in its stead. The old Ram Air engine was replaced by a new 370 horsepower Ram Air IV powerplant that was the most powerful ever put into a GTO. Then, in January, a special GTO Judge model was announced. The Judge came standard with the 366 horsepower Ram Air engine plus a host of other appearance goodies. In addition to functional hood scoops, the Judge featured unusual, and intentionally garish, striping and decals, as well as a 60-inch floating rear deck air foil with the Judge emblem on the upper surface. Most early units were painted a bright red-orange.

Prices rose a bit in 1969. The Hardtop Coupe now listed at $3,156, while the Convertible base price was $3,382. The Judge option cost around $400 more.

Total production sagged to 72,287. Of this number, 58,126 were Hardtop Coupes, 7,328 were Convertibles, 6,725 were Judge Hardtop Coupes and 108 were Judge Convertibles.

The literature, as before, included a GTO section in the main catalogue (pages 51-52), high performance cars catalogue (pages 46-50) and color and trim brochure (page 53), as well as a small color card on the Judge (page 50).

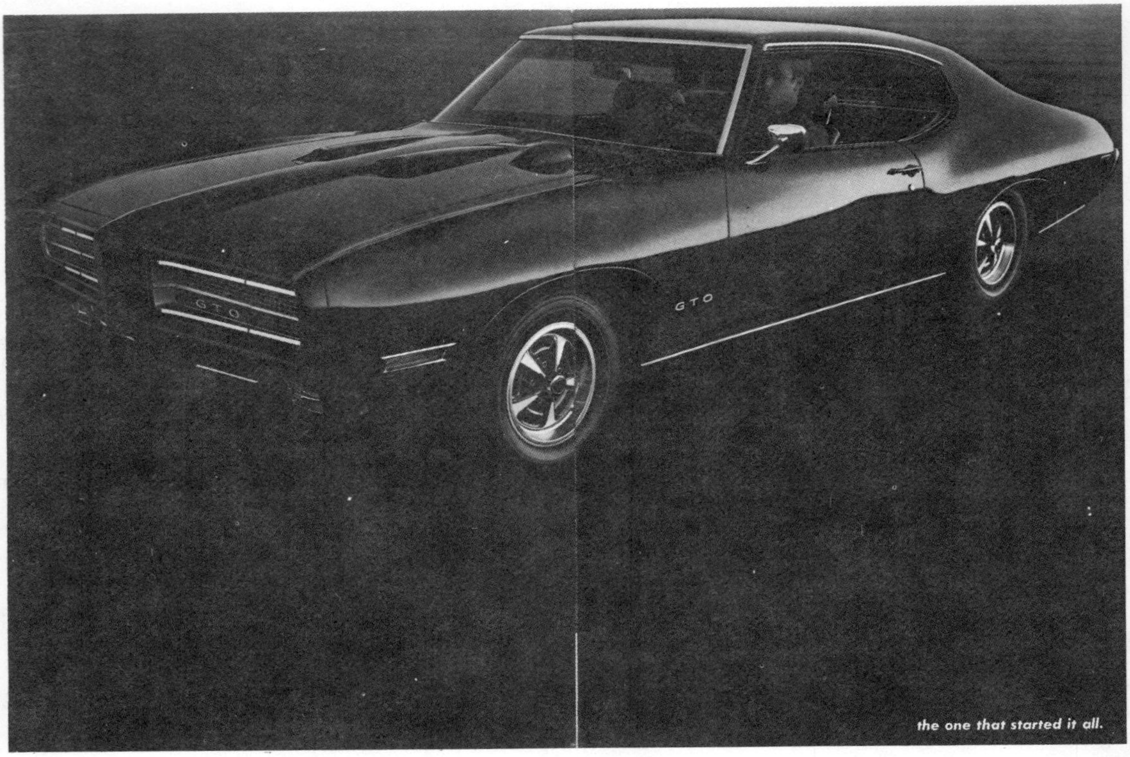
GTO
GTO
the one that started it all.

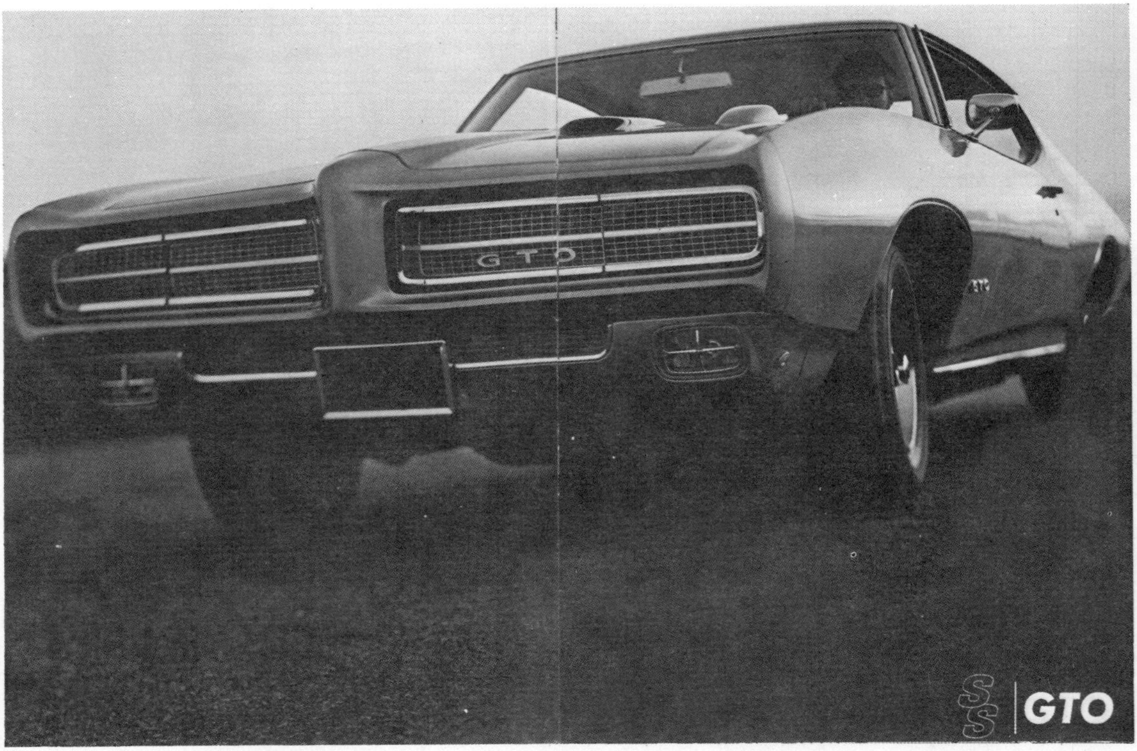
GTO
SS GTO

Jim McCraw's belief in performance cars is as deep and abiding as his interest in editing the magazine Super Stock*—an authoritative and responsible voice in the world of motor sports. We arranged for Jim to give our '69 GTO a special pre-new-car-announcement, behind-the-scene run-through at Ubly Dragway and asked for reactions. He reacted.*

Once upon a time, a division of General Motors decided to factory-build what a lot of barked-knuckle chaps were trying to glue together in their backyards.

Under the unwieldy title of Gran Turismo Omologato, the first GTO saw the light of day in 1964.

Ever since, that GM division, Pontiac, has been adding to the stature of this very particular car, and we have watched the rest of the industry fielding their own versions with varying degrees of success.

Even so, it's a pleasure to get back to the original—The Great One, Pontiac calls it—and find out what GTO has done for us lately. We weren't disappointed with the '69 version.

Our test car might have been equipped with a few more items than we'd normally prefer for our kind of work. But it seemed none of them got in the way of the GTO's ability to make tracks.

What we were really glad to have was the 400-cubic-inch Quadra-jet Ram Air V-8, fitted with 4-speed Hurst-stirred box and a 3.55 at rear. New for '69 are manually controlled flaps for the carb ducts. Very useful in bad weather.

We also felt good about the beautifully quick power steering and the powered single-piston discs at front.

The strip at Ubly, Michigan provided the pavement. And the result of our week's sojourn leads us to believe The Great One is intent on hanging on to its years-old reputation when the '69s are available in quantity. So much so, we sincerely doubt that GTO fans are going to look elsewhere for their automotive kicks.

One other thing. GTO's competing brethren are not as solicitous of creature comfort as was our Limelight Green edition. Comforts like big, cushy bucket seats either side of the center-mounted console. Like upper-level ventilation that lets you have outside air with the windows up. Like a special handling package and Wide-oval Redlines that firm up beautifully in the corners to inspire real confidence.

This is truly an automobile that reacts in a very positive fashion . . . the way anybody who loves cars reacts when he watches The Great One at work.

Some of the equipment illustrated, described in copy or referred to above is available at extra cost. Consult your local Pontiac dealer for model availability and costs.

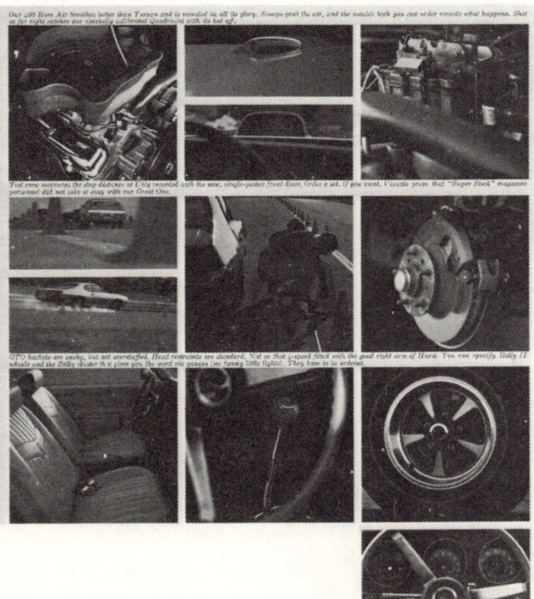

Our 400 Ram Air breathes better than Tarzan and is revealed in all its glory. Scoops grab the air, and the outside tach you can order records what happens. Shot at far right catches our specially calibrated Quadra-jet with its hat off.

Test crew measures the stop distance at Ubly recorded with the new, single-piston front discs. Order a set, if you want. Visuals prove that "Super Stock" magazine personnel did not take it easy with our Great One.

GTO buckets are cushy, but not overstuffed. Head restraints are standard. Not so that 4-speed fitted with the good right arm of Hurst. You can specify Rally II wheels and the Rally cluster that gives you the word via gauges (no funny little lights). They have to be ordered.

Engines:	Standard	Optional 2-BBL	400 Ram Air		400 Ram Air IV
Bhp @ rpm	350 @ 5000	265 @ 4600	366 @ 5100		370 @ 5500
Torque (lb.-ft.)	455 @ 3000	355 @ 2800	445 @ 3600		445 @ 3900
Type	OHV V-8	OHV V-8	OHV V-8		OHV V-8
Bore & Stroke	4.12 x 3.75	4.12 x 3.75	4.12 x 3.75		4.12 x 3.75
Displacement (cu. in.)	400	400	400		400
Compression Ratio	10.75:1	9.2:1	10.75:1		10.75:1
Minimum Allowable Combustion Chamber Volume (cc.)	65.0	90.0	65.0		65.0
Carburetion	4-BBL	2-BBL	4-BBL		4-BBL
Camshaft Duration (deg.)			Man.	Auto.	
—intake	273	269	288	273	308
—exhaust	289	277	302	289	320
—overlap	54	47	63	54	87
Camshaft Lift @ Zero Lash—intake	.410 ± .011	.376 ± .011	.414 ± .011		.520 ± .011
—exhaust	.413 ± .011	.412 ± .011	.413 ± .011		.520 ± .011

Heavy-duty Moraine-400 main and rod bearings. Flat-top pistons with valve indents. High-performance hydraulic valve lifters and springs. Manual transmission lash, limited-travel hydraulic lifters standard on Ram Air IV engine. Large diameter valves—2.11" intake, 1.77" exhaust (1.96" and 1.66" on 2-BBL). Dual exhausts, low-restriction mufflers. Power-Flex fan. Low-restriction air cleaner on 350 and 366. Functional hood scoop and air trap option on Ram Air and Ram Air IV's. High-output cam and springs. 4-bolt main-bearing caps.

Transmissions: *A fully synchro, heavy-duty, 3-speed with Hurst floor shifter is standard. Ratios are 2.42:1, 1.61:1, and 1.00:1.*

Next come two versions of the fully synchronized, aluminum-case 4-speed with Hurst floor shifter: Wide-ratio—2.52:1, 1.88:1, 1.46:1 and 1.00:1. Close-ratio (available only with 3.90:1 and 4.33:1 axle ratios for special driving)—2.20:1, 1.64:1, 1.28:1 and 1.00:1.

Then there's our new heavy-duty, 3-speed torque converter Turbo Hydra-matic, its lever mounted on the steering column. Ratios are 2.48:1, 1.48:1 and 1.00:1, with a total torque multiplication at the start of 5.70:1 (5.09:1 with 2-BBL). The governor is set for a maximum automatic upshift at 5000 rpm.

Console will accommodate the shift lever for all floor-shift transmissions when ordered.

Steering: *Recirculating ball bearing steering gear. Standard ratio is 24:1. Power steering is 17.5:1.*

Suspension: *Heavy-duty coil springs have wheel rates of 91 and 110 pounds per inch, front and rear. Diameter of stabilizer bar is 1".*

We'd suggest you try this already heavy-duty standard suspension before you make up your mind about the stiffer shock absorbers we have available.

Brakes: *Diameter of finned drum is 9.5", with a swept area of 269.2 sq. in. Power front disc brakes are available. Diameter: 11.1"; swept area: 323.6 sq. in.*

Capacities: *The gas tank holds 21.5 gallons. Oil capacity is 5 quarts, 6 with filter. Radiator holds 17.8 quarts.*

Axle Ratios:

Engine	Transmission	Standard Axle Ratio	Special-order Axle Ratios					
265 bhp	automatic only	2.93	2.56	2.78†	3.23			
350 bhp	3- or 4-speed	3.55	3.08	3.23†	3.36*	3.90*	4.33*	
	automatic	3.36	3.23†	3.23	3.55*	3.90*	4.33*	
360 bhp Ram Air	3- or 4-speed	3.55	3.08	3.23†	3.36*	3.90*	4.33*	
	automatic	3.55		3.23†	3.36*	3.90*	4.33*	
366 bhp Ram Air IV	3- or 4-speed	3.90*			4.33*			
	automatic	3.90*			4.33*			

† Standard axle ratio with air conditioning. * Air conditioning not available.

Special 4.11:1 axle ratio is available, dealer-installed, but make sure you order the car with the heavy-duty 3-speed or close-ratio 4-speed and 3.90:1 axle ratio. Certain special-order combinations require extra-cost items such as a heavy-duty radiator, limited-slip differential, special brakes and speedometer gear adapters. Be sure to see your dealer's detailed power train specifications for this information.

The Judge

Total Final Drive Ratios:

Axle Ratios	Wide-ratio 4-speed 1 2.52	2 1.88	3 1.46	4 1.00	Close-ratio 4-speed 1 2.20	2 1.64	3 1.28	4 1.00	MPH per 1000 rpm in high gear
3.08	7.76	5.79	4.50	3.08	N.A.	N.A.	N.A.	N.A.	24.5
3.23	8.14	6.07	4.72	3.23	N.A.	N.A.	N.A.	N.A.	23.4
3.36	8.47	6.32	4.90	3.36	N.A.	N.A.	N.A.	N.A.	22.5
3.55	8.95	6.67	5.18	3.55	N.A.	N.A.	N.A.	N.A.	21.3
3.90	9.83	7.33	5.69	3.90	8.58	6.40	4.99	3.90	19.4
4.11	10.36	7.73	6.00	4.11	9.04	6.74	5.26	4.11	18.4
4.33	10.91	8.14	6.32	4.33	9.53	7.10	5.54	4.33	17.4

Estimated Shipping Weight, lbs.

Model	Engine	Stick	lbs./hp	Auto.	lbs./hp
Hardtop	265 bhp	3525	13.30	3557	13.42
	350 bhp	3515	10.04	3547	10.13
	360 bhp & Ram Air IV	3513	9.76	3547	9.85
Convertible	265 bhp	3579	13.30	3611	13.62
	350 bhp	3569	10.20	3601	10.28
	360 bhp & Ram Air IV	3569	9.91	3601	10.00

One day, you, too, may become Feature Editor of Hot Rod magazine. But you better work hard. Or change your name to Steve Kelly, the guy who presently holds the job and likes it very much. Which includes such joy as being the first to test the newest of Pontiac's Break Away Squad at Ubly Dragway. Listen to what he's got to say after our specially arranged test session.

So here it come. A Pontiac bountifully endowed with red-orange paint, blackened grille, exposed headlights and a spoiler (yep, a spoiler) running more than the full width of the rear deck, and looking every tough inch of it like older brother Billy.

Here come the Judge. The Judge—Pontiac's special version of the car that started it all. A new name, but also a new game that's bound to discourage the performance-minded competition for many months to come.

We first met the Judge at Ubly Dragway, about 100 miles north of Detroit, an attractively remote spot, where one can get familiar with just about anything without the rest of the world looking over one's shoulder. We were impressed with the way this Pontiac newcomer looked. With the way it went.

The Ubly asphalt permitted some great results! Even though this car was absolutely showroom.

All testing was accomplished with the *standard*, 366-hp, 400-

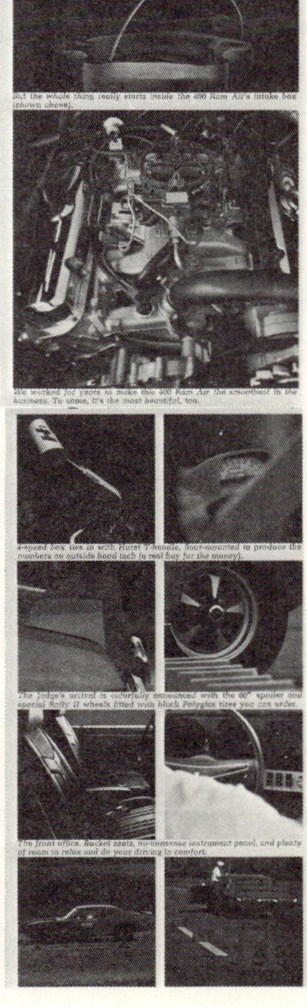

But the whole thing really starts inside the 400 Ram Air's intake box (shown above).

We worked for years to make this 400 Ram Air the smoothest in the business. To some, it's the most beautiful, too.

4-speed box ties in with Hurst T-handle, floor-mounted to produce the numbers on outside hood tach (a real buy for the money).

The Judge's arrival is colorfully announced with the 60" spoiler and special Rally II wheels fitted with black Polyglas tires you can order.

The front office. Bucket seats, no-nonsense instrument panel, and plenty of room to relax and do your driving in comfort.

VEHICLE

Pontiac GTO/The Judge

ENGINE

Cylinders 8
Bore and stroke .... 4.12 x 3.75
Displacement 400
Compression ratio 10.75:1
Horsepower .... 366 @ 5100
Torque .... 445 @ 3600
Valves: Intake .... 2.11 in.
Exhaust .... 1.77 in.
Camshaft:
Lift .... .414 intake, .413 exhaust
Duration ...... 288° intake, 302° exhaust
Carburetion .... 1 4-bbl. Quadra-jet
Exhaust system.. Dual w/low-restriction muffler

TRANSMISSION

Type: Close-ratio 4-speed w/Hurst shifter
Ratios: 1st 2.20:1
2nd 1.64:1
3rd 1.28:1
4th 1.00:1

BRAKES

Type .... Disc, front; Drum, rear
Dimensions: Front .... 11.1 in.
Swept area .... 323.6 sq. in.
Rear .... 9.5 in.
Swept area .... 269.2 sq. in.

SUSPENSION

Front .... Heavy-duty coil
Rear .... Heavy-duty coil
Stabilizer .... 1.00-in. diameter
Tires G78-14
Rims 6-in.-wide
Steering gear:
Type .... Saginaw power
Ratio 17.5:1
Turning circle .... 40.9 ft.
Turns of steering wheel, lock to lock 4.2

DIFFERENTIAL

Type .... Limited Slip
Ring gear diameter .... 8.125 in.
Ratio 3.90:1

DIMENSIONS

Wheelbase .... 112 in.
Front track .... 60 in.
Rear track .... 60 in.
Overall height .... 52.3 in.
Overall width .... 75.8 in.
Overall length .... 201.5 in.
Shipping weight .... 3513 lbs.
Test weight, pre-production car ..... N.A.
Crankcase capacity .... 5 qt.
Cooling system .... 17.8 qt.
Fuel tank .... 21.5 gal.

Some of the equipment illustrated, described in copy or referred to above is available at extra cost. Consult your local Pontiac dealer for availability and costs.

cubic-inch V-8 with Ram Air, attached to a 4-speed box with Hurst arm (the latter two items for your ordering)—a combination which strikes us as the ideal setup.

We're told there's a floor-mounted 3-speed or an automatic job available. But we wouldn't expect the same flexibility or enjoyment inherent in the 4-speed.

So here it is. Pontiac's newest method of putting the competition in deep thought. Customer reaction will play the ultimate role in planning this car's future. But we'll be so bold as to say it won't take very long for the Judge to reach top rating. And if the popularity of the new breed of performance car starts to slide, this one will be there until the very last.

Remember that name—the Judge.

1969 THE JUDGE

boasts these performance features:

- Functional, Driver-controlled, Air-intake Scoops on Hood
- Quadrajet Carb
- Hurst "T" Handle Stick Shift
- Chromed Rocker Arm Covers, Oil Filler Cap and Air Cleaner
- Free-flowing Dual Exhausts
- Full-width Rear Deck Airfoil
- Heavy-duty Springs and Shocks
- Heavy-rated Stabilizer Bar
- Variable-pitch 5-Blade Fan
- Dechromed Safety Rim Rally II Wheels
- G70—14 Wide-tread Fiberglass Belted Tires (Black)
- Body Rally Stripes
- 400-cu.-in. Ram Air V-8

performance and convenience options:

- 4-speed Stick Shift
- Rally Sports Shifter with Turbo Hydra-matic
- Driver-controlled Ram Air IV Package
- Rally Gauge Cluster—Rally Clock
- Hood-mounted Tach
- Custom Sports Steering Wheel
- Small-diameter, Leather-covered Steering Wheel
- Front-wheel Discs, with Power Assist
- G70—14 Redline or Whiteline Tires
- Left-side Power Bucket Seat
- Fast-ratio Power Steering

The Judge standard features:

- Front Buckets or Bench Seat with Folding Center Armrest
- Expanded Morrokide Interior
- Carpeted Lower Door Panels
- Dark Walnut Appearance Instrument Panel Trim
- Stainless Steel Pedal Trim
- "Endura" Front Bumper
- Concealed Windshield Wipers—Pulse Wiper System
- Upper-level Ventilation
- Identification: Ram Air Decal on side of Hood Scoops; "The Judge" on Front Fenders; Three-color Vinyl Stripe on upper edge of Front Fender, Door and Quarter.

GTO—THE JUDGE SPECIFICATIONS

Wheelbase	Tread		Length	Width	Tire Size
	Front	Rear			
112"	61"	60"	201.5"	75.8"	G70—14

standard engine:

400-cu.-in., 366-hp, 4-bbl. Ram Air V-8

available engine:

400-cu.-in., 370-hp, 4-bbl. Ram Air IV V-8

standard transmission:

Heavy-duty 3-speed Manual—Stick Shift

available transmissions:

4-speed Manual—Stick Shift
Turbo Hydra-matic—Column Shift
Turbo Hydra-matic—Stick Shift (with console only)

GTO CONVERTIBLE

GTO

There are leaders. There are followers. And The Great One—Pontiac GTO—is still kingpin. No matter how the Johnny-come-latelys try, they have yet to snatch the reins from our ultimate road car.

Small wonder. With its long hood, lean lines and short deck, it looks like a French curve on wheels. There's the front bumper, too. Made of energy absorbing Endura in the same color as the car.

And GTO handles as if it were an extension of your mind. You want to negotiate a snaky piece of blacktop? It does so. With finesse.

You feel like biting off Lookout Mountain at the knees? It does so. With alacrity.

Sure, there are plenty of reasons why GTO is the master of macadam. Wide-Tracking, to single out but one.

The front tread is 61″ and the rear, 60″. This way, you don't act like a worn squeegee bending into a turn.

Know what else makes GTO the one to reckon with? This page was made for turning.

GTO HARDTOP COUPE

GTO CONVERTIBLE

What else makes GTO The Great One is a 400-cubic-inch V-8 with Quadra-jet carburetor that gives you some 350 horses. If you want to economize on fuel outlay—and that's not to say our standard engine hangs around gas stations a lot—there's a 265-hp version available that does wonders with regular.

GTO sports a fully synchronized, floor-mounted 3-speed with Hurst shifter, dual exhaust system, G78—14 redlines with wide-oval appearance, stiff suspension, buckets or notch-back front bench seat with fold-down center armrest, full instrument panel padding with recessed instrumentation and controls, plus an inlay of walnut-grained vinyl along the panel's lower section.

There's also an option list for GTO that lets you rig yours up like nobody else's business. A 370-hp Ram Air IV engine installation with functional hood air scoops. Hood-mounted tach. Front power disc brakes. Four-speed cogbox. Three-speed Turbo Hydra-matic. Mag-type Rally II wheels. Stereo tape system and—well, you get the message. What it all shapes up to is: GTO is still The Great One.

GTO

Hardtop Coupe (4237)
Convertible (4267)
Strato Bucket Seats

Expanded Morrokide

Interior	Recommended Exterior Colors
250 BLUE	A, C, D, E, P
252 GOLD	A, B, C, G, H, M, Q, S, Y
254 RED	A, C, N, P, R
256 GREEN	A, B, C, G, H, M, Q, S
257 PARCHMENT	A, B, C, D, E, G, H, K, M N, P, Q, R, S, Y
258 BLACK	A, B, C, D, E, G, H, K, M N, P, Q, R, S, Y

Hardtop Coupe (4237)
Convertible (4267)
Notch Back Front Seat with Center Armrest

Expanded Morrokide

Interior	Recommended Exterior Colors
267 PARCHMENT	A, B, C, D, E, G, H, K, M N, P, Q, R, S, Y
268 BLACK	A, B, C, D, E, G, H, K, M N, P, Q, R, S, Y

††A Starlight Black Two-tone Combinations C, D, H, P

††B Expresso Brown Two-tone Combinations A*, C* *(*Upper only)*

C Cameo White Two-tone Combinations A, D, E, G, K, P

D Warwick Blue Two-tone Combinations A, C, E

E Liberty Blue Two-tone Combinations A*, C, D *(*Upper only)*

G Antique Gold Two-tone Combinations A*, C *(*Upper only)*

H Limelight Green Two-tone Combinations A, C*, M *(*Upper only)*

K Crystal Turquoise Two-tone Combinations A*, C *(*Upper only)*

M Midnight Green Two-tone Combinations A*, C*, H *(*Upper only)*

N Burgundy Two-tone Combinations A*, C* *(*Upper only)*

P Palladium Silver Two-tone Combinations A, C

Q Verdoro Green Two-tone Combinations A*, C* *(*Upper only)*

R Matador Red Two-tone Combinations A*, C *(*Upper only)*

S Champagne Two-tone Combinations A*, C* *(*Upper only)*

††Y Mayfair Maize Two-tone Combinations A*, C* *(*Upper only)*

††Not available Firebird except at additional cost and Special Order

1969 Convertible Top Usage Chart

Firebird (2367), Custom S (3567), LeMans (3767), GTO (4267), Catalina (5267) and Bonneville (6267).

Top Color Code Number: 1 Ivory-White 2 Black 3 Dark Blue 9 Dark Green

Black Interior Trim Numbers: 208‡, 218‡, 248, 258, 268, 538, 239, 568, 539, 569

A—1,2	M—1,2,9
B—1,2	N—1,2
C—1,2	P—1,2
D—1,2,3	Q—1,2,9
E—1,2,3	R—1,2
‡F—1,2,3	S—1,2
G—1,2	‡T—1,2
H—1,2,9	‡W—1,2
K—1,2	Y—1,2

Parchment Interior Trim Numbers: 207‡, 217‡, 257, 267, 567

A—1,2	M—1,2,9
B—1,2	N—1,2
C—1,2	P—1,2
D—1,2,3	Q—1,2,9
E—1,2,3	R—1,2
‡F—1,2,3	S—1,2
G—1,2	‡T—1,2
H—1,2,9	‡W—1,2
K—1,2	Y—1,2

Blue Interior Trim Numbers: 200‡, 210‡, 241, 250, 531, 560

A—1,2,3	E—1,2,3
C—1,2,3	‡F—1,2,3
D—1,2,3	P—1,2

Red Interior Trim Numbers: 214‡, 254, 534, 564

A—1,2	P—1,2
C—1,2	R—1,2
N—1,2	‡T—1,2

Green Interior Trim Numbers: 206‡, 216‡, 256, 566

A—1,2	M—1,2,9
B—1,2	S—1,2
C—1,2	Q—1,2,9
G—1,2	
H—1,2,9	

Gold Interior Trim Numbers: 202‡, 212‡, 252, 293‡, 532, 563

A—1,2	M—1,2,9
B—1,2	Q—1,2,9
C—1,2	S—1,2
G—1,2	‡W—1,2
H—1,2,9	Y—1,2

‡Firebird only.

Cordova Top Options. Vinyl coated, fabric roof covering in a "grain" texture in (2) Black, (3) Dark Blue, (5) Parchment, (8) Dark Fawn and (9) Dark Green, available on all models except Custom S and LeMans Safari Station Wagons. Decor Option required on Tempest, Custom S and Catalina Series.

1970

1970

Pontiac had a bad year in 1970 as production fell by a couple hundred thousand units and third place in sales was lost for the first time since 1961. The GTO didn't do so well, either. The performance car market was really in a tailspin now, and GTO production fell by almost 45% over the already depressed 1969 level. Production was less than half what it had been in 1968.

All Pontiac intermediates received a face lift in 1970. The sheet metal was new, even if the basic body and chassis was not. The front end received a snub-nosed grille that was a cross between the Firebird and the 1969 Grand Prix. The tail light treatment was very much like that on the 1968 Grand Prix. The cars looked like Pontiacs, and they were pleasant enough, but just didn't seem to do much for the buyers. The GTO still sported a unique Endura front bumper, but the concealed headlights were gone and the rear end treatment was scarcely altered from the other intermediates. Mechanically, the economy V-8 was discarded and there was a new 455 cubic inch, 360 horsepower engine available. The other 1969 powerplants returned with reduced compression ratios.

Prices were up again, although not by much. The standard GTO Hardtop Coupe now listed for $3,267. The Convertible listed for $3,492.

Production dropped to 40,149 units. The Hardtop Coupe accounted for 32,737 of these, the Convertible for 3,615, the Judge Hardtop Coupe for 3,629 and the Judge Convertible for 168.

The literature repeated familiar patterns for 1970, except that there was no separate Judge card. The GTO section from the main catalogue is featured on pages 56-57. The GTO section in the color and trim brochure is reproduced on page 58. A gorgeous 32 page high performance cars catalogue was also issued. There was no specific GTO section in it as in years past. Rather, all high performance models were covered on all pages, feature by feature. It made for an impressive catalogue, but one that is prohibitively expensive to reproduce. The cover appears below.

GTO

The Humbler's here. Wielding a tough new Endura snout. Rumbling through a split dual exhaust. Just sitting there, it's a mind-bender.

But the 1970 GTO really earns its new nickname on the road. Try the beefed-up suspension on a few curves and you'll see what those new stabilizer bars and firmer shocks are for.

The Humbler's even better at putting down long straightaways. It cranks 350 horses out of the standard 400 V-8. For stunting an interstate's ego, order the 366-horsepower Ram Air or 370-horsepower Ram Air IV. Specify a wide- or close-ratio 4-speed cogbox. Then go by-by.

So now you've got this tough, tough car. But you want to hang on an air conditioner. And lots of other available stuff like variable-ratio power steering and power front disc brakes. Good-bye performance? Not if you order our compensator V-8. 455 cubes. 360-horsepower. It puts out incredible torque while barely turning over.

Inside, you really start to get that GTO feeling, without even touching the key. For one thing, those buckets make most so-called, sporty car seating arrangements resemble so many park benches. And the padded and vinyl-trimmed instrument panel has a deeply recessed array of dials that know how to talk your language.

While you're taking it all in, try the air scoop handle. It controls the flow of outside air to either of the Ram Air engines. That way it's up to you whether those two bulges on the hood mean business or not.

That third bulge is a tach you can get, by making the right marks on the order form. You can also specify it inside instead of a clock, if you're more interested in rpm's than the time of day.

But enough of this talk. Where's the nearest mountain road?

This quiet little beauty, to begin with, is a GTO. And you know what that means. (If you don't, you just flunked your speed-reading course. Go back four pages.) But it's a very special GTO—The Judge. Just about the wildest looking package ever to hit the street.

The list of standard equipment reads like a performance catalog. 366-horsepower, Ram Air V-8. 3-speed, heavy-duty transmission. Hurst shifter with a T-handle. Get the idea? We've taken every choice piece of gear we could get, including Rally II wheels wrapped in fiberglass-belted blackwalls, and laid it all on The Judge.

We've also done a little modifying here and there. Blacked out the grille. Put on an airfoil and a front air dam. Even used wild stripes that almost glow, so nobody will miss you.

Just in case kibitzers still don't get the message, there are "The Judge" decals liberally displayed. Fair warning to armchair enthusiasts, jalopy jockeys and other would-be performance cars. All rise for The Judge! (After a few moments of respectful silence, you may turn the page.)

Standard Engine	Available Transmissions	Standard Axle Ratios	Available Axle Ratios (1)
V-8—400 cu. in. 4-bbl, 350 hp Torque: 445 lb. ft. Compression ratio: 10.25:1 Premium fuel	3-speed (standard) 4-speed (wide-ratio) 4-speed (close-ratio) Turbo Hydra-matic	3.55:1 3.23:1 (2)	3.23:1 3.08:1 (3) 3.90:1 (3, 4) 4.33:1 (3, 4)
Available Engines			
V-8—455 cu. in. (5) 4-bbl, 360 hp Torque: 500 lb. ft. Compression ratio: 10.25:1 Premium fuel	3-speed 4-speed (close-ratio)	3.31:1	3.55:1 (3)
	Turbo Hydra-matic	3.07:1	3.31:1 (3)
V-8—400 cu. in. Ram Air 366 hp Torque: 445 lb. ft. Compression ratio: 10.5:1 Premium fuel	3-speed 4-speed (wide-ratio) 4-speed (close-ratio) Turbo Hydra-matic	3.55:1 3.23:1 (2)	3.90:1 (3, 4) 4.33:1 (3, 4)
V-8—400 cu. in. Ram Air IV 370 hp Torque: 445 lb. ft. Compression ratio: 10.5:1 Premium fuel	4-speed (close-ratio) Turbo Hydra-matic	3.90:1 (4)	4.33:1 (3, 4)

(1) Special ratios for trailer hauling also available (2) Standard with air conditioning (3) Special order (4) Not available with air conditioning. Close-ratio 4-speed only (5) Not available with "The Judge"

Dimensions	Hardtop Coupe	Convertible
Wheelbase	112"	112"
Overall Length	202.9"	202.9"
Overall Width	76.7"	76.7"
Front Tread	61"	61"
Rear Tread	60"	60"
Overall Height	52.0"	52.3"
Front Seat Leg Room (1)	42.4"	42.4"
Rear Seat Leg Room (2)	31.9"	31.9"
Front Head Room (3)	37.7"	38.5"
Rear Head Room (3)	36.3"	36.9"

(1) Maximum effective (2) Minimum effective (3) Seat depressed

1970 Convertible Top Usage Chart

Pontiac Convertibles available: LeMans Sport (3767), GTO (4267), Catalina (5267) and Bonneville (6267).

Top Color Code Number: 1 White 2 Black 5 Sandalwood 7 Dark Gold

Black Interior Trim Numbers: 258, 268, 538, 568

A—1,2	M—1,2,5
B—1,2,5	N—1,2
C—1,2	P—1,2
D—1,2	Q—1,2,5
E—1,2	R—1,2
G—1,2,5,7	Y—1,2,5,7
H—1,2,5	Z—1,2,5,7
K—1,2	

Sandalwood Interior Trim Numbers: 257, 267, 537, 567

A—1,2,5	M—1,2,5
B—1,2,5	N—1,2,5
C—1,2,5	P—1,2
D—1,2	Q—1,2,5
E—1,2	R—1,2
G—1,2,5,7	Y—1,2,5,7
H—1,2,5	Z—1,2,5,7
K—1,2	

Saddle Interior Trim Numbers: 255, 535, 565

A—1,2,5	M—1,2,5
B—1,2,5	N—1,2
C—1,2,5	Q—1,2,5
E—1,2	R—1,2
G—1,2,5,7	Y—1,2,5,7
H—1,2,5	Z—1,2,5,7

Blue Interior Trim Number: 250

A—1,2	E—1,2
C—1,2	P—1,2
D—1,2	

Green Interior Trim Numbers: 256, 536, 566

A—1,2	M—1,2,5
C—1,2	Q—1,2,5
G—1,2,5,7	Y—1,2,5,7
H—1,2,5	Z—1,2,5,7

Red Interior Trim Number: 254

A—1,2	R—1,2
C—1,2	

Brown Interior Trim Number: 563

A—1,2	M—1,2,5
B—1,2,5	N—1,2,5
C—1,2	Q—1,2,5
G—1,2,5,7	Y—1,2,5,7
H—1,2,5	Z—1,2,5,7

Cordova Tops (available at extra cost). Vinyl-coated, fabric roof covering in a "grain" texture in (1) White, (2) Black, (5) Sandalwood, (7) Dark Gold and (9) Dark Green, available on all models except LeMans and LeMans Sport Safari Station Wagons.

Recommended exterior colors with Cordova Tops:

(1) White—**A, B, C, D, E, G, H, K, M, N, P, Q, R, Y, Z**
(2) Black—**A, B, C, D, E, G, H, K, M, N, P, Q, R, Y, Z**
(5) Sandalwood—**A, B, C, G. H, M, N, Q, Y, Z**
(7) Dark Gold—**A, C, G, Y, Z**
(9) Dark Green—**A, C, H, M, Q**

1970 Pontiac Exterior Finishes

Code	Color	Two-tone Combinations
A	Starlight Black	C, D, H, P
B	Palomino Copper	A*, C* (*upper only)
C	Polar White	A, D, E, G, K, P
D	Bermuda Blue	A, C, E
E	Atoll Blue	A*, C, D (*upper only)
G	Baja Gold	A*, C (*upper only)
H	Palisade Green	A, C*, M (*upper only)
K	Mint Turquoise	A*, C (*upper only)
M	Pepper Green	A*, C*, H (*upper only)
N	Burgundy	A*, C* (*upper only)
P	Palladium Silver	A, C
Q	Verdoro Green	A*, C* (*upper only)
R	Cardinal Red	A*, C* (*upper only)
Y	Sierra Yellow	A*, C* (*upper only)
Z	Granada Gold	A*, C* (*upper only)

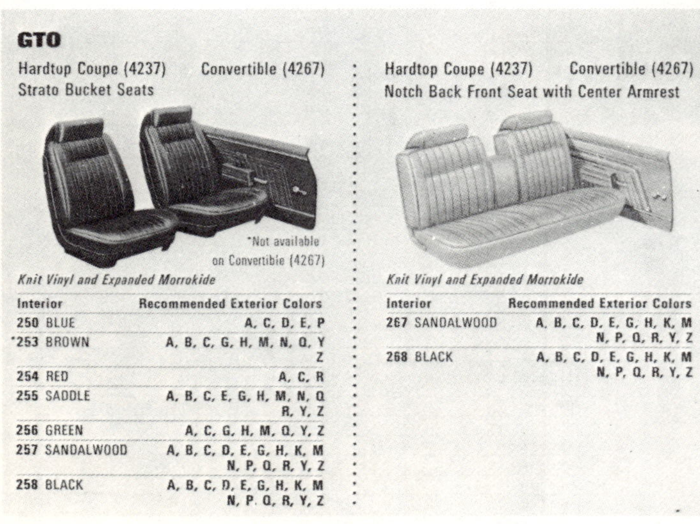

GTO

Hardtop Coupe (4237) Convertible (4267)
Strato Bucket Seats

*Not available on Convertible (4267)

Knit Vinyl and Expanded Morrokide

Interior	Recommended Exterior Colors
250 BLUE	A, C, D, E, P
*253 BROWN	A, B, C, G, H, M, N, Q, Y, Z
254 RED	A, C, R
255 SADDLE	A, B, C, E, G, H, M, N, Q, R, Y, Z
256 GREEN	A, C, G, H, M, Q, Y, Z
257 SANDALWOOD	A, B, C, D, E, G, H, K, M, N, P, Q, R, Y, Z
258 BLACK	A, B, C, D, E, G, H, K, M, N, P, Q, R, Y, Z

Hardtop Coupe (4237) Convertible (4267)
Notch Back Front Seat with Center Armrest

Knit Vinyl and Expanded Morrokide

Interior	Recommended Exterior Colors
267 SANDALWOOD	A, B, C, D, E, G, H, K, M, N, P, Q, R, Y, Z
268 BLACK	A, B, C, D, E, G, H, K, M, N, P, Q, R, Y, Z

1971

Total Pontiac production fell to the lowest level in years in 1971 and the GTO suffered even more than the rest of the line. GTO production fell by 74% from the already miserable 1970 figure.

The appearance of the GTO was little changed from 1970 except for the grille and bumper, which were restyled. There was significant mechanical news, however, as the Ram Air engine options were deleted, and the other powerplants were revised. The standard engine was now a 400 cubic inch V-8 rated at only 300 horsepower. Two 455 V-8s were optional at horsepower ratings of 325 and 335.

Prices were up to $3,446 for the Hardtop Coupe and $3,676 for the Convertible. Production fell to 10,532 for all models. The Hardtop Coupe was still the most popular model, such as it was, as 9,497 units were built. The Convertible accounted for only 661 units, the Judge Hardtop Coupe accounted for only 357 units and the Judge Convertible, the rarest GTO of all, accounted for a piddling 17 units.

The literature followed traditional formats. The GTO section of the main catalogue is reproduced on pages 63-65, the GTO section of the high performance cars catalogue is reproduced on pages 60-62, and the color and trim section appears on page 66.

Shown above: GTO Convertible with standard knit vinyl and expanded Morrokide upholstery in Sandalwood.

The GTO

It was back in 1964 when it all began. Out of a shop in Pontiac, Michigan, swaggered a car with a slightly ungainly name . . . and a legend to build.

Gran Turismo Omologato. The ultimate American road car.

What made the GTO right then is what makes it right now. Power. Handling. Comfort. The totality of the vehicle.

Power translates as engines. Standard is a 400-CID V-8 delivering 300 gross horsepower (255 net).†

There's also an available 455-CID V-8 that develops 325 gross horsepower (260 net). And the biggest news for 1971. A new Pontiac engine. The 455 H.O. LS5.

The new LS5 has cylinder heads with 2.18" x 1.15" intake ports (less radiused corners). A big combustion chamber. And 1.76" diameter exhaust ports for quicker purging of the combustion chamber.

A lightweight aluminum intake manifold has smoother surfaces for better fuel flow. And aluminum gives the manifold a more uniform temperature; radiates heat rapidly to stay cooler.

Our high-lift, long-duration 068 camshaft was tailored by computer for the exact specs of the LS5. It's ground to a tolerance of one-millionth of an inch.

The LS5's standard hydraulic valve lifters are quieter than solids. And never need adjustment. Crankshaft bearing caps with four bolts on the mains give the LS5 the best strength-to-weight ratio in the business.

One final item on the LS5 that

†Gross horsepower/torque figures represent maximum output of the bare engine *without* fan, air cleaner or exhaust system *before* engine is installed. Net figures are derived from engine after installation in the

helps produce 335 gross horsepower (310 net): We made an extra cut in the combustion chamber. To unshroud the intake valves. This allows air to flow from the valve into the combustion chamber with less restriction.

Installed performance of the LS5 is better than any Pontiac engine in history. Both bottom and top ends.

All of which is a little astounding when you consider that the LS5, like every '71 Pontiac engine, has a relatively low compression ratio to allow the use of low-lead or unleaded gas. And, as you know, lowering the compression ratio lowers the general performance curve of an engine.

The key to this seemingly paradoxical situation is what our engineers call "tractive force."

You see, what comes out of the crankshaft is only one function of a car's performance. Even on the straightaway, a car's performance is determined by the net result of all its drive-train components. And that's what tractive force is. The force exerted by the turning of the drive wheels.

To keep the tractive force of every Pontiac up to snuff, we've lowered the axle ratios, which multiplies the lowered engine torque and results in a tractive force as good as, or better than, last year's cars equipped with higher compression engines.

Because of the lower compression, Pontiac's '71 engines should require tuning less often. And since low-lead fuel is usually less expensive than premium, you should save money every time you fill it up.

Order the LS5, and you can make GTO's new scoops scoop. Last year's scoops were efficient, but this year's are more so. They're longer. And they open in the high-pressure area just above GTO's tough Endura bumper. So they're able to ram colder, denser air to the waiting 4-bbl. carb. Screened openings and baffles with drains to trap rain and snow eliminate the need for manually operated inlet doors.

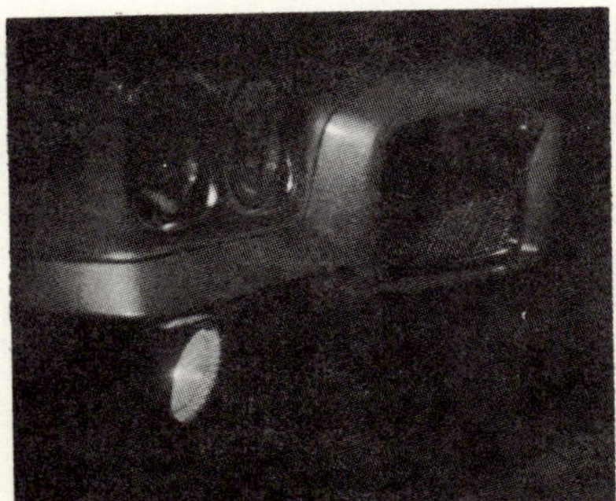

Transmissions are pretty important to tractive force, too. And, as usual, GTO has the best.

Standard is a heavy-duty Muncie 3-speed with a floor-mounted Hurst shifter. You can order close-or wide-ratio Hurst-shifted Muncie 4-speeds. Or the Turbo Hydra-matic that's available.

Since we claim the GTO is the ultimate road car, maybe we should explain exactly how it handles a road.

The suspension includes high-rate coil springs. Heavy-duty shocks. A 1.125" stabilizer bar in the front. A .875" bar in the rear. So it can handle any road. Without a rock-hard ride.

While we're on the suspension. Pontiac would like to introduce a new automotive term. Ridge-nibble. Some wry engineering-type thought it up. Just so we could tell you GTO isn't bothered by it.

Ridge-nibble happens when one of your front tires is running right on the edge of two pavement surfaces of different heights. The tire can't decide whether to drop down to the lower level . . . or climb up to the higher one. So it does neither. And both. It just sort of waddles back and forth between the two.

GTO's front suspension geometry is now designed to overcome this problem and make the car go exactly where you point it. Not off in some direction of its own. For proof, just try to nibble a ridge sometime. Or go through a turn. GTO has a way of Wide-Tracking around it like the car was locked in a slot.

If you drive where tight turns and severe braking are commonplace, we highly recommend the available front disc brakes. They're outstanding because they stay drier when you run in the wet. And they're great if you get on them a lot.

Of course, if you're primarily a straight-ahead driver, you'll appreciate the fact that GTO comes standard with drum brakes. The no-drag factor makes them great for straight lines.

Now some people have a notion that a tough car has to be tough to ride in. We scoff. Remember, we promised a total car and two-thirds of our name is Grand Touring. So you have a right to expect nothing less.

GTO's bucket seats are upholstered in knit vinyl and expanded Morrokide. They breathe. No goose bumps in the winter—or heat rash in the summer.

You get nylon-blend carpeting. Castillian leather textured vinyl and engine-turned aluminum accents on the vinyl-covered instrument panel.

Hood and instrument panel tachs, clocks, sound systems and a whole array of instruments are also available for your GTO.

But no matter how you order it, you'll know something very right is happening every time you take it out. Totality. That's why GTO is the ultimate American road car. It's Pure Pontiac!

The Judge

In spite of its name, we just can't see many parental types gently nudging The Judge into their parking spots at work.

Subtle it's not. It comes in some of the keenest colors this side of a light show. And with some equally keen features.

First of all, it's a GTO. Which is a nice place for any car to begin. But The Judge is a very special GTO.

The 455-CID H.O. LS5 engine is standard. With functional hood Ram

Air. And a heavy-duty Muncie 3-speed transmission with a floor-mounted Tee-handle Hurst shifter.

Outside, special Rally II wheels are tucked inside G70—14 bias-belted, white-lettered tires. There's a 60" fiberglass rear-deck airfoil. Big Judge decals. And body striping that'd put a first sergeant to shame.

The Judge. If anybody asks how you ever came up with a car like that, tell him it happened with a little help from your friends. At Pontiac.

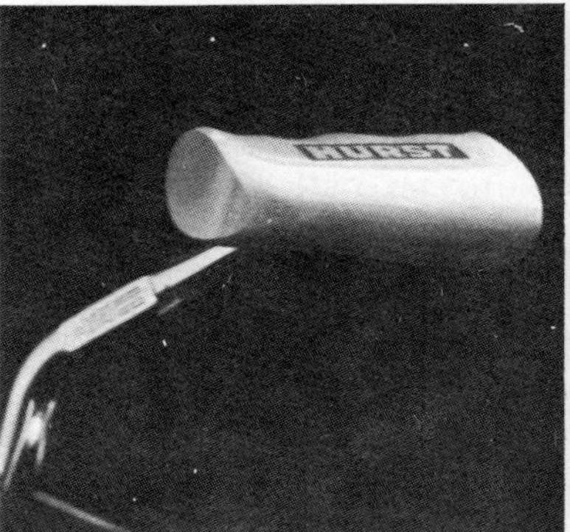

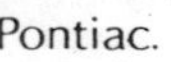

GTO

Engine—Transmission—Chassis—Tires
400-CID, 4-bbl. V-8 • Power-Flex fan • dual exhausts with extensions through valance panel • 3-speed heavy-duty manual transmission with floor shifter • 1⅛" front stabilizer bar • ⅞" rear stabilizer bar • high-rate springs and shocks • G70—14 bias-belted tires.

Interior
Knit vinyl front bucket seats or notch-back bench seat • nylon-blend loop-pile carpet • safety rear armrests with ash-trays • pedal trim plates • ashtray and glove box lamps • courtesy lamps (convertible) • 3-spoke custom cushion steering wheel • engine-turned aluminum instrument panel.

Exterior
Dual-speed parallel-action concealed windshield wipers • hood rear-edge moldings • roof drip moldings (hardtop only) • rocker panel moldings • exclusive front end with Endura front bumper • special hood with forward-mounted simulated air-intake scoops • GTO identification.

THE JUDGE

Engine—Transmission—Chassis—Tires
455-CID, 4-bbl. H.O. V-8 • functional hood Ram Air • Power-Flex fan • dual exhausts with extensions through valance panel • 3-speed heavy-duty manual transmission with Hurst Tee-handle floor shifter • 1⅛" front stabilizer bar • ⅞" rear stabilizer bar • high-rate springs and shocks • G70—14 bias-belted, white-lettered tires.

Interior
Knit vinyl front bucket seats or notch-back bench seat • nylon-blend loop-pile carpet • safety rear armrests with ash-trays • pedal trim plates • ashtray and glove box lamps • 3-spoke deluxe steering wheel • engine-turned aluminum instrument panel • The Judge emblem on glove box door.

Exterior
Dual-speed parallel-action concealed windshield wipers • hood rear-edge moldings • special Rally II wheels • blacked-out grille • roof drip moldings • Ram Air decals on hood scoops • rocker panel moldings • The Judge stripes and decals • low-gloss black hood air scoop bezels • exclusive front end with Endura front bumper • full-width rear-deck airfoil

Engines	400 V-8 4-bbl.	455 V-8 4-bbl.	455 H.O. V-8 4-bbl.
Standard on	GTO	—	The Judge
Available on	GT-37	GTO, GT-37	GTO, GT-37
Gross Horsepower @ rpm†	300 @ 4800	325 @ 4400	335 @ 4800
Net Horsepower @ rpm†	255 @ 4400	260 @ 4000	310 @ 4400
Gross Torque @ rpm (lb.-ft.)†	400 @ 3600	455 @ 3200	480 @ 3600
Net Torque @ rpm (lb.-ft.)†	340 @ 3200	380 @ 2800	410 @ 3200
Displacement (cu. in.)	400	455	455
Bore and Stroke (in.)	4.12 x 3.75	4.15 x 4.21	4.15 x 4.21
Compression Ratio	8.2:1	8.2:1	8.4:1
Carburetor Barrels (no.)	4	4	4
Carburetor Bore Diameter—Primary	1.38	1.38	1.38
—Secondary	2.25	2.25	2.25
Camshaft Duration, Degrees—Intake	273	273	288
—Exhaust	289	289	302
—Overlap	54	54	63
Camshaft Lift @ Zero Lash Intake	.410 ± .011	.410 ± .011	.410 ± .011
Exhaust	.413 ± .011	.414 ± .011	.413 ± .011
Valve Head Diameter Intake	2.11	2.11	2.11
Exhaust	1.77	1.77	1.77
Exhaust System (type)	Dual	Dual	Dual
Fuel Tank Capacity (gal.)	19	19	19
Cooling System Capacity (qt.)	18.6	17.9	17.9
Crankcase Oil Capacity (qt.)	5	5	5
Spring Rates, (lbs./in.) Deflection—Front	280*	280*	280*
—Rear	122	122	122
Axle Ratios Manual Transmission	3.55:1	N.A.	3.55:1
Turbo Hydra-matic	3.55:1**	3.31:1	3.55:1

*310 with air conditioning on GT-37 **3.23:1 on GT-37

Dimensions	GTO	The Judge	GT-37
Overall Length (in.)	203.3	203.3	202.8
Overall Width (in.)	76.7	76.7	76.7
Overall Height (in.)	52.0	52.0	52.0
Wheelbase (in.)	112.0	112.0	112.0
Track Front/Rear (in.)	61.0/60.0	61.0/60.0	61.0/60.0
Turning Diameter (curb-to-curb, ft.)	37.5	37.5	37.5
Head Room, Front/Rear (in.)	37.7/36.3*	37.7/36.3*	37.9/36.3
Leg Room, Front/Rear (in.)	42.4/31.6	42.4/31.6	42.4/32.2
Shoulder Room, Front/Rear (in.)	58.4/57.0**	58.4/57.0**	58.4/57.0
Hip Room, Front/Rear (in.)	59.7/58.3	59.7/58.3	59.6/58.1
Trunk Capacity (cu. ft.)	14.0***	14.0***	14.6

*38.5/36.9 on convertible **58.4/47.9 on convertible ***10.3 on convertible

'71 GTO

If ever a car were born for the road, it's Pontiac's new GTO. Sure, it's a fine city car too. But get one out where the gophers begin and there's just no way to beat it.

Where else except in GTO would you get a 400-CID V-8, dual exhausts, high-rate springs, thick front and rear stabilizer bars, firm shocks and Wide-Track—all standard?

And if you want a little extra behind that great new Endura front bumper, two new 455-cubic-inch V-8's are available.

Both have four-barrel carburetion. And one can be ordered with a nifty air-induction system that rams air into the carburetor from efficient new forward-mounted hood scoops. It's called Ram Air.

Now you might think these engines would perform like turtles on the low-lead gas they use.

Quite the contrary. In fact, extensive testing has proved they actually outperform their predecessors.

Since not everyone thinks alike about transmissions, we've served up four to choose from. The standard floor-mounted 3-speed. Which is heavy-duty, by the way. Two 4-speeds (close- and wide-ratios). And Turbo Hydra-matic. Check the specifications at the end of this section for engine availability.

Okay, you've got a bunch of car now. But a great road car has to be more. It has to be comfortable—enough, say, to take you through a 500-mile day without grinding off all your nerve endings.

Answer: GTO's interior.

With most vinyl seats, a person contends with the elements. When it's cold, goose bumps. When it's hot, you squirm a lot.

35

GTO HARDTOP COUPE

34

GTO CONVERTIBLE

But GTO has a special knit vinyl in the body-contact areas that actually breathes. No sweat. No frostbite.

GTO's comfort quotient comes from other things, too. The deep wall-to-wall carpet. Thick padding. Upper-level ventilation. It goes on and on.

Maybe you never thought about it before, but the way a car handles has a lot to do with how refreshed—or how beat—you are after X number of hours on the road.

If the wheel is sloppy, you get fatigued trying to keep the car constantly pointed in the right direction. If the steering is too heavy, you plain get armweary. Answer? GTO, of course, with variable-ratio power steering you can order.

On straight turnpikes you get precise handling and a solid feel of the road. But if you're winding up a snaky byway or pulling off often, the steering gets faster the further you turn the wheel.

As you know, comfort can also be a state of mind. Which is precisely why we make a number of intriguing items available to keep you unbored.

If you're an rpm reader, a hood-mounted or dash-mounted tach.

If gauges get you, a special Rally Gauge Cluster with clock.

Radios? AM. AM/FM. AM/FM with FM stereo multiplex. And rear-seat speaker.

Stereo tape player. And on GTO it's conveniently placed in the front of the center console you can specify.

Well, that's it, sports fans. GTO. What are you waiting for?

Standard Engine	Available Transmissions	Standard Axle Ratios	Available Axle Ratios
V-8, 400-cu.-in. 4-bbl. 300 hp. gross* 255 hp. net Compression ratio: 8.2:1	3-speed (heavy-duty, standard)	3.55:1 3.23:1 (1)	3.23:1 (3) 3.55:1 3.90:1 (2,3) 4.33:1 (2,3)
	4-speed (wide-ratio)		
	4-speed (close-ratio)	3.90:1 (3)	4.33:1 (2,3)
	Turbo Hydra-matic	3.55:1 3.23:1 (1)	3.08:1 3.55:1
Available Engines			
V-8, 455-cu.-in. 4-bbl. 325 hp. gross 280 hp. net Compression ratio: 8.2:1	Turbo Hydra-matic	3.31:1 3.07:1 (1)	
V-8, 455-cu.-in. H.O. 4-bbl., 335 hp. gross* 310 hp. net Compression ratio: 8.4:1	3-speed (heavy-duty)	3.55:1 3.31:1 (1)	
	4-speed (close-ratio)	3.55:1 3.31:1 (1)	
	Turbo Hydra-matic	3.55:1 3.07:1 (1)	

(1) Standard with air conditioning (2) Special order (3) Not available with air conditioning
*For an explanation of gross and net figures, see footnote on back cover

Dimensions	Hardtop Coupe	Convertible
Wheelbase	112.0"	112.0"
Overall Length	203.3"	203.3"
Overall Width	76.7"	76.7"
Front Tread	61.0"	61.0"
Rear Tread	60.0"	60.0"
Overall Height	52.0"	52.3"
Front Seat Leg Room (1)	42.4"	42.4"
Rear Seat Leg Room (2)	31.6"	31.6"
Front Head Room (3)	37.7"	38.5"
Rear Head Room (3)	36.3"	36.9"

(1) Maximum effective (2) Minimum effective (3) Seat depressed

THE JUDGE

The '71 Judge

A word of advice to the demure and meek.

Unless you're ready to change your image, pass over this section. What you see here is an extrovert's car. Something for the movers. Our very special GTO—The Judge.

Its credentials are impressive. A hefty 455-CID H.O. V-8 that develops 335 gross horsepower, 310 hp. net.*

An air-induction system that takes in oxygen from those front-mounted scoops and tamps it down the mouth of a big 4-bbl. carburetor.

A T-handle shifter for the heavy-duty 3-speed transmission.

On the outside, The Judge demonstrably reinforces our assertion that it isn't for sensitive types.

Special Rally II mag-type wheels. Blacked-out grille. Wild fender stripes. A full-width rear-deck air spoiler. And some strategically placed good words about our most brazen GTO—"455 H.O." and "The Judge."

*For an explanation of gross and net figures, see footnote on back cover

Standard Engine	Available Transmissions	Standard Axle Ratios
V-8, 455-cu.-in. H.O. 4-bbl., 335 hp. gross* 310 hp. net Compression ratio: 8.4:1	3-speed (heavy-duty, standard)	3.55:1 3.31:1 (1)
	4-speed (close-ratio)	3.55:1 3.31:1 (1)
	Turbo Hydra-matic	3.55:1 3.07:1 (1)

(1) Standard with air conditioning
*For an explanation of gross and net figures, see footnote on back cover

Dimensions. Same as GTO, page 37.

GTO

(Standard)
Hardtop Coupe (4237)
Convertible (4267)

Knit Vinyl and Expanded Morrokide	
261 BLUE	A, C, D, F, P
262 IVORY	A, B, C, D, F, H, L, M, N, P, R, S, T, Y, Z
*263 SADDLE	A, B, C, D, H, L, M, N, P, R, S, T, Y, Z
264 SIENNA	A, B, C, H, S, T, Y, Z
*266 JADE	A, B, C, H, L, M, Y, Z
*267 SANDALWOOD	A, B, C, H, L, M, N, P, R, S, T, Y, Z
269 BLACK	A, B, C, D, F, H, L, M, N, P, R, S, T, Y, Z

**N.A. on Convertible*

GTO

(Standard)
Hardtop Coupe (4237)
Notch Back Bench Seat

Knit Vinyl and Expanded Morrokide	
277 SANDALWOOD	A, B, C, H, L, M, N, P, R, S, T, Y, Z
279 BLACK	A, B, C, D, F, H, L, M, N, P, R, S, T, Y, Z

1971 Pontiac Exterior Finishes

A Starlight Black
Two-tone Combination
C, P, D, H
Available all Models

B Sandalwood
Two-tone Combination
A*, C*
*(*upper only)*
Available all Models

C Cameo White
Two-tone Combination
A, D, H, P, S
Available all Models

D Adriatic Blue
Two-tone Combination
A, C, E
Available all Models

E Regency Blue
Two-tone Combination
A*, C, D
*(*upper only)*
N.A. Firebird, Esprit, Formula, Trans Am, T-37, LeMans, LeMans Sport and GTO

F Lucerne Blue
Two-tone Combination
A*, C*
*(*upper only)*
N.A. Catalina, Safari, Catalina Brougham, Bonneville, Grand Safari, Grand Ville and Grand Prix

G Baja Gold
Two-tone Combination
A*, C
*(*upper only)*
N.A. Firebird, Esprit, Formula, Trans Am, T-37, LeMans, LeMans Sport and GTO

H Limekist Green
Two-tone Combination
A, C, M
Available all Models

K Aquarius Aqua
Two-tone Combination
A*, C*
*(*upper only)*
N.A. on Firebird, Esprit, Formula, Trans Am, T-37, LeMans, LeMans Sport, GTO and Grand Prix

L Tropical Lime
Two-tone Combination
A*, C*
*(*upper only)*
N.A. Catalina, Safari, Catalina Brougham, Bonneville, Grand Safari and Grand Ville

M Laurentian Green
Two-tone Combination
A*, C*, H
*(*upper only)*
Available all Models
N.A. Catalina, Safari, Catalina Brougham, Bonneville, Grand Safari, Grand Ville and Grand Prix

N Rosewood
Two-tone Combination
A*, C*
*(*upper only)*
Available all Models
N.A. Firebird, Esprit, Formula, Trans Am, T-37, LeMans, LeMans Sport and GTO

P Nordic Silver
Two-tone Combination
A, C, V
Available all Models

R Cardinal Red
Two-tone Combination
A*, C*
*(*upper only)*
N.A. Grand Prix
N.A. Catalina, Safari, Catalina Brougham, Bonneville, Grand Safari, Grand Ville and Grand Prix

S Castillian Bronze
Two-tone Combination
A*, B*, C
*(*upper only)*
Available all Models

T Canyon Copper
Two-tone Combination
A*, C*
*(*upper only)*

V Bluestone Gray
Two-tone Combination
C*, P
*(*upper only)*

W Bronzini Gold
Available Grand Prix only

Y Quezal Gold
Two-tone Combination
A*, C*
*(*upper only)*

Z Aztec Gold
Two-tone Combination
A*, C*
*(*upper only)*
Available all Models

1971 Convertible Top Usage Chart

Pontiac Convertibles Available:
LeMans Sport (3767), GTO (4267),
Catalina (5267) and Grand Ville (6867)

Top Color Code Numbers:
1. White 2. Black 5. Sandalwood
9. Dark Green

Black Interiors:
A—1,2 M—1,2,9
B—1,2,5 N—1,2,5
C—1,2 P—1,2
D—1,2 R—1,2
E—1,2 S—1,2,5
F—1,2 T—1,2,5
G—1,2,5 V—1,2
H—1,2,9 Y—1,2
K—1,2 Z—1,2,5
L—1,2,9

Blue Interiors:
A—1,2 F—1,2
C—1,2 P—1,2
D—1,2

Ivory Interiors:
A—1,2 L—1,2,9
B—1,2,5 M—1,2,9
C—1,2 N—1,2,5
D—1,2 P—1,2
E—1,2 R—1,2
F—1,2 S—1,2,5
G—1,2,5 T—1,2,5
H—1,2,9 V—1,2
K—1,2 Y—1,2,5
Z—1,2,5

Saddle Interiors:
A—1,2,5 K—1,2
B—1,2,5 M—1,2,5,9
C—1,2,5 N—1,2,5
D—1,2 P—1,2
E—1,2 R—1,2
G—1,2,5 S—1,2,5
H—1,2,5,9 V—1,2
Z—1,2,5

Sienna Interiors:
A—1,2,5 S—1,2,5
B—1,2,5 T—1,2,5
C—1,2,5 Y—1,2,5
H—1,2 Z—1,2,5

NOTE: All Ivory Interiors Will Feature Black Carpeting, Seat Belts, Instrument Panel, Kick Panels, etc.

1971 Cordova Top Usage Chart

Vinyl-coated, fabric roof covering is available at extra cost in a pebble-grain texture on all models except Trans-Am and LeMans Station Wagons. Roof drip moldings are included if not already standard.

Top Color Code Numbers:
1. White 2. Black 5. Sandalwood
7. Dark Brown 9. Dark Green

Black Interiors:
A—1,2 M—1,2,9
B—1,2,5,7 N—1,2,5,7
C—1,2 P—1,2
D—1,2 R—1,2
E—1,2 S—1,2,5,7
F—1,2 T—1,2,5,7
G—1,2,5,7 V—1,2
H—1,2,9 W—1,2,5,7
K—1,2 Y—1,2,7
L—1,2,9 Z—1,2,5,7

Blue Interiors:
A—1,2 F—1,2
C—1,2 P—1,2
D—1,2 V—1,2
E—1,2

Jade Interiors:
A—1,2,9 L—1,2,9
B—1,2,5,7 M—1,2,5,9
C—1,2,9 Y—1,2
H—1,2,9 Z—1,2,5

Saddle Interiors:
A—1,2 N—1,2,5,7
B—1,2,5,7 P—1,2
C—1,2,5,7 R—1,2
D—1,2 S—1,2,5,7
E—1,2 T—1,2,5,7
G—1,2,5,7 V—1,2
H—1,2,9 W—1,2,5,7
K—1,2 Y—1,2,5,7
L—1,2,9 Z—1,2,5,7
M—1,2,5,9

Sandalwood Interiors:
A—1,2,5 N—1,2,5,7
B—1,2,5,7 P—1,2
C—1,2,5,7 R—1,2
G—1,2,5,7 S—1,2,5,7
H—1,2,9 T—1,2,5,7
K—1,2 V—1,2
L—1,2,9 W—1,2,5,7
M—1,2,5,9 Y—1,2,5,7
Z—1,2,5,7

Sienna Interiors:
A—1,2,5 T—1,2,5,7
B—1,2,5,7 W—1,2,5,7
C—1,2,5,7 Y—1,2,5,7
H—1,2 Z—1,2,5,7
S—1,2,5,7

Ivory Interiors:
A—1,2,5 M—1,2,5,9
B—1,2,5,7 N—1,2,5,7
C—1,2,5,7 P—1,2
D—1,2 R—1,2
E—1,2 S—1,2,5,7
F—1,2 T—1,2,5,7
G—1,2,5,7 V—1,2
H—1,2,9 W—1,2,5,7
K—1,2 Y—1,2,5,7
L—1,2,9 Z—1,2,5,7

1972

The GTO lost a lot in 1972, both literally and figuratively. Most importantly, it ceased to be an independent series, and was reduced once more to being an option on the LeMans or the LeMans Sport. It could be had either as a Hardtop Coupe or as a Coupe, but the Convertible was no longer available. Gone, too, was the Judge. As if to add insult to injury, the distinctive GTO front end was now available as an option on any LeMans or LeMans Sport equipped with a V-8 engine. After all this, it was not surprising that GTO production fell to a record low level.

Styling was not greatly changed for 1972. The only meaningful differences were inside. The basic GTO on the down-graded LeMans body was quite a bit plainer than in years past, although the more traditional LeMans Sport trim could be had, too, at extra cost. Standard and optional engines were essentially the same as in 1971.

The price of the basic LeMans GTO was about 8% below the base price in 1971, and even lower for the Coupe, which had not been available the previous season. The LeMans GTO Coupe listed at $3,066, while the LeMans GTO Hardtop Coupe listed at $3,195. Only 5,807 GTOs were built.

There was no Pontiac high performance cars catalogue after 1971. The relevant section of the main Pontiac catalogue is reproduced on page 68, and the relevant sections of the color and trim brochure are reproduced on pages 69-70.

GTO

You'll be seeing a lot more of this great road car in 1972. Because Pontiac has made the GTO much easier to own. By letting you decide just how grand you want your Gran Turisimo Omologato to be. Here's the plan.

One way we made GTO more affordable. It's now available as a coupe, as well as a hardtop.

We give you a great road engine as standard equipment. A 400-CID, 4-bbl V-8.

However, you may want to order more cubic inches. Such as our 455-CID, 4-bbl V-8 or the 455 H.O. with Ram Air.

Transmissions affect GTO's price, too. We drop in a 3-speed. Not an ordinary 3-speed, you understand. A heavy-duty job. With a Hurst floor shifter. If you want more speeds, you can order a close- or wide-ratio 4-speed. If you want less work, order Turbo Hydra-matic.

We think the interior we give you in the '72 GTO is just right for a road car. Bench seats covered with cloth and Morrokide. Very businesslike. Very comfortable. There are those who prefer bucket seats, however. So buckets are available.

Without certain things, GTO wouldn't be GTO. Things like front and rear stabilizer bars. Firm shocks. G70—14 tires. Hood scoops. A protective Endura bumper.

We've added a few new niceties for '72. Front-fender air extractors. They keep the engine compartment cooler and reduce air-pressure buildup. New performance dual exhausts with side outlets. They help make sure GTO's classic burble is on pitch.

Of course, there also exists a list of items you might want to order. Tach. Gauges. A rear spoiler. New side stripes. It's all there if you want it. But only if you want it.

Affordability, remember?

Standard Engine	Available Transmissions	Standard Axle Ratios	Available Axle Ratios
V-8, 400-cu.-in. 4-bbl. Compression ratio: 8.2:1	3-speed manual (standard)	3.55:1 3.23:1 (1)	3.23:1
	4-speed close-ratio	3.55:1 (2)	
	Turbo Hydra-matic	3.55:1 3.23:1 (1)	3.08:1
Available Engines			
V-8, 455-cu.-in. 4-bbl. Compression ratio: 8.2:1	Turbo Hydra-matic	3.31:1 3.07:1	
V-8, 455-cu.-in. H.O. 4-bbl. Compression ratio: 8.4:1	4-speed close-ratio	3.55:1 3.31:1 (1)	
	Turbo Hydra-matic	3.55:1 3.07:1 (1)	
(1) Standard with air conditioning	(2) Not available with air conditioning		

Dimensions. GTO Hardtop Coupe and Coupe have the same dimensions as LeMans Hardtop Coupe and Coupe, page 39.

GTO HARDTOP COUPE

GTO COUPE

1972 PONTIAC RECOMMENDED TWO-TONE COMPATIBILITY CHART

EXTERIOR COLORS	
LOWER	UPPER
A—Starlight Black	C,N,L
C—Cameo White	A,G,F,J,M,P,U
D—Adriatic Blue	A,C,U
E—Quezal Gold	C
F—Lucerne Blue	C
G—Brittany Beige	A,C,J
H—Shadow Gold	A,C,J

EXTERIOR COLORS	
LOWER	UPPER
J—Brasilia Gold	A,C,H
K—Julep Green	C
L—Springfield Green	A,C,M
M—Wilderness Green	A,C,L
N—Revere Silver	A,P,C
P—Antique Pewter	A,C,N
R—Cardinal Red	A,C

EXTERIOR COLORS	
LOWER	UPPER
S—Anaconda Gold	C
T—Cinnamon Bronze	A,C
U—Cumberland Blue	A,C
V—Spice Beige	A,C
W—Arizona Gold	A,C,J
Y—Monarch Yellow	C
Z—Sundance Orange	C

1972 CONVERTIBLE TOP USAGE CHART

Pontiac Convertibles available: LeMans Sport, Catalina, Grand Ville

Top Color Code Numbers: (1) White, (2) Black, (6) Beige (Covert)

EXTERIOR COLOR CODE	INTERIOR TRIM COLORS									
	BLACK		WHITE		SADDLE		GREEN		PEWTER	BEIGE (Covert)
	LeMans Sport	Catalina & Grand Ville	LeMans Sport	Catalina & Grand Ville	LeMans Sport	Catalina & Grand Ville	LeMans Sport	Grand Ville	LeMans Sport	Grand Ville
A		1,2,6		1,2,6		1,2,6		1,2,6		1,2,6
C	1,2,6	1,2,6	1,2,6	1,2,6	1,2,6	1,2,6	1,2,6	1,2,6	1,2	1,2,6
D		1,2		1,2		1,2				
E	1,2,6		1,2,6		1,2,6					
F	1,2		1,2						1,2	
G	1,2,6	1,2,6	1,2,6	1,2,6	1,2,6	1,2,6	1,2,6	1,2,6		1,2,6
H	1,2,6	1,2,6	1,2,6	1,2,6	1,2,6	1,2,6	1,2,6	1,2,6		1,2,6
J	1,2,6	1,2,6	1,2,6	1,2,6	1,2,6	1,2,6				1,2,6
K	1,2		1,2		1,2					
L	1,2,6	1,2,6	1,2,6	1,2,6	1,2,6	1,2,6	1,2,6	1,2,6		1,2,6
M	1,2,6	1,2,6	1,2,6	1,2,6	1,2,6	1,2,6	1,2,6	1,2,6		1,2,6
N	1,2,6	1,2,6	1,2,6	1,2,6	1,2,6	1,2,6	1,2,6	1,2,6	1,2,	1,2,6
P	1,2,6	1,2,6	1,2,6	1,2,6					1,2	1,2,6
R	1,2	1,2	1,2	1,2	1,2	1,2				1,2
S	1,2		1,2		1,2					
T		1,2,6		1,2,6		1,2,6				1,2,6
U		1,2		1,2		1,2				
V		1,2		1,2		1,2				
W		1,2,6		1,2,6		1,2,6				1,2,6
Y	1,2,6		1,2,6		1,2,6					
Z	1,2,6		1,2,6		1,2,6					

1972 CORDOVA TOP USAGE CHART

Vinyl-coated, fabric roof covering is available at extra cost in the new "wet look" on all models except Trans Am and LeMans Station Wagons. Roof drip moldings are included if not already standard.

Top Color Numbers: (1) White, (2) Black, (4) Pewter, (6) Beige (Covert), (7) Tan

EXTERIOR COLOR CODE	INTERIOR COLORS							
	BLACK	WHITE	BLUE	GREEN	PEWTER	SADDLE	BEIGE (Covert)	TAN
A	1,2,4,7	1,2,4,7	1,2,4	1,2,7	1,2,4	1,2,4,7	1,2,6,7	
C	1,2,4,6	1,2,4,6	1,2,4	1,2,6,7	1,2,4	1,2,6	1,2,6	1,2,6,7
D	1,2,4	1,2,4	1,2,4		1,2,4	1,2,4		
E	1,2,6	1,2,6				1,2,6	1,2,6	1,2,6
F	1,2,4	1,2,4	1,2,4		1,2,4			
G	1,2,6	1,2,6		1,2,6		1,2,6	1,2,6	1,2,6
H	1,2,6	1,2,6		1,2,6		1,2,6	1,2,6	
J	1,2,6	1,2,6				1,2,6	1,2,6	
K	1,2,7	1,2,7				1,2,7	1,2,7	1,2,6,7
L	1,2,6	1,2,6		1,2,6		1,2,6	1,2,6	1,2,6
M	1,2,6,7	1,2,6,7		1,2,6,7		1,2,6,7	1,2,6,7	1,2,6,7

EXTERIOR COLOR CODE	INTERIOR COLORS							
	BLACK	WHITE	BLUE	GREEN	PEWTER	SADDLE	BEIGE (Covert)	TAN
N	1,2,4	1,2,4	1,2,4	1,2,4	1,2,4	1,2,4	1,2,4	
P	1,2,4	1,2,4	1,2,4		1,2,4		1,2,4	
R	1,2	1,2				1,2	1,2	1,2,6
S	1,2,6	1,2,6				1,2,6	1,2,6	1,2,6
T	1,2,6,7	1,2,6,7				1,2,6,7	1,2,6,7	
U	1,2,4	1,2,4	1,2,4		1,2,4	1,2,4		
V	1,2,7	1,2,7				1,2,7		
W	1,2,6	1,2,6				1,2,6	1,2,6	
Y	1,2,6,7	1,2,6,7				1,2,6,7	1,2,6,7	1,2,6,7
Z	1,2,6,7	1,2,6,7				1,2,6,7	1,2,6,7	1,2,6,7

Ventura II Sunroof Option is available in the same *colors* and *usage* as Cordova Tops.

LeMans

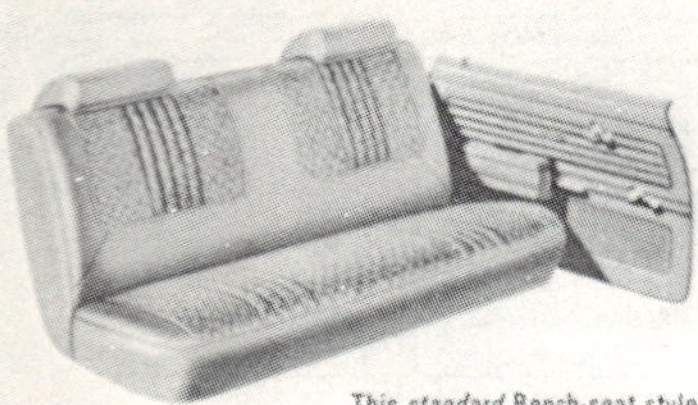

This *standard* Bench-seat style is available in Piccard Pattern Cloth and Madrid Morrokide(1)

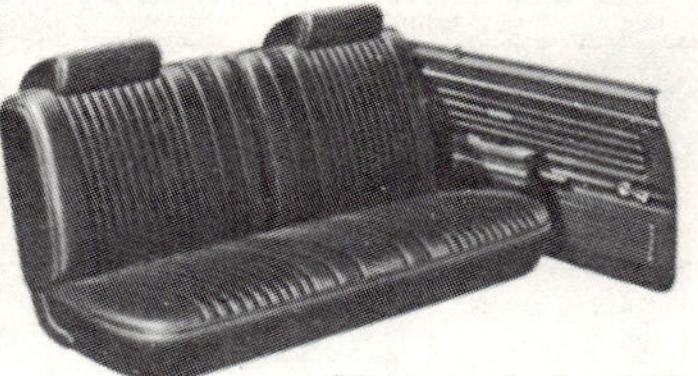

This *extra-cost* Bench-seat style is available in Madrid Morrokide(2)

Style	Material	2-DOOR COUPE, HARDTOP COUPE, 4-DOOR SEDAN	
(1) Bench Seat (standard)	Cloth and Morrokide	**412 Blue, 442 Green, 452 Beige (Covert)**	
(2) Bench Seat (extra cost)	Morrokide	**522 Ivory, 532 Saddle, 542 Green, 562 Black**	
(3) Bench Seat (standard)	Morrokide		

C—CAMEO WHITE
Recommended Interior Colors: Beige (Covert), Black, Blue, Green, Ivory, Pewter, Saddle, Tan

D—ADRIATIC BLUE
Recommended Interior Colors: Black, Blue, Ivory, Pewter, Saddle

E—QUEZAL GOLD
Recommended Interior Colors: Beige (Covert), Black, Ivory, Saddle, Tan

F—LUCERNE BLUE
Recommended Interior Colors: Black, Blue, Ivory, Pewter

G—BRITTANY BEIGE
Recommended Interior Colors: Beige (Covert), Black, Green, Ivory, Saddle, Tan

H—SHADOW GOLD
Recommended Interior Colors: Beige (Covert), Black, Green, Ivory, Saddle, Tan

J—BRASILIA GOLD
Recommended Interior Colors: Beige (Covert), Black, Ivory, Saddle, Tan

L—SPRINGFIELD GREEN
Recommended Interior Colors: Beige (Covert), Black, Green, Ivory, Saddle, Tan

M—WILDERNESS GREEN
Recommended Interior Colors: Beige (Covert), Black, Green, Ivory, Saddle, Tan

N—REVERE SILVER
Recommended Interior Colors: Beige (Covert), Black, Blue, Green, Ivory, Pewter, Saddle

R—CARDINAL RED
Recommended Interior Colors: Beige (Covert), Black, Ivory, Saddle, Tan

S—ANACONDA GOLD
Recommended Interior Colors: Beige (Covert), Black, Ivory, Saddle, Tan

Y—MONARCH YELLOW
Recommended Interior Colors: Beige (Covert), Black, Ivory, Saddle, Tan

Z—SUNDANCE ORANGE
Recommended Interior Colors: Beige (Covert), Black, Ivory, Saddle, Tan

1973

Pontiac produced a record 919.000 cars in 1973, but this success did not extend to the GTO. It was continued as an option on the LeMans and LeMans Sport but now had potent in-house competition from the all-new Pontiac Gran Am series. The Grand Am was designed to be a high performance, European style sports sedan and was available in two and four-door configurations featuring luxury trim shared in large part with the Grand Prix. With all that to contend with it is a wonder they sold as many GTOs as they did.

The Pontiac intermediates were entirely new in 1973. They had dramatic new bodies that were not especially well styled in the opinion of most observers. Front and rear end designs seemed to have little in common other than meeting in the middle. The rear end treatment was particularly offensive to many people. The top and bottom of the car came together at the rear bumper in a pronounced point. This effect was substantially modified with the 1974 models, but of course, by then the intermediate sized GTO was no more.

The 1973 GTO was available as an option on either the LeMans Two-Door Colonnade Hardtop or the LeMans Sport Coupe Two-Door Colonnade Hardtop. The term "hardtop" was a misnomer, since these models had a definite center pillar and rear side windows that did not even retract. The Endura bumper was gone, but new hood scoops were featured. These scoops were among the strangest ever used on a production car, and were also available as an option on the Gran Am with the 455 SD engine. The standard GTO engine was, again, a 400 cubic inch V-8. Two 455 V-8s were optional on GTOs as well as on other LeMans and LeMans Sport Coupe models. The base GTO option listed for $354 with air conditioning and $368 without. The whole GTO concept was clearly in its death throes and only 4,806 were built.

The GTO related sections from the full-line Pontiac catalogue are reproduced on pages 72-73, and the related sections from the color and trim brochure are reproduced on page 74.

LeMans Sport Coupe

Pontiac's sporty new mid-sized car.

Our 2-Door Colonnade Hardtop in Regatta Blue.

Pontiac's been building sporty looking cars for some time. You expect them from the Wide-Track people. And for 1973, we've got a new one. One that's not only sporty looking, but affordable, too. It's the new 1973 LeMans Sport Coupe.

Just seeing it is enough to make you want it sitting in your driveway. What with that great new LeMans styling and those sporty new louvered rear quarter windows.

But you've got to look deeper to get really turned on. To the sharp new interior with loop-pile carpeting. To the notch-back bench seat with pull-down center armrest or bucket seats. To the sporty new instrument panel. To the front disc brakes and 4-wheel, coil-spring suspension. Obviously, we didn't skimp.

But to keep it affordable, we left plenty of decisions up to you. You can add more performance. V-8s up to 455 cubic inches are available. You can add more plush. Air conditioning, AM-FM stereo, tilt steering wheel, whatever. Fact is, more options are available on the Sport Coupe than on any other '73 Wide-Track. Even our legendary GTO is alive and well as an option.

Affordable. And equipped any way you want it. That's what we think a sporty looking car should be. If you agree, there's a 1973 LeMans Sport Coupe waiting.

Dimensions (inches)

Overall length	207.4
Overall width	77.7
Overall height	52.9
Wheelbase	112.0
Track, front/rear	61.5/60.7
Head room, front/rear	37.8/36.9
Leg room, front/rear	42.4/33.7
Shoulder room, front/rear	59.6/57.5
Trunk capacity (cu. ft.)	15.1

Morrokide notch-back bench seat. Shown in blue—also available in white, saddle, black and burgundy.

Standard Engine	Transmissions	Axle Ratios Std.	Axle Ratios Avail.
6-cyl., 250-cu.-in. 1-bbl.	Std: 3-speed Manual	3.23:1	
	Avail: Turbo Hydra-matic	3.08:1	3.23:1
Available Engines			
V-8, 350-cu.-in. 2-bbl.	Std: 3-speed Manual	3.23:1	3.08:1 (1)
	Avail: 3-speed Heavy-duty Manual	3.23:1	3.08:1 (1)
	Avail: 4-speed Manual	3.23:1	3.08:1 (1)
	Avail: Turbo Hydra-matic	2.73:1 (4)	3.08:1
V-8, 400-cu.-in. 2-bbl.	Avail: Turbo Hydra-matic	2.73:1 (2)	3.08:1
V-8, 400-cu.-in. 4-bbl.	Avail: 3-speed Heavy-duty Manual	3.42:1	3.23:1 (1,3)
	Avail: 4-speed Manual	3.42:1	3.23:1 (1,3)
	Avail: Turbo Hydra-matic	3.42:1	3.23:1 (3) 3.08:1 (1)
V-8, 455-cu.-in. 4-bbl.	Avail: Turbo Hydra-matic	3.23:1	3.08:1 (3)
V-8, SD 455-cu.-in. 4-bbl.	Avail: 4-speed Manual	3.42:1	
	Avail: Turbo Hydra-matic	3.42:1	

(1) Economy ratio (2) California 2.93:1 only
(3) Air conditioning (4) California 3.08:1 only

2-Door Colonnade Hardtop in Golden Olive.

LeMans

Pontiac's lowest priced mid-sized car.

LeMans is the lowest priced mid-sized car we Wide-Track people build. But it's so packed with Pontiac quality, it'll take you years to appreciate everything we built into it.

Sure, the new styling's sensational. But LeMans' sound design includes things far more substantial. Like a strong new frame for a better tuned ride. Effective new sound insulation. Improved body mounts to help keep that new car ride. A new improved front bumper system. The kinds of things that satisfy long after the new car smell is gone.

The seats are handsomely upholstered. But beneath the beauty are thick foam cushions with springs molded inside. They'll stay comfortable. The thick nylon-blend, loop-pile carpeting will take years of wear, too.

The standard 250-cu.-in. engine and 3-speed transmission are rugged units designed for dependable operation.

Now, LeMans comes pretty well equipped. But that doesn't mean you can't add more. The list of available gear is very complete.

For example. You can turn LeMans into Pontiac's legendary GTO. Just by ordering the GTO package. You get a scooped hood, blacked-out grille, firm suspension, wide tires and a lot of performance.

1973 LeMans. It's nice to know that a car with so much going for it is so affordable. Because we have a way with cars.

Dimensions (inches)	2-Dr.	4-Dr.
Overall length	207.4	211.4
Overall width	77.7	77.7
Overall height	52.9	54.3
Wheelbase	112.0	116.0
Track, front/rear	61.5/60.7	61.5/60.7
Head room, front/rear	37.8/36.9	38.5/37.2
Leg room, front/rear	42.4/33.7	42.4/38.4
Shoulder room, front/rear	59.6/57.5	59.6/58.9
Trunk capacity (cu. ft.)	15.1	15.1

Our 4-Door Colonnade Hardtop in Florentine Red.

Morrokide upholstered split bench seat. Shown in saddle—also available in blue and black.

Standard Engine	Transmissions	Axle Ratios Std.	Axle Ratios Avail.
6-cyl., 250-cu.-in. 1-bbl.	Std.: 3-speed Manual	3.23:1	
	Avail.: Turbo Hydra-matic	3.08:1	3.23:1
Available Engines			
V-8, 350-cu.-in. 2-bbl.	Std.: 3-speed Manual	3.23:1	3.08:1 (1)
	Avail.: 3-speed Heavy-duty Manual	3.23:1	3.08:1 (1)
	Avail.: 4-speed Manual	3.23:1	3.08:1 (1)
	Avail.: Turbo Hydra-matic	2.73:1 (4)	3.08:1
V-8, 400-cu.-in. 2-bbl.	Avail.: Turbo Hydra-matic	2.73:1 (2)	3.08:1
V-8, 400-cu.-in. 4-bbl.	Avail.: 3-speed Heavy-duty Manual	3.42:1	3.23:1 (1,3)
	Avail.: 4-speed Manual	3.42:1	3.23:1 (1,3)
	Avail.: Turbo Hydra-matic	3.42:1	3.23:1 (3) 3.08:1 (1)
V-8, 455-cu.-in. 4-bbl.	Avail.: Turbo Hydra-matic	3.23:1	3.08:1 (3)
V-8, SD 455-cu.-in. 4-bbl. (2-dr. only)	Avail.: 4-speed Manual	3.42:1	
	Avail.: Turbo Hydra-matic	3.42:1	

(1) Economy ratio (2) California 2.93:1 only
(3) Air conditioning (4) California 3.08:1 only

LeMans 2-Door Colonnade Hardtop in Porcelain Blue.

LeMans 2-Door Colonnade Hardtop with available GTO package in Ascot Silver.

Shown on the cars on these pages are some of the options and accessories offered by Pontiac at extra cost.

LEMANS SPORT COUPE
(Standard and Available at No Extra-cost Interiors)

NOTCHBACK BENCH SEAT
Caribou and Madrid Morrokides

STANDARD—ALL MORROKIDE		
Models	Interior Trims	Exterior Colors
2-DR. COLONNADE H.T.	515 (BLUE)	A, C, D, E, F
	525 (WHITE)	A, C, D, E, F, G, H, J, K, L, M, S, V, W, Y, Z
	535 (SADDLE)	A, C, G, H, J, L, M, V, W, Y, Z
	565 (BLACK)	A, C, D, E, F, G, H, J, K, L, M, S, V, W, Y, Z
	575 (BURGUNDY)	A, C, E, S, V

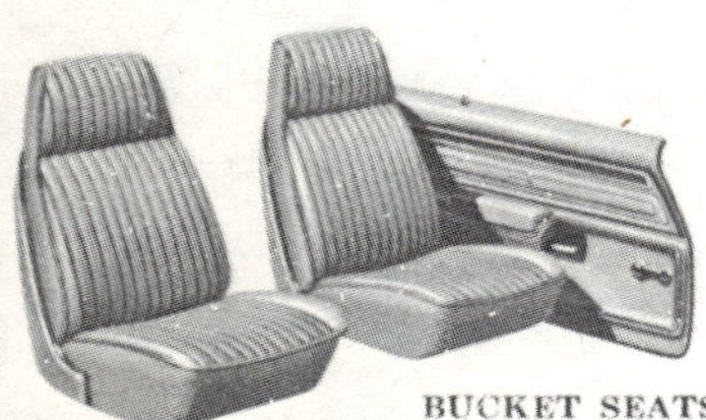

BUCKET SEATS (Available)
Caribou and Madrid Morrokides

AVAILABLE—ALL MORROKIDE		
Models	Interior Trims	Exterior Colors
2-DR. COLONNADE H.T.	511 (BLUE)	A, C, D, E, F
	521 (WHITE)	A, C, D, E, F, G, H, J, K, L, M, S, V, W, Y, Z
	531 (SADDLE)	A, C, G, H, J, L, M, V, W, Y, Z
	561 (BLACK)	A, C, D, E, F, G, H, J, K, L, M, S, V, W, Y, Z
	571 (BURGUNDY)	A, C, E, S, V
	581 (CHAMOIS)	A, C, G, H, J

LEMANS (Standard and Extra-cost Interiors)

FULL BENCH SEAT
Pingree Cloth and Madrid Morrokide or Oxen and Madrid Morrokides

STANDARD—CLOTH AND MORROKIDE		
Models	Interior Trims	Exterior Colors
4-DR. COLONNADE H.T.	612 (BLUE)	A, C, D, E, F
	642 (GREEN)	A, C, G, K, L, M
	652 (BEIGE)	A, C, E, G, H, J, K, L, M, S, V, W, Y, Z
EXTRA COST—ALL MORROKIDE		
4-DR. COLONNADE H.T.	732 (SADDLE)	A, C, G, H, J, L, M, V, W, Y, Z
	742 (GREEN)	A, C, G, K, L, M
	752 (BEIGE)	A, C, E, G, H, J, K, L, M, S, V, W, Y, Z

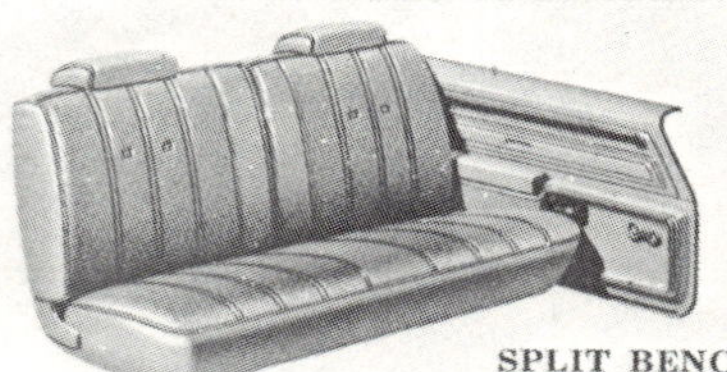

SPLIT BENCH SEAT
Pingree Cloth and Madrid Morrokide or Oxen and Madrid Morrokides

STANDARD—CLOTH AND MORROKIDE		
Models	Interior Trims	Exterior Colors
2-DR. COLONNADE H.T.	642 (GREEN)	A, C, G, K, L, M
	652 (BEIGE)	A, C, E, G, H, J, K, L, M, S, V, W, Y, Z
EXTRA COST—ALL MORROKIDE		
2-DR. COLONNADE H.T.	712 (BLUE)	A, C, D, E, F
	722 (WHITE)	A, C, D, E, F, G, H, J, K, L, M, S, V, W, Y, Z
	732 (SADDLE)	A, C, G, H, J, L, M, V, W, Y, Z
	762 (BLACK)	A, C, D, E, F, G, H, J, K, L, M, S, V, W, Y, Z

COLOR USAGE CHARTS

1973 CORDOVA TOP USAGE CHART

Available at extra cost is vinyl-coated fabric roof covering in "wet look" appearance on all models except Trans Am and LeMans Safaris. Bright roof drip moldings are included if not already standard.

EXTERIOR COLORS	CORDOVA TOP COLORS						
	(1) White	(2) Black	(3) Beige	(4) Chamois	(5) Green	(6) Dark Burgundy	(7) Blue
R—Buccaneer Red	X	X					
T—Sunlight Yellow	X	X					
U—Navajo Orange	X	X	X	X			
C—Cameo White	X	X	X	X	X	X	X
D—Porcelain Blue	X	X					X
E—Admiralty Blue	X	X					X
F—Regatta Blue	X	X					X
H—Desert Sand	X	X	X	X			
J—Golden Olive	X	X	X				
K—Verdant Green	X	X	X				
L—Slate Green	X	X	X		X		
M—Brewster Green	X	X	X		X		
S—Florentine Red	X	X	X			X	
V—Ascot Silver	X	X	X			X	
Y—Valencia Gold	X	X	X	X			
Z—Burma Brown	X	X	X				
A—Starlight Black	X	X	X	X		X	
G—Mesa Tan	X	X	X	X			
W—Burnished Umber	X	X	X	X			

1973 PONTIAC RECOMMENDED TWO-TONE COMPATIBILITY CHART

EXTERIOR COLORS	
Lower	Upper
R—Buccaneer Red	C
T—Sunlight Yellow	C
U—Navajo Orange	C
C—Cameo White	A, D, E, H, L, M, S
D—Porcelain Blue	A, C, E
E—Admiralty Blue	A, C, D, V
F—Regatta Blue	A, C, D, E, V
H—Desert Sand	A, C, G
J—Golden Olive	A, C, M

EXTERIOR COLORS	
Lower	Upper
K—Verdant Green	A, C, L, V
L—Slate Green	A, C, M
M—Brewster Green	A, C, L, V
S—Florentine Red	A, C, V
V—Ascot Silver	A, C, M, W
Y—Valencia Gold	A, C
Z—Burma Brown	C, V
A—Starlight Black	C, V
G—Mesa Tan	A, C, H
W—Burnished Umber	C, V

1973 PONTIAC EXTERIOR FINISHES

Available all Pontiac models except Trans Am.

Special note: Trans Am model is available only in—
C—Cameo White
M—Brewster Green
R—Buccaneer Red

C—CAMEO WHITE
Recommended Interior Colors: Black, White, Beige, Saddle, Green, Blue, Burgundy, Chamois

D—PORCELAIN BLUE
Recommended Interior Colors: Black, White, Blue

E—ADMIRALTY BLUE
Recommended Interior Colors: Black, White, Beige, Blue, Burgundy

F—REGATTA BLUE
Recommended Interior Colors: Black, White, Blue, Burgundy

H—DESERT SAND
Recommended Interior Colors: Black, White, Beige, Saddle

J—GOLDEN OLIVE
Recommended Interior Colors: Black, White, Beige, Saddle, Chamois

K—VERDANT GREEN
Recommended Interior Colors: Black, White, Beige, Green

L—SLATE GREEN
Recommended Interior Colors: Black, White, Beige, Saddle, Green

M—BREWSTER GREEN
Recommended Interior Colors: Black, White, Beige, Saddle, Green

S—FLORENTINE RED
Recommended Interior Colors: Black, White, Beige, Burgundy

V—ASCOT SILVER
Recommended Interior Colors: Black, White, Beige, Burgundy, Saddle

Y—VALENCIA GOLD
Recommended Interior Colors: Black, White, Beige, Saddle

Z—BURMA BROWN
Recommended Interior Colors: Black, White, Beige, Saddle

1974

The shriek heard across the country in the fall of 1973 was the sound of GTO enthusiasts upon learning what had happened to the car of their dreams. As if it hadn't been insulting enough to see it down-graded until it was little more than a trim option on the LeMans—for 1974 the GTO became a trim option on the Ventura. To be fair, the division has been getting something of a bum rap for what it did with the GTO in 1974. The GTO had fallen on hard times in terms of public acceptance long before the 1974 models were announced, and Pontiac marketing people genuinely felt that there was an important market developing for compact high performance cars. Ford, Chevrolet, Plymouth and Dodge all had interesting entries in this field by 1973 and seemed to be reaching increasing numbers of buyers. The GTO was supposed to crack the field wide open. It didn't quite do that, although production did rise about 47% over 1973 levels. This figure is all the more respectable when it is considered in the light of the kind of year 1974 was. The Arab Oil Embargo and the recession combined to reduce auto production to the lowest levels in years.

The 1974 GTO was essentially the same as the Ventura Sprint with the addition of parking lights set in the grille, a hood scoop and a standard four-barrel 350 cubic inch V-8 engine. It was available either as a Coupe or as a Hatchback. A total of 7,058 GTOs were built during this final year of production.

In 1974, as in in the first year of GTO production, there was a separate GTO brochure. It is reproduced on pages 76-78. The GTO related sections of the color and trim brochure are reproduced on pages 78-79.

Available all-Morrokide bucket seats. Shown in red—also available in white, saddle and green.

Available Radial Tuned Suspension Package (RTS).

You can't inherit a name like GTO. You have to earn it. And we built our compact '74 GTO to do just that.

Our new GTO is a quick-handling, agile Wide-Track. It comes in either a 2-Door Coupe or roomy Hatchback Coupe.

GTO's styling really gets down to business. There's a blacked-out split grille with inset parking lamps. Pontiac's tough-looking shaker hood that scoops up cold, dense air. Body-colored sport mirrors. Mag-type Rally II wheels. And contemporary GTO I.D.

Underneath, GTO is just as tough as its reputation. It comes with a beefy suspension that includes front and rear stabilizer bars and firm shocks.

A special Radial Tuned Suspension with FR78—14 steel-belted radials is also available.

GTO's performance comes from Pontiac's new cold-air induction 350 4-bbl. V-8, teamed with a tough, floor-shifted 3-speed and a 3.08:1 rear axle that relays the

n on the cars on these pages are some of the options and accessories offered by Pontiac at extra cost.

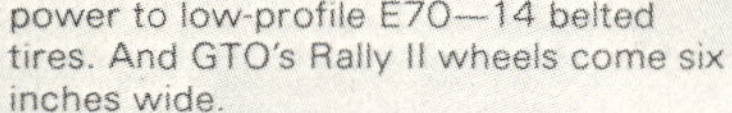

Standard bench seat upholstered in cloth and Morrokide. Shown in black/white/red plaid—also available in black/white/green plaid.

Custom bench seat upholstered in cloth and Morrokide. Shown in green—also available in black.

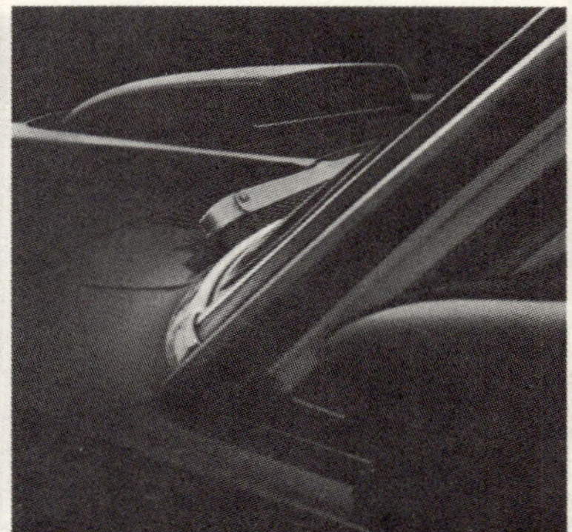

Functional engine-mounted shaker hood scoop.

power to low-profile E70—14 belted tires. And GTO's Rally II wheels come six inches wide.

Low-restriction dual exhausts dump at the sides, behind the rear wheels.

Power front disc brakes are available for the ordering.

You can also order bucket seats and a console to go along with the special GTO identification plates on the inner doors.

If you do, full rally instrumentation is available, including an electric tach. To keep closer tabs on the way things are going.

1974 GTO. The tough little road car that's earned a big name for itself.

After all, the Wide-Track people have a way with cars.

GTO 2-Door Coupe in Buccaneer Red.

GTO FACTS AND FIGURES

MODELS

2-Door Coupe and Hatchback Coupe.

POWER TEAMS

Standard engine: 350-cu.-in. 4-bbl. V-8.
Standard transmission: 3-speed floor-shifted manual.
Available transmissions: 4-speed floor-shifted manual, Turbo Hydra-matic. Manual transmissions not available in California.
Standard axle ratio: 3.08:1.

STANDARD INTERIOR FEATURES

Front bench seat upholstered in cloth trimmed with Morrokide. Black deluxe 2-spoke steering wheel. Wood-grained vinyl door trim accents. Front and rear armrests. Low-level ventilation. Vinyl-coated rubber floor covering. Rear seat ash trays. Right-hand front doorjamb dome light switch. Fold-down rear seat (Hatchback only). Fully trimmed side walls in cargo area (Hatchback only). Lamp in cargo area activated by doorjamb switch (Hatchback only). GTO identification on door panels.

STANDARD EXTERIOR FEATURES

Improved bumper systems. Blacked-out grille with parking lamps. Functional shaker hood scoop. Body-colored sport mirrors, left-hand remote control. Windshield and back-light reveal moldings. Slit-style tail lamps. GTO identification.

STANDARD CHASSIS FEATURES

Computer-selected front coil springs and rear multileaf springs. Firm shocks. Front .812" dia. and .562" dia. rear stabilizer bars. Front and rear drum-type brakes. Space-saver spare tire (Hatchback only). 14x6" Rally II wheels (less trim rings). E70—14 belted blackwall tires. Dual exhausts.

Dimensions (inches)	2-Door Coupe	2-Door Hatchback
Overall length	199.4	199.4
Overall width	72.5	72.5
Wheelbase	111.0	111.0
Track, front/rear	59.9/59.6	59.9/59.6
Head room, front/rear	38.2/36.8	38.2/36.8
Leg room, front/rear	41.7/33.4	41.7/33.4
Shoulder room, front/rear	55.8/55.3	55.8/55.3
Hip room, front/rear	55.2/55.0	55.2/55.0

The GTO Hatchback hatch.

CAPACITIES

Fuel tank—20.5 gals.
Cooling system—20.1 qts.
Oil, less filter refill—5.0 qts.

POPULAR EQUIPMENT AVAILABLE

Bucket seats on both models. Space-saver spare tire. AM, AM/FM, or AM/FM stereo radios. Custom Sport steering wheel. Variable-ratio power steering. Power front disc brakes. Radial Tuned Suspension Package, which includes: FR78—14 whitewall or white-lettered steel-belted radial tires, front and rear stabilizer bars, Pliacell shock absorbers and specific springs. Rally gauge cluster (V-8s with bucket seats and console only), which includes: instrument panel tachometer and clock and console-mounted ammeter, fuel, oil pressure and water temp gauges. Wheel trim rings. Air conditioning. Vinyl accent stripes. Protective rubber bumper strips. Front bumper guards.

GTO SAFETY FEATURES

OCCUPANT PROTECTION

Seat belts with pushbutton buckles for all passenger positions. Two front combination seat and shoulder belts for driver and right front passenger (with reminder light and buzzer, inertia reel and starter interlock). Two front-seat head restraints. Energy-absorbing steering column. Passenger-guard door locks. Safety door latches and hinges. Folding seat-back latches. Energy-absorbing padded instrument panel and front seat-back tops. Contoured windshield header. Thick laminate windshield. Padded sun visors. Safety armrests. Safety steering wheel. Cargo-Guard. Side-Guard beams.

ACCIDENT PREVENTION

Side marker lights and reflectors (front side marker lights flash with directional signal). Parking lamps that illuminate with headlamps. Four-way hazard warning flasher. Backup lights. Lane-change feature in direction signal control. Windshield defrosters, washers and dual-speed wipers. Wide-view inside mirror (vinyl edged, shatter-resistant glass and deflecting support). Outside rearview mirror. Dual master cylinder brake system with warning light. Starter Safety Switch. Dual-action safety hood latches. Improved bumper systems.

ANTI-THEFT

Anti-theft ignition key warning buzzer. Anti-theft steering column lock.

Shown on the cars and described in this catalog are some of the many options and accessories offered by Pontiac. They're available at extra cost, and well worth it in driving comfort and convenience. Pontiac Motor Division of General Motors Corporation reserves the right to make changes at any time, without notice, in colors, equipment, specifications, prices and models—and also to discontinue models. The right is also reserved to change any specifications, parts or equipment at any time without incurring any obligation to equip same on cars built prior to date of such change.

Pontiac Motor Division, General Motors Corporation, One Pontiac Plaza, Pontiac, Michigan 48053.

COLOR USAGE CHARTS

1974 CORDOVA TOP USAGE CHART

Available at extra cost is vinyl-coated fabric roof covering for all models except Pontiac LeMans and Luxury LeMans Safaris. Also available is special Landau Cordova Top for Pontiac LeMans, Luxury LeMans, LeMans Sport Coupe and Grand Am 2-door Colonnade Hardtops and Grand Prix Hardtop Coupe only. Order Code 451. Bright roof drip moldings are included if not already standard.

EXTERIOR COLORS	CORDOVA TOP COLORS									
	(1) White	(2) Black	(3) Beige*	(4) Russet*	(5) Green	(6) Burgundy	(7) Blue	(8) Brown	(9) Saddle	(0) Taupe*
H—Denver Gold	X	X	X					X	X	
M—Fernmist Green	X	X			X					
R—Buccaneer Red	X	X								
T—Sunstorm Yellow	X	X								
C—Cameo White	X	X	X	X	X	X	X	X	X	X
E—Admiralty Blue	X	X					X			
F—Regatta Blue	X	X					X			
G—Carmel Beige	X	X	X	X				X	X	
J—Limefire Green	X	X			X					
K—Gulfmist Aqua	X	X								
N—Pinemist Green	X	X			X					
S—Honduras Maroon	X	X				X				
V—Ascot Silver	X	X				X		X		X
W—Fire Coral Bronze	X	X	X	X					X	
Y—Colonial Gold	X	X	X					X		
Z—Crestwood Brown	X	X	X					X	X	
A—Starlight Black	X	X	X	X	X	X	X	X	X	X
D—Porcelain Blue	X	X					X			
L—Lakemist Green	X	X			X					
U—Shadowmist Brown	X	X	X					X	X	X

*Beige (3), Russet (4) and Taupe (0-zero) colors are not available on Catalina, Bonneville and Grand Prix Hardtop Coupes.

Pontiac

VENTURA (Extra-cost Bucket Seats)

BUCKET SEATS (Extra Cost)
Oxen and Madrid Morrokides

EXTRA COST—ALL MORROKIDE

Models	Interior Trims	Exterior Colors
COUPE & HATCHBACK COUPE	621 (White)	C, E, F, G, H, J, K, M, N, R, S, T, V, W, Y, Z
	651 (Saddle)	C, G, H, J, S, T, V, W, Z
	671 (Green)	C, J, M, N
	681 (Red)	C, E, R, V

AVAILABLE—COLORED INTERIOR WITH WHITE SEATS

Models	Interior Trims	Seat Color
COUPE & HATCHBACK COUPE	671 (Green)	White (Order Code 331)
	681 (Red)	

AVAILABLE—COLORED APPOINTMENTS* WITH WHITE INTERIOR

Models	Interior Trim	Appointment Color
COUPE & HATCHBACK COUPE	621 (White)	Red (Order Code 338)

**Floor Covering, Instrument Panel, Steering Column, Package Shelf.*

Pontiac

VENTURA (Standard Interiors)

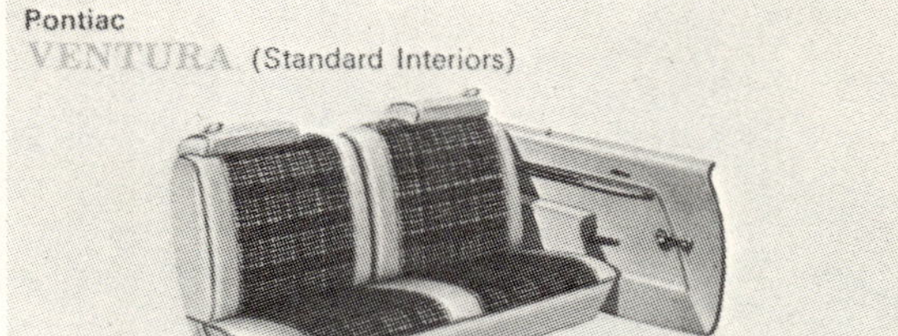

SPLIT BENCH SEAT
Plaid Premier Cloth and Madrid Morrokide
or Knit and Madrid Morrokides

STANDARD—CLOTH & MORROKIDE

Models	Interior Trims	Exterior Colors
COUPE & HATCHBACK COUPE	022 (Black/White/Red—Plaid w/White trim)	C, E, F, G, R, S, V, W
	232 (Black/White/Green—Plaid w/Green trim)	C, G, H, J, M, N, T, Y, Z

STANDARD—ALL MORROKIDE

Models	Interior Trims	Exterior Colors
COUPE & HATCHBACK COUPE	032 (Saddle/Orange)	C, G, H, J, S, T, V, W, Z
	522 (Black/White/Red)	C, E, F, G, R, S, V, W
	742 (Green/Yellow)	C, J, M, N

AVAILABLE—COLORED APPOINTMENTS* WITH COMPATIBLE INTERIOR

Models	Interior Trims	Appointment Color
COUPE & HATCHBACK COUPE	022 (Black/White/Red—Plaid)	Red (Order Code 338)
	522 (Black/White/Red)	

**Floor Covering, Instrument Panel, Steering Column, Package Shelf.*

Pontiac

VENTURA CUSTOM (Standard Interiors)

SPLIT BENCH SEAT
Meridian Cloth and Madrid Morrokide
or Oxen and Madrid Morrokides

STANDARD—CLOTH AND MORROKIDE

Models	Interior Trims	Exterior Colors
COUPE & HATCHBACK COUPE	222 (Black)	C, E, F, G, H, J, K, M, N, R, S, T, V, W, Y, Z
	642 (Green)	C, J, M, N

STANDARD—ALL MORROKIDE

Models	Interior Trims	Exterior Colors
COUPE & HATCHBACK COUPE	422 (White)	C, E, F, G, H, J, K, M, N, R, S, T, V, W, Y, Z
	632 (Saddle)	C, G, H, J, S, T, V, W, Z
	842 (Green)	C, J, M, N

AVAILABLE—COLORED INTERIOR WITH WHITE SEATS

Models	Interior Trims	Seat Color
COUPE & HATCHBACK COUPE	222 (Black)	White (Order Code 331)
	842 (Green)	

AVAILABLE—COLORED APPOINTMENTS* WITH WHITE INTERIOR

Models	Interior Trim	Appointment Colors
COUPE & HATCHBACK COUPE	422 (White)	Green (Order Code 336)
		Red (Order Code 338)

**Carpeting, Instrument Panel, Steering Column, Package Shelf.*

Pontiac

VENTURA CUSTOM (Extra-cost Bucket Seats)

BUCKET SEATS (Extra Cost)
Oxen and Madrid Morrokides

EXTRA COST—ALL MORROKIDE

Models	Interior Trims	Exterior Colors
COUPE & HATCHBACK COUPE	421 (White)	C, E, F, G, H, J, K, M, N, R, S, T, V, W, Y, Z
	501 (Red)	C, E, R, V
	631 (Saddle)	C, G, H, J, S, T, V, W, Z
	841 (Green)	C, J, M, N
4-DOOR SEDAN	661 (Black)	C, E, F, G, H, J, K, M, N, R, S, T, V, W, Y, Z

AVAILABLE—COLORED INTERIOR WITH WHITE SEATS

Models	Interior Trims	Seat Color
COUPE & HATCHBACK COUPE	501 (Red)	White (Order Code 331)
	841 (Green)	

AVAILABLE—COLORED APPOINTMENTS* WITH WHITE INTERIOR

Models	Interior Trim	Appointment Colors
COUPE & HATCHBACK COUPE	421 (White)	Green (Order Code 336)
		Red (Order Code 338)

**Carpeting, Instrument Panel, Steering Column, Package Shelf.*

Accessories

Pontiac had helped to pioneer the concept of factory accessories as early as the 1930s. Almost every year, at least since 1934, Pontiac has issued a comprehensive accessory brochure which has both listed and illustrated virtually every regular factory installed item. Accessory catalogues were issued during every year of GTO production. The front covers of these catalogues are reproduced below.

All GTO factory accessories are listed in chronological order exactly as they were featured in the factory accessory catalogues. Where options are repeated from one year to the next, illustrations (if used) are not repeated, only the text portion of the original catalogue. Accessories within each yearly section are grouped roughly as they were grouped in the original catalogues.

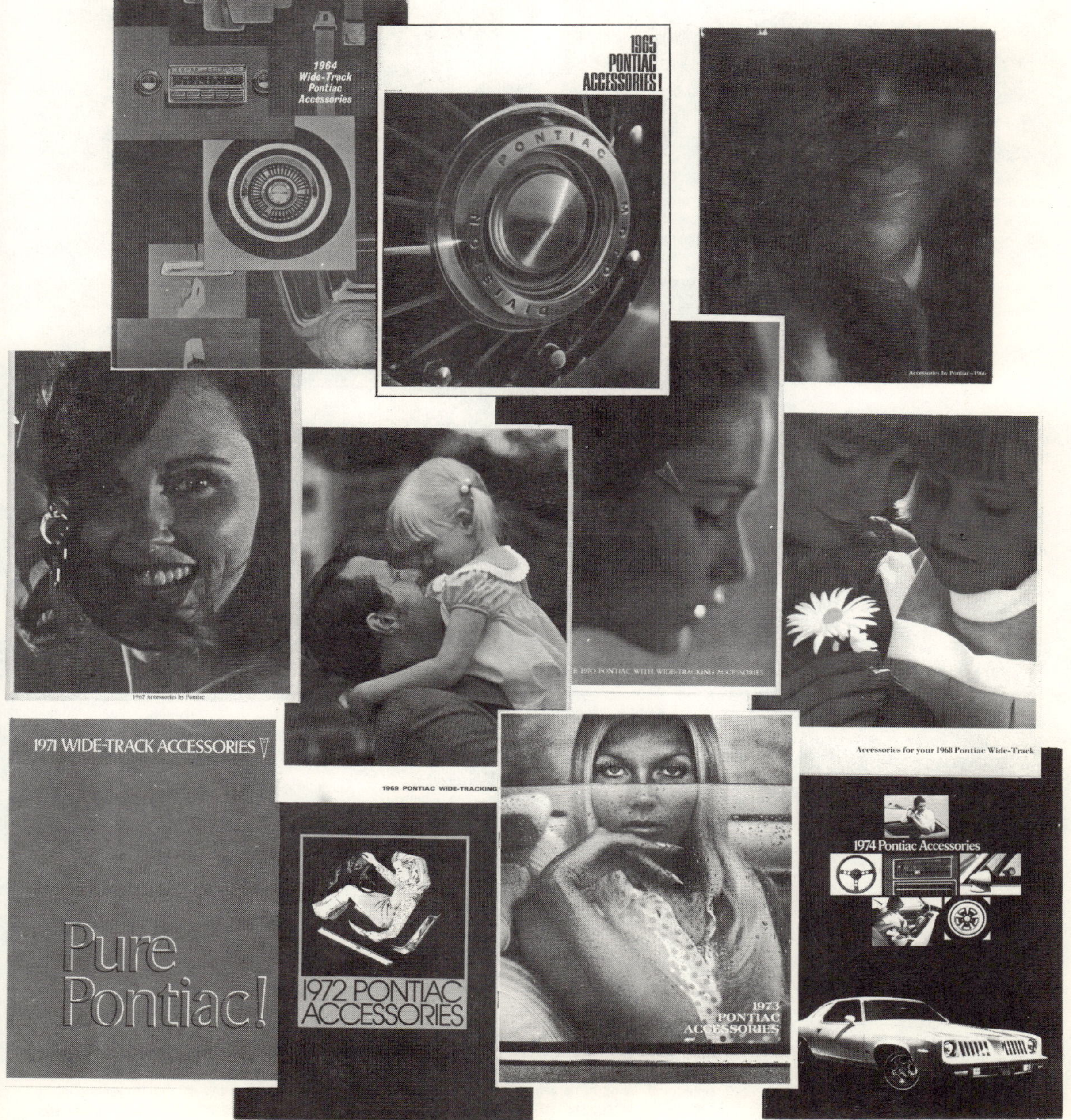

BASIC GROUP

(061)

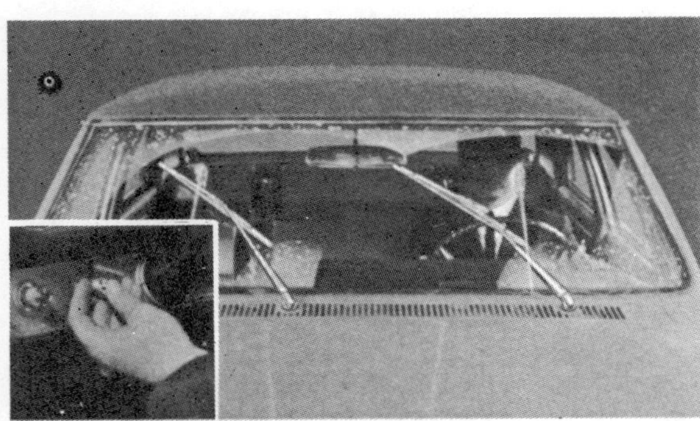

Windshield Washers and Dual Speed Wipers (Code 421) . . . wipers operate at two speeds. Washers operate from push of button—two streams of fluid spray onto windshield; wipers clean away dirt. Unit includes extra-tough plastic fluid jar.

Back-Up Lamps (Code 471) . . . light up automatically as you shift into reverse. Illuminate area behind car to make backing up at night much easier, safer . . . warn pedestrians, other cars. **(D)**

Radio & Antenna (Code 392) . . . to bring you excellent listening enjoyment. Push-button tuning radio with 57-inch stretch antenna mounted on right front fender.

Dome Reading Lamp (Code 484) . . . passenger can read without light disturbing driver. Concentrated beam from lamp on ceiling swings 360° . . . independent switch.

Luggage Lamp (Code 481) . . . automatically turns on when trunk is lifted (sedans and coupes only). **Underhood Lamp (Code 404)** . . . automatically turns on when hood is opened. **(D)**

Parking Brake Warning Lamp (Code 494) . . . guards against driving with parking brake on. Light on instrument cluster flashes bright red warning when ignition is turned on and parking brake set, continues until brake is released. **(D)**

Glove Compartment Lamp (Code 482) . . . lights automatically to help you find any item quickly and easily when glove compartment door is opened. **(D)**

Ashtray and Lighter Lamps (Code 492) . . . they are visible when ashtray is pulled out, or when cigar lighter is removed. Lamp lights automatically when parking lights or headlights go on. **(D)**

Courtesy Lamp (Code 491) . . . driver and passengers enter and leave car safely and conveniently at night . . . lamp flashes on when front door is opened. Can be operated manually by switch on instrument panel. **(D)**

1964 PROTECTION GROUP

(062)

Seat Belts and Seat Belt Retractor (Code 624) . . . outboard belts retract to compact roll when not in use, extend to needed length when in service. **Standard Belts Without Retractors (Code 411)** also available. All belts meet highest safety standards. Choice of harmonizing colors. **(D)**

Instrument Panel Pad (Code 424) . . . new design, new styling . . . in beautiful, durable Morrokide to harmonize with interior. Pad is cushioned with resilient, long lasting foam.

Door Edge Guards (Code 512) . . . an extra measure of protection for your new Tempest's exterior. Help prevent nicks and scratches on door edges. **(D)**

Rear Window De-Fogger (Code 541) . . . blower under rear package shelf directs air through grille to rear window for clearer view. **(D)**

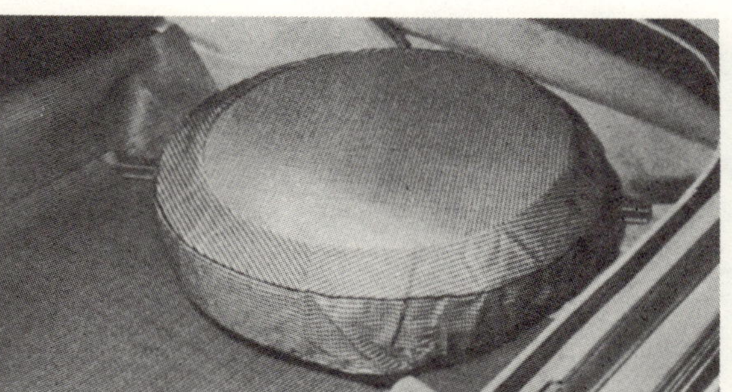

Spare Tire and Wheel Cover (Code 572) . . . protects luggage from becoming marred or damaged, slips on and off easily. Dresses up luggage compartment. (All models except Safari) **(D)**

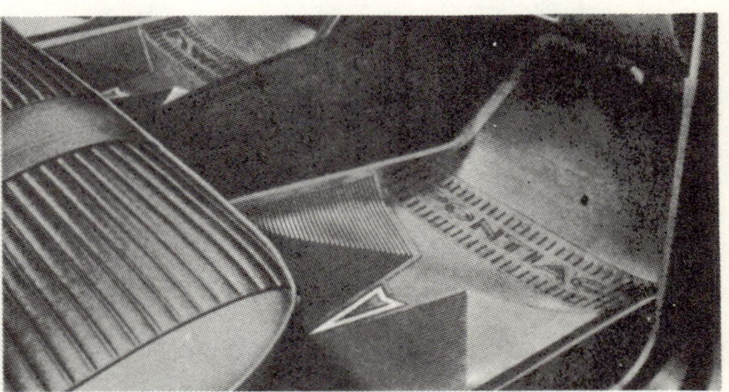

Floor Mats (Code 633) . . . protect both front and rear floor covering against soil and wear. Especially useful during bad weather months. Easily removed for washing. **(D)**

MIRROR GROUP

(081)

Remote-Control Outside Mirror (Code 444) . . . controlled from inside the car—especially appreciated when more than one person drives the same car. Simple control knob lets you make any adjustment desired. **(D)**

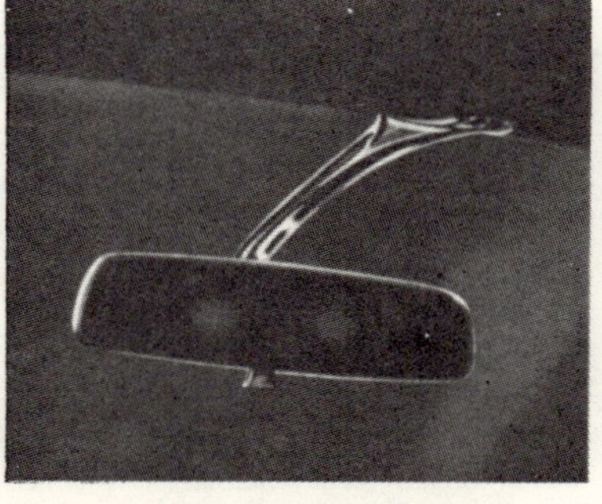

Non-Glare Inside Rear-View Mirror (Code 442) . . . has special finger tab to permit easy adjustment to non-glare or nighttime driving position. **(D)**

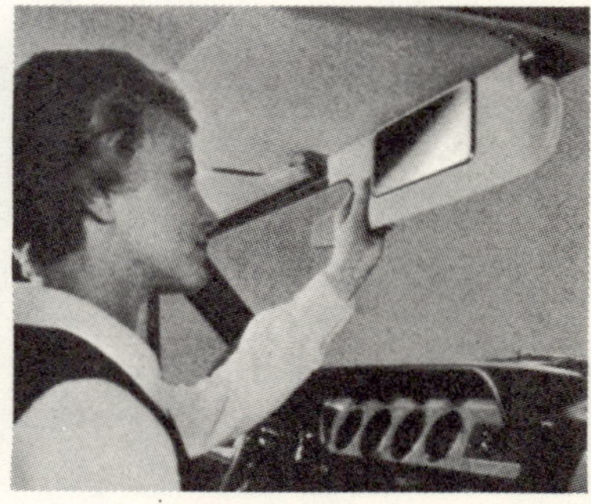

Visor Vanity Mirror (Code 441) . . . a greatly appreciated item in any car. Clips neatly to back of visor. Out of sight when not in use. Ideal for checking makeup, combing hair, etc. **(D)**

INDIVIDUAL OPTIONS AND ACCESSORIES

New Tempest Power Brakes (Code 502) . . . new design for increased braking capacity. Positive braking and car control with a light touch of the toe. Braking is easier, but feel of control is still there. (**D**)

Power Steering (Code 501) . . . drive, shift and park with almost effortless ease, yet feel of control is still there. (**D**)

New Power Window Lifts (Code 551) . . . for automatic control of all vertically opened windows from single control on door trim at driver's position. Individual controls at each window.

Power Tilt Front Seat (Code 564—Bucket Seat L. H. only; Code 561—Bench Seat) . . . moves seat forward and backward, raises and lowers rear of seat only for safer driving and comfort.

Soft Ray Glass (Code 531) . . . all windows fully tinted for reduced glare, with upper area of windshield shaded for added glare reduction. Reduced eyestrain permits safer driving and added comfort to all passengers. Also available windshield only. (**Code 532**)

Safe-T-Track Differential (Code 701) . . . all new design assures necessary amount of pull when very low traction conditions are encountered at one wheel. Also provides smooth transfer of torque from one rear wheel to another.

New Tilt Steering Wheel (Code 454) . . . 7 different vertical positions easily selected to meet individual requirements. Maximum steering comfort and safety, easier entry and exit from car.

Tachometer (Code 452) . . . tells exact number of engine RPM's and how hard engine is working, helps you attain optimum driving performance. A "must" for the sports-minded driver. (**D**)

Power Tilt Bucket Seat (Code 564) for driver's seat only.

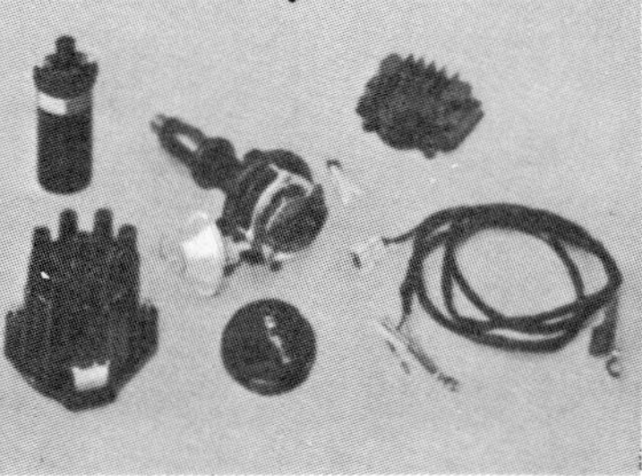

Transistor Ignition System (Code 671) . . . available on all premium fuel engines, provides ignition without metal contacts. Fully transistorized, provides lifetime operation with longer spark life and quicker starting.

Console (Code 601) . . . available with bucket seats and 3-Speed and optional 4-Speed Manual Transmissions and optional Automatic Transmission. Has locked storage compartment and rear courtesy lamp. Shown is console with optional Automatic Transmission and Manifold Vacuum Gauge. (Vacuum Gauge Dealer Installed only)

Manual Control Radio and Antenna (Code 398) . . . excellent listening enjoyment at a modest cost. Design changes minimize channel interference from adjacent stations. Broader bass response for wide tonal range. Improved antenna for better capacity control. (**D**)

Tonneau Cover . . . helps protect the interior of your Tempest convertible from dirt, dust, sun and rain. Ideal for daytime parking—keeps seats cool. Sturdy vinyl cover snaps off or on in a jiffy. Can be left on when driver is alone in car. (**D**)

Trunk Light (Code 481) . . . automatically turns on when trunk lid is lifted! Reflecting shade directs light to every area of trunk . . . frees hands for loading, unloading luggage. (**D**)

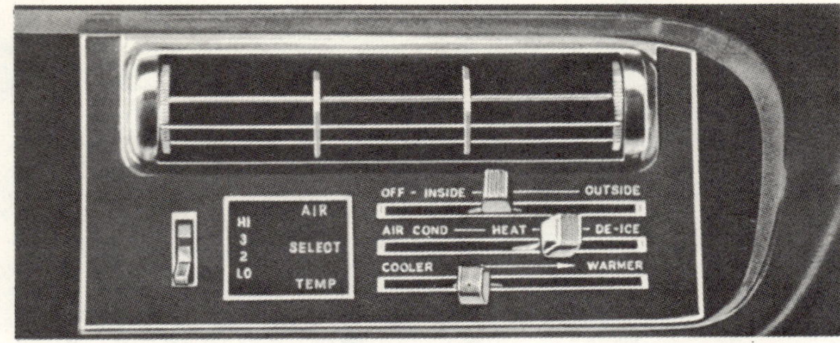

Tri-Comfort Circ-L-Aire Conditioner (Code 581) . . . vastly improved, all new system combines heater and air conditioner to provide year-round controlled humidity comfort. Supplies air heated to desired degree to lower part of passenger area, or air cooled to desired temperature to upper passenger area.

Custom Wheel Discs (Code 521) . . . fully cover the wheel. New 3-piece design (retaining band, wheel cover, die cast spinner). Discs are of bright chrome-flashed stainless steel. **(D)**

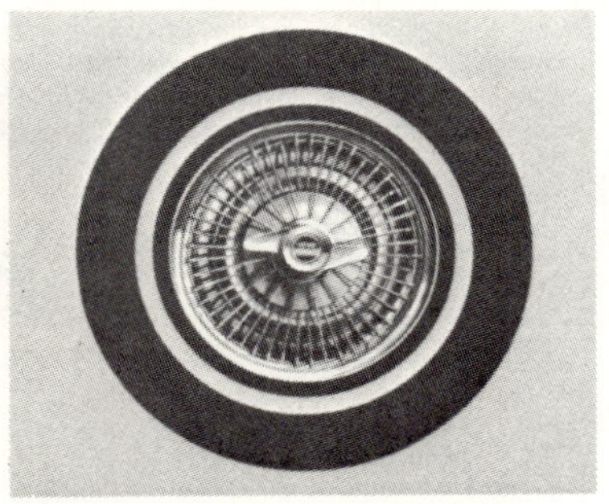

Wire Wheel Discs . . . give your Tempest a sports car look. Wire wheel discs are boldly styled, structurally strong and elegant. A "must" for the sports-minded driver. **(D)**

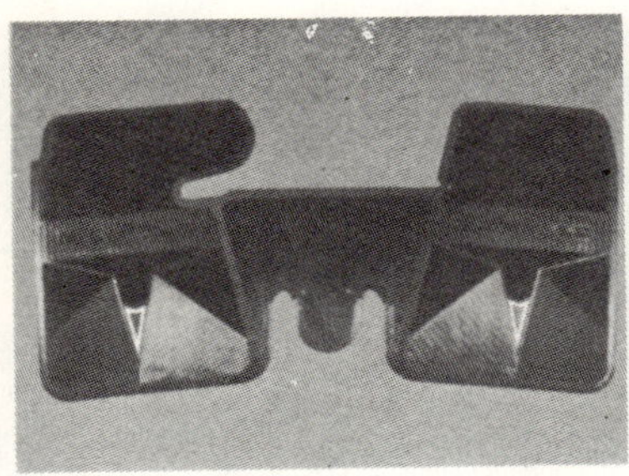

Full-Width Floor Mat (front only) . . . extends over center hump, easily removed for cleaning. Attractively styled in 6 colors that complement Tempest interiors. **(D)**

Verbra-Phonic Rear Speaker System (Code 474) . . . a new dimension in sound, delays sound from rear speaker a fraction of a second, just enough to simulate acoustics in an auditorium. 3-step switch on instrument panel plays through front, rear or both speakers. All models except Safari and convertibles. **(D)**

Separa-Phonic Speaker (Code 401) . . . brings stereo-quality sound to your car. Brilliant tone depth and control. 3-step switch lets you play through front, rear or both speakers. **(D)**

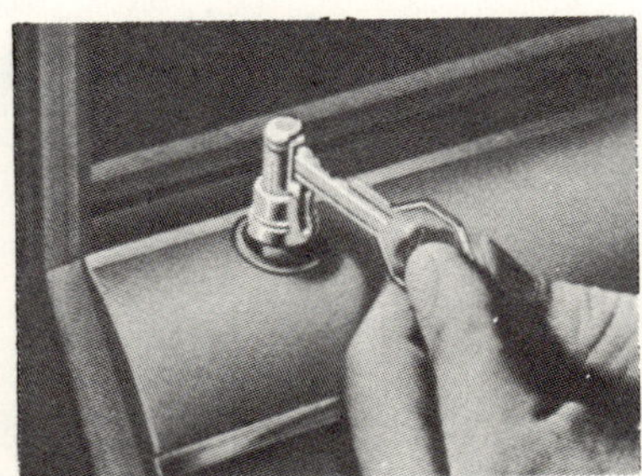

Rear Door Safety Locks (4-door only) . . . prevent children from opening rear door. When lock button is pushed down, rear doors cannot be opened without inserting key in lock button. **(D)**

Rear Deck Lid Release (Code 451) . . . lets you open trunk from driver's seat without removing key from ignition. Trunk can be opened by key if so desired. Convenient for pickup service stops. All models except Safari. **(D)**

Gas Cap Lock . . . helps prevent fuel theft and possible damage to fuel system by youngsters' pranks. Lock on gas cap is coded to separate key. **(D)**

INDIVIDUAL OPTIONS AND ACCESSORIES

Tempest Rally Clock (Code 604) . . . smartly restyled, features sweep second hand, built-in self-regulator and illuminated dial. (Note: Not available with tachometer option.) **(D)**

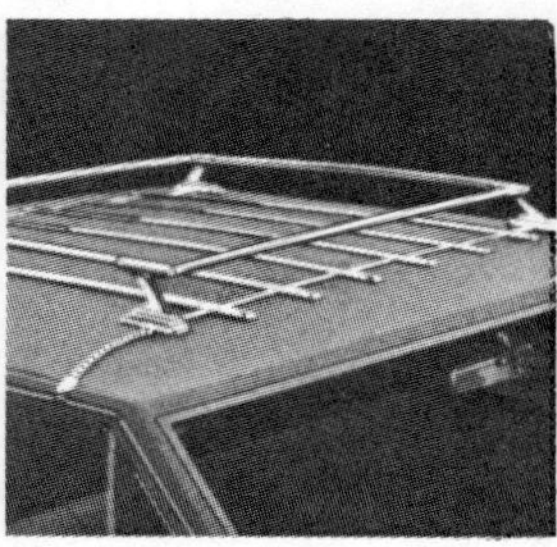

Removable Luggage Carrier . . . this new accessory is lightweight and may be easily and quickly installed on roof, or as easily removed. Available all models except Safaris and convertibles. **(D)**

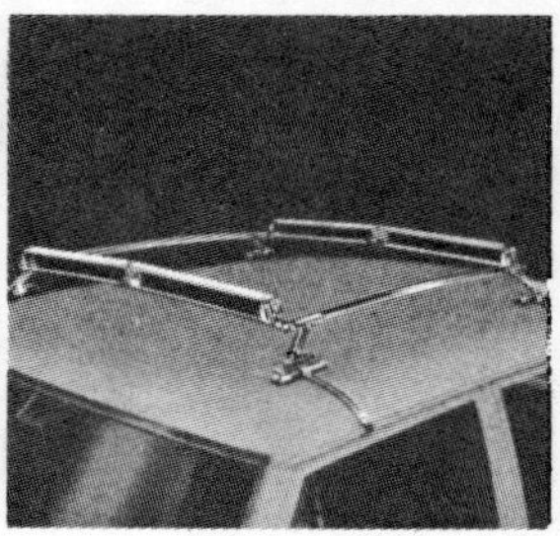

Removable Ski Carrier . . . skiers will like this easy-to-put-on-and-take-off ski rack. **Optional Platform** converts unit to luggage carrier. Available all models except Safaris and convertibles. **(D)**

Rear Deck Ski & Luggage Carrier . . . makes use of that empty space atop the rear deck. Can be installed or removed in a few minutes. Available all models except Safari. **(D)**

BASIC GROUP [code 061]

Windshield Washers and Dual Speed Wipers (Code 421). Wipers operate at two speeds. Washers operate from push button on instrument panel. Two jets of washer solution spray onto windshield. Extra-tough plastic jar for fluid. (F)

Backup Lamps (Code 471) . . . light up automatically as you shift into reverse. Illuminate area behind car to make backing up at night much easier, safer . . . warn pedestrians, other cars. (F,D)

Deluxe Push-button Radio & Antenna (Code 392). Refinements in circuit design bring superior tone and fidelity. Wider dial for more precise tuning. New shallow basket speaker is more compact while having same power and response. New oval antenna reduces wind noise. (F,D)

LAMP GROUP [code 084]

Luggage Lamp (Code 481) . . . automatically turns on when trunk is lifted (sedans and coupes only). **Under-hood Lamp (Code 404)** . . . automatically turns on when hood is opened. (D)

Parking Brake Warning Lamp (Code 494) . . . guards against driving with parking brake on. Light on instrument cluster displays bright red warning when ignition is turned on with parking brake set, continues until brake is released. (F,D)

Glove Compartment Lamp (Code 482) . . . lights automatically to help you find any item quickly and easily when glove compartment door is opened. (F,D)

Ashtray and Lighter Lamps (Code 492) . . . visible when ashtray is pulled out or when cigar lighter is removed. Lamp lights automatically when parking lights or headlights go on. (F,D)

Courtesy Lamp (Code 491) . . . driver and passengers enter and leave car more conveniently at night . . . lamp flashes on when front door is opened. Can be operated manually by headlamp switch on instrument panel. (F,D)

PROTECTION [code 062] GROUP

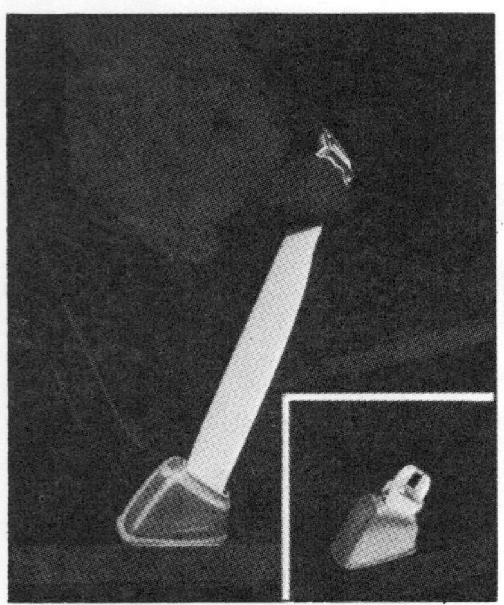

Custom Front Seat Belts with Retractor and Housing (Code 624) . . . outboard belts retract into compact housing when not in use, extend to needed length when in service. 7 new colors harmonize with interiors. New buckles feature bright metal finish, greater locking-unlocking ease and greater holding power. **(F)**

Instrument Panel Pad (Code 424) . . . new design, new styling . . . in beautiful, durable Morrokide to harmonize with interior. Pad is cushioned with resilient, long lasting foam. **(F)**

Door Edge Guards (Code 512) . . . Pontiac's narrow design helps prevent nicks and scratches on door edges yet does not interfere with sleek exterior appearance. **(F,D)**

Spare Tire and Wheel Cover (Code 572) . . . protects luggage from becoming marred or damaged, slips on and off easily. Dresses up luggage compartment. (All models except Safari.) **(F,D)**

Floor Mats, Front & Rear (Code 633). Protect both front and rear floor covering against soil and wear. Especially useful during bad weather. Easily removed for washing. Available in 9 colors that harmonize with interiors. **(F,D).** Front only **(Code 631). (F,D)**

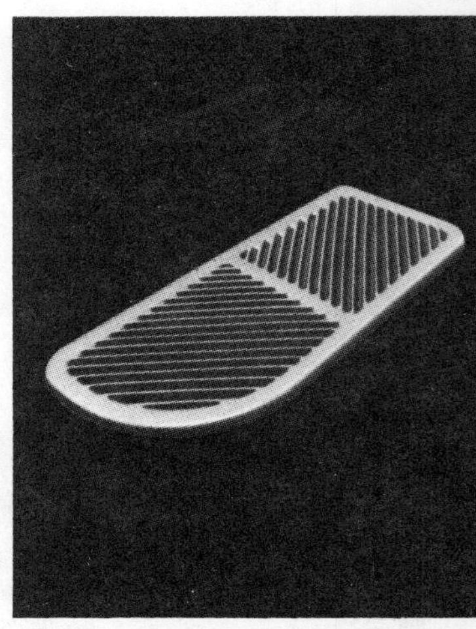

Rear Window Defogger (Code 541) . . . blo under rear package shelf directs air thro grille to rear window for clearer view. (N available on convertible or Safari.) **(F,D)**

MIRROR [code 081] GROUP

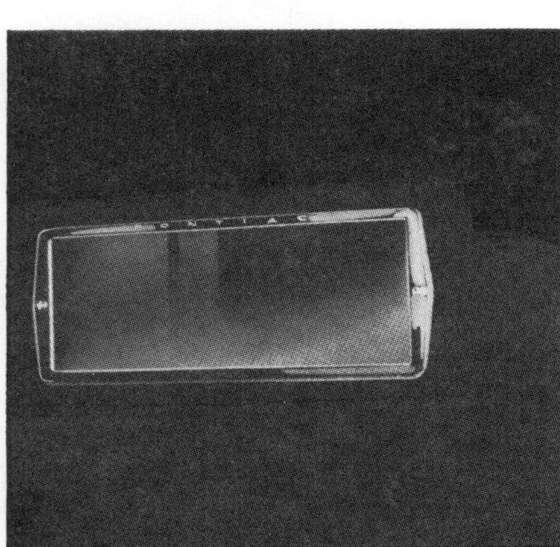

Visor Vanity Mirror (Code 441) . . . an appreciated item in any car. Securely attached to back of visor. Out of sight when not in use. Ideal for checking makeup, combing hair, etc. **(F,D)**

Non-glare Inside Rearview Mirror (Code 442) . . . has special finger tab to permit easy adjustment to non-glare or nighttime driving position. **(F,D)**

Remote-control Outside Mirror (Code 444) . . . mounted on door for maximum rear visibility—controlled from inside the car—especially appreciated when more than one person drives the same car. Simple control knob lets you make any adjustment desired. **(F,D)**

INDIVIDUAL OPTIONS & ACCESSORIES

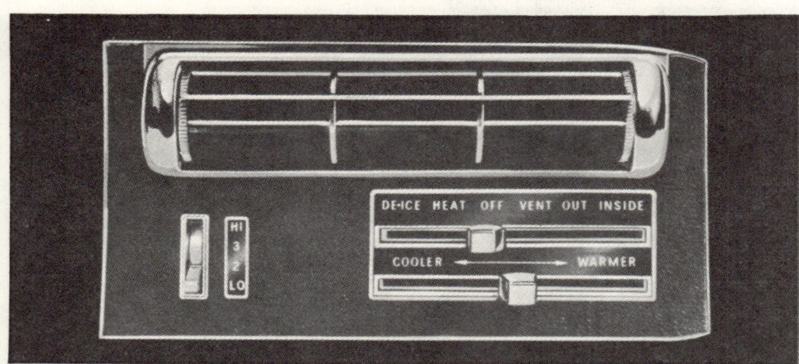

Tri-Comfort Air Conditioner (Code 582). Combined with the Circ-L-Aire Heater, provides a full range of comfort control over heat, cold and humidity—that's why it's called "Tri-Comfort." Controls have been simplified and are power operated for easier operation. Low speed cooling—important in slow traffic driving—has been substantially improved. Air is distributed from five adjustable air outlets on instrument panel. **(F,D)**

AM-FM Radio (Code 394). Completely transistorized. Push buttons can be set to AM or FM or combination of both. Unusual fidelity of sound for those who appreciate music. **(D)**

Power Tilt Front Seat (Code 564, Left Bucket Seat only) (Code 561, Bench Seat). Moves seat forward and back, raises and lowers front seat for safer driving and comfort. **(F)**

Tonneau Cover. Protects convertible interior when top is down and car is parked. Sturdy vinyl cover snaps off or on in a jiffy. Can be left on when driver is alone in car. **(D)**

Soft-Ray Glass (Code 531) . . . all windows fully tinted for reduced glare, with upper area of windshield shaded for added glare reduction. Reduced eyestrain permits safer driving and added comfort to all passengers. Also available windshield only **(Code 532). (F)**

Manual Control Radio and Antenna (Code 398). Refinements in circuit design provide superior tone quality and fidelity. Wider dial width for more precise tuning. New oval antenna reduces wind noise. **(F,D)**

Separa-Phonic Speaker (Code 401) . . . brings concert-hall sound to your car. Brilliant tone depth and control. 3-step switch lets you play through front, rear or both speakers. (All models except Safaris and convertibles.) **(F,D)**

Verbra-Phonic Rear Speaker System (Code 474). Delays sound from rear speaker a fraction of a second, to simulate acoustics in an auditorium. 3-step switch on instrument panel plays through front, rear or both speakers. (All models except Safaris and convertibles.) **(F,D)**

Power Window Lifts (Code 551) . . . for automatic control of all vertically opened windows from single control on door trim at driver's position. Individual controls at each window. **(F)**

Tempest Power Brakes (Code 502) . . . positive braking and car control with a light touch of the toe. Braking is easier, but feel of control is still there. **(F,D)**

Power Steering (Code 501) . . . drive and park with almost effortless ease, yet feel of control is still there. **(F,D)**

Luggage Lamp (Code 481) . . . automatically turns on when trunk lid is lifted. Reflecting shade directs light to every area of trunk . . . frees hands for loading, unloading luggage. **(F,D)**

INDIVIDUAL OPTIONS & ACCESSORIES

Rear Deck Lid Release (Code 451) . . . lets you open trunk from driver's seat without removing key from ignition. Trunk can be opened by key if so desired. Convenient for pickup service stops. All models except Safari. **(F,D)**

Outside Rearview Mirror (Code 602). Beautifully styled. Chrome reflecting glass gives sharp, clear picture without ghosting or blurring. **(F,D)**

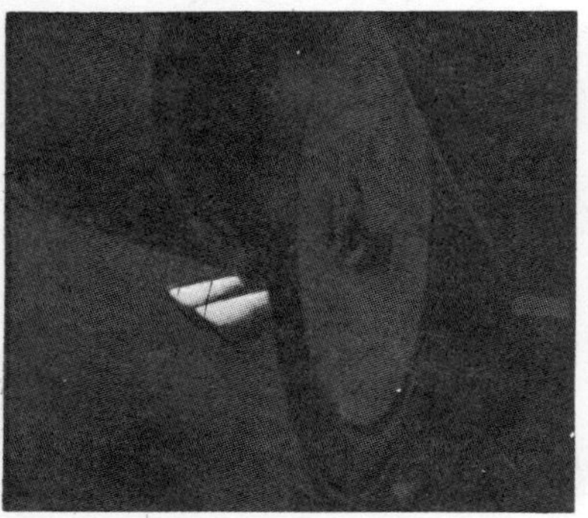

Dual Exhaust Splitters (Code 422) . . . two bright metal extension pipes are attached to the end of each outlet of the Dual Exhaust System. They enhance the "go!" look of a performance car. **(F,D)**

Car Compass . . . dependable, with special compensator for car use. Illuminated dial. **(D)**

Rear Door Safety Locks (4-door models only) . . . prevent children from opening rear door. When lock button is pushed down, rear doors cannot be opened without inserting key in lock button. **(D)**

Full-width Floor Mat (front only) . . . extends over center hump, easily removed for cleaning. Attractively styled in 9 colors that complement Tempest interiors. **(D)**

Tissue Dispenser. Holds a regular-size Kleenex box. Mounts under instrument panel. Swings out for use, swings back when not needed. **(D)**

Safe-T-Track Differential (Code 701) . . . design assures necessary amount of pull when very low traction conditions are encountered at one wheel. Also provides smooth transfer of torque from one rear wheel to another. **(F)**

Tilt Steering Wheel (Code 454) . . . 7 different vertical positions easily selected to meet individual requirements. Maximum steering comfort, easier entry and exit from car. **(F)**

Superlift Shock Absorbers (Code 622). Help maintain level ride when trunk or trailer-tongue loads are extra heavy. Tire-type air-filler valve makes Superlift easy to re-adjust for normal loads. **(F,D)**

Full Transistor Ignition System (Code 671). Available all 8-cyl. prem. fuel engines. Provides ignition without metal contacts or condenser. Std. on V-8 engines when ordered with transistor ignition together with air conditioning. **(F)**

Full Transistor Voltage Regulator (Code 662). Increases battery life, provides more accurate voltage regulation. No breaker points. Std. on V-8 engines when ordered with transistor ignition or Air Conditioning. **(F)**

Wire Wheel Discs (Code 411) . . . give your Tempest a sports car look. Wire wheel discs are boldly styled, structurally strong and elegant. A must for the sports-minded driver. **(F,D)**

Custom Wheel Discs (Code 521). Fully cover the wheel. New design has die cast spinner. Discs are of bright chrome-flashed stainless steel and feature six large cooling slots. **(F,D)**

Rally Wheels (Code 691) . . . with special 7.75 x 14 tires only. Highly functional as well as extra sporty. Large openings provide maximum cooling for brakes. Includes stainless steel cap, chrome plated wheel nuts and stainless steel full trim ring. **(F)**

INDIVIDUAL OPTIONS & ACCESSORIES

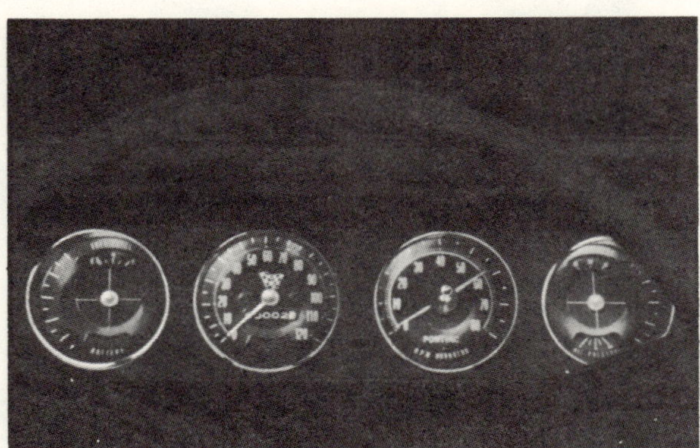

Rally Cluster (Code 504). Includes 250° sweep tachometer, speedometer, oil pressure and water temperature gauges—plus fuel indicator and battery tell-tale light. Tachometer not available without Cluster. **(F)** Electric Clock (Code 604) not available with Rally Cluster.

Roof or Deck Lid Ski Carrier . . . makes use of that empty space. Can be installed or removed in a few minutes. Available all models. **(D)**

Tempest Rally Clock (Code 604) . . . smartly restyled, features sweep second hand, built-in self-regulator and illuminated dial. (Note: Not available with Rally Cluster option.) **(F,D)**

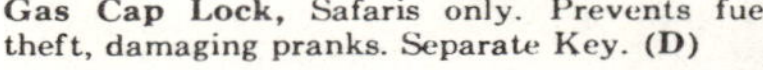

Gas Cap Lock, Safaris only. Prevents fuel theft, damaging pranks. Separate Key. **(D)**

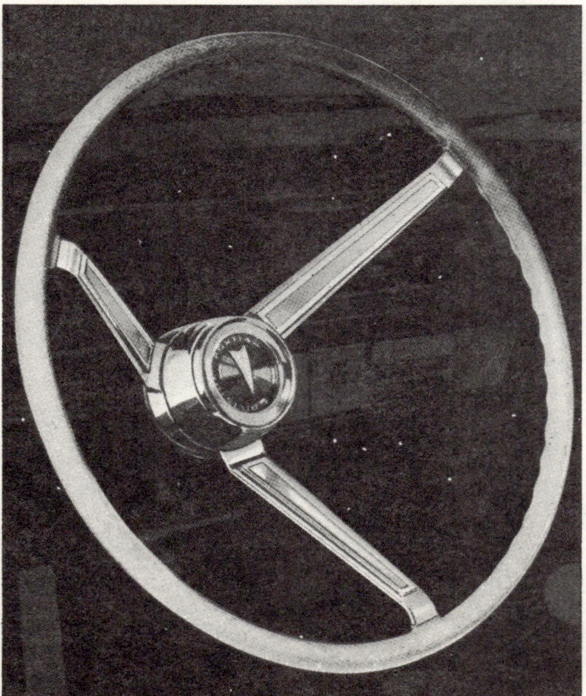

Custom Sports Steering Wheel (Code 524) . . . completely redesigned for 1965 to present a more symmetrical and pleasing appearance. Three equally spaced stainless steel spokes. Optionally available on all Tempest models, it can be ordered also when the tilt-wheel is selected. **(F)**

Safeguard Speedometer & Fuel Warning Lamp (Code 634). Warns of excess speed and low fuel. Control knob lets you select desired speed limit. Buzzer signals you when car exceeds this speed. Light tells you when to refuel. Not available with Rally Instrument Cluster. **(F)**

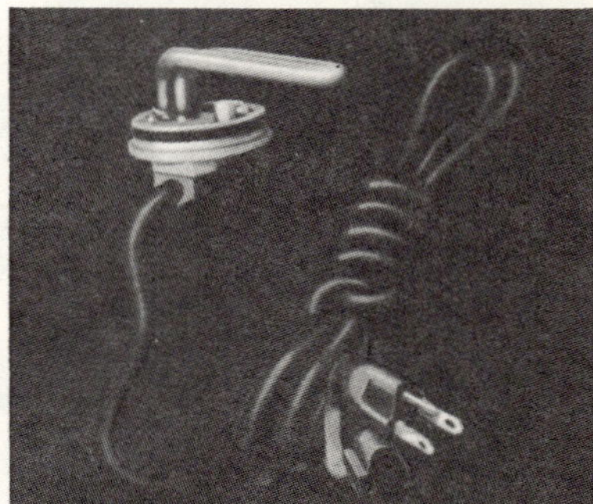

Engine Block Water Heater. Electric engine-coolant warm-up units are designed to provide fast starts and quick heater action in severe cold. Overnight, single unit raises engine coolant temperature from 0°F. to 50°F., dual unit to about 90°F. Plugs into cord from standard house outlet. **(D)**

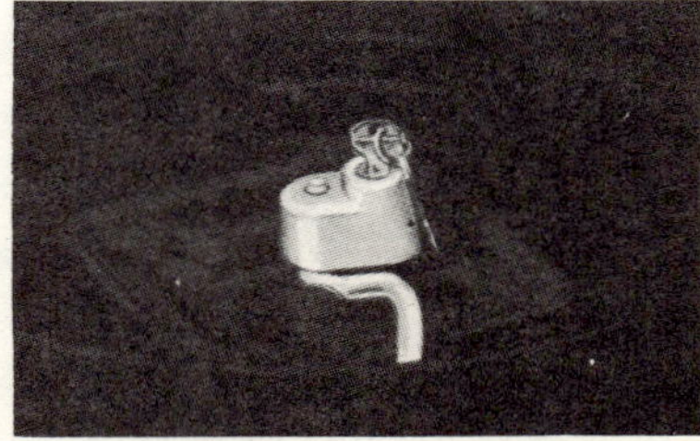

Spare Tire Lock. Prevents theft of spare tire and wheel in trunk. **(D)**

HERE ARE SOME ADDITIONAL PONTIAC ACCESSORIES YOU MIGHT LIKE TO CONSIDER...

"Car Pak" Roof Luggage Carrier . . . can be easily installed or removed in a few moments. Heavy-duty vinyl-coated fabric protects your good luggage from dirt, wind and rain. Lockable zipper door . . . strong fiber board floor. Available all models except Safari. **(D)**

Rear Seat Belts . . . for the outstanding Custom Seat Belts with bright metal-finish buckles, available in 7 colors to harmonize with interiors, use **Code 788 plus 624.** For Standard Rear Seat Belts, available in 4 colors, use **Code 788** only. **(F,D)**

Guide-Matic Headlamp Control . . . automatically dims or flicks up bright lights when needed. Also available for Tempest, Tempest Custom and Le Mans Series. **(D)**

Seat Belt Retractors . . . neatly retracts belt into compact roll when not in use, extends to needed length when belts are being used. Keep belts from dangling. Available for Front and Rear Seat Belts. **(D)**

Basic Group (code 061)

Push-button Radio with Manual Antenna.

Electric Clock for all cars, except when equipped with Code 448 Rally Gauge Cluster and Tachometer.

Lamp Group (code 074)

Luggage Compartment Lamp except on Station Wagon models.
Glove Box Lamp.
Roof Rail and Reading Lamp.
Courtesy Lamp except on Convertible models.
Ashtray and Lighter Lamp.
Parking Brake Warning Lamp.
Underhood Lamp (not illustrated).

Protection Group (code 062)

Spare Tire Cover for all models except Station Wagons.
Rear Window Defogger for all models except Station Wagons and Convertibles.
Door Edge Guards.
Custom Seat Belts, Front and Rear.
Floor Mats, Front and Rear.

Rear Window Defogger (Code 374)

Blower under rear package shelf directs air through grille to rear window to remove condensation for clearer view. (Not available on Station Wagons or Convertibles.) (F,D)

Custom Air Conditioner (Code 582)

Combined with Circ-L-Aire heater gives full range of comfort control for any weather . . . heats or cools air, controls humidity, removes pollen from air. Permits riding in cool, clean, noise-free comfort when it's hot, dusty and noisy outside. (F,D)

Soft-Ray Glass (Code 531)

All windows fully tinted except convertible back window for reduced glare, with upper windshield area shaded for added glare reduction. Reduced eye strain permits added comfort. Recommended with air conditioning. (Code 532) Also available for windshield only. (F)

Mirror Group (code 071)

Visor Vanity Mirror.
Non-glare Inside Rear View Mirror.
Outside Remote-control Mirror.

Power Steering (Code 501)

Drive, turn, park with ease. One to two pounds effort sufficient for steering yet retains feel of control. (F,D)

Power Brakes (Code 502)

Positive braking with light touch of toe. Includes bright metal trim on brake and accelerator pedal when factory installed. (F,D)

Rear Deck Lid Release (Code 422)

Provides the conveniences of opening trunk from the driver's seat. Manual control located inside glove box. Trunk may also be opened by key. All models except Station Wagons. (F,D)

Power 4-Way Bench Seat (Code 561)

Variable seat positions for greater comfort and safer driving. Makes it easier for tall or short person to conveniently drive same car. Available full-width seat only. (F)

Power Bucket Seat (L.H. only) (Code 564)

Moves seat forward, backward—raises and lowers rear of seat to positions for greater driving comfort. (F)

Rear Door Safety Lock

Prevents children from opening rear door. When lock button is pushed down, rear doors can't be opened without inserting key into lock button. (D)

Power Windows (Code 551)

For remote control of all vertical side windows from single control on driver's door. Individual control at each window. (F)

Push-button AM-FM Radio with Manual Antenna (Code 344)

Offers dual listening enjoyment on either FM or AM frequencies. Completely transistorized. Push buttons can be set to either AM or FM or combination of both. Unusually fine quality and fidelity. (F,D)

Push-button Radio & Manual Antenna (Code 342)

Superior tone and fidelity. Completely transistorized. Wide dial provides space for precise tuning. (F,D)

Manual Control Radio and Manual Antenna (Code 348)

Completely transistorized. Excellent tone quality and fidelity. Wide dial for precise tuning. (F,D)

Rear Speaker (Code 351)

Brilliant tone and depth control. 3-step switch lets you play front, rear or both speakers. All models except Convertibles. (F,D)

Verbra-Phonic Rear Speaker System (Code 352)

Fine reverberation-quality listening. Brilliant tone simulates acoustics in an auditorium when both speakers are operating. 3-step switch lets you play through front, rear or both speakers. All models except Station Wagons and Convertibles. (F,D)

Electric Power Antenna

Available with all radios. Raised or lowered by switch on instrument panel. Mounted on right rear fender on all models. Not available on Station Wagons. (F,D)

Luggage Lamp (Code 401)

Lights automatically when trunk is lifted. Permits free use of both hands for loading or unloading luggage. (Not available on Station Wagons). (F,D)

Underhood Lamp (Code 421)

Unit similar to luggage lamp but located under engine hood . . . available on all models. (F,D) (Not illustrated)

Electric Power Antenna ▼

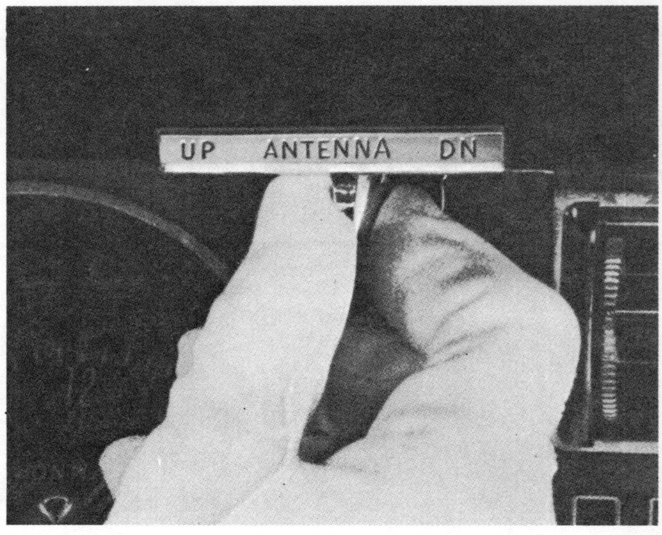

Side Roof Rail and Reading Lamps (Code 404)

Mounted on interior side of roof rails, one lamp on each side. Light up when door is opened. Each lamp has an individual switch. Not available on Convertibles. (F)

Traffic Hazard Warning Flasher Switch (Code 521)

Parking lamps and stop lamps flash on and off repeatedly. Excellent precaution for emergency off-highway stops. (F,D)

Safeguard Speedometer and Fuel Warning Lamp (Code 441)

Warns of excess speed and low fuel. Control knob lets you select desired speed limit. Buzzer signals when car exceeds this speed. Not available with Rally Gauge Cluster. (F)

Parking Brake Warning Lamp (Code 414)

Mounted on instrument panel to show red light when ignition is turned on and parking brake is set. Lamp stays on until brake is fully released. (F,D)

Glove Compartment Lamp (Code 402)

Lights automatically when glove compartment door is opened. (F,D)

Ashtray and Lighter Lamps (Code 412)

Glow automatically when parking lamps or head lamps go on. Plainly seen when ashtray is pulled out or when lighter is removed. (F,D)

Instrument Panel Courtesy Lamp (Code 411)

Lights when front door is opened. Also manually operated by instrument panel switch. Located under instrument panel. Standard on Convertibles. (F,D)

Remote-control Outside Mirror (Code 394)

Mounts on left-hand door. Easily adjusted from inside car. Provides sharp, clear image. (F, D)

Visor Vanity Mirror (Code 391)

Mounts on back of visor. Out of sight when not in use. Ideal for checking makeup, combing hair, etc. (F,D)

Non-glare Inside Rearview Mirror (Code 392)

Has special finger knob to permit easy adjustment to non-glare or nighttime driving position. (F,D)

Visor Vanity Mirror ▼

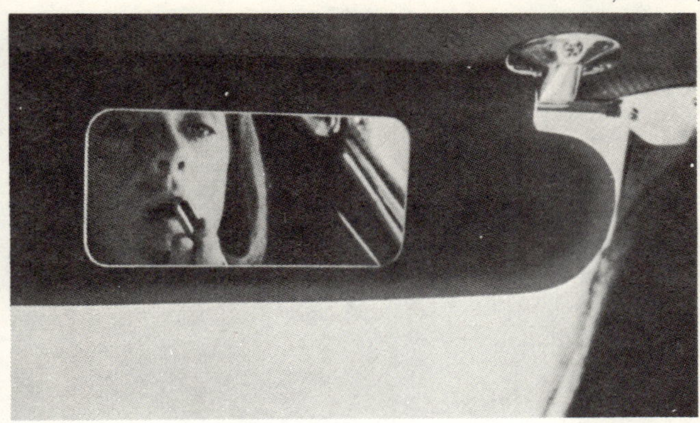

Spare Tire and Wheel Cover (Code 372)

Protects trunk contents and tire. Slips on, off easily. Dresses up luggage compartment. (All models except Station Wagons.) (F,D)

Safe-T-Track Differential (Code 731)

Power is directed from one driving wheel to the other, always the one with the best grip on the road surface. Controlled ride through rutted roads on sand or gravel, over bumps or chuckholes, through heavy snow, on wet or icy roads. Minimizes the hazard of getting stuck. (F)

Custom Sports Steering Wheel (Code 471)

Handsome wood-grain appearance. Has three equally spaced brushed stainless steel spokes. Horn button is in center. (F)

Exhaust Tailpipe Extensions (Code 482)

Two gleaming extension pipes for dual exhaust system;

Custom Front and Rear Seat Belts with Retractors (Code 431)

On 4-door models—custom seat belts with retractors in both front and rear . . . on 2-door models—custom seat belts with retractors on front seat, custom seat belts less retractors on rear seat. Push-button on buckle releases belt which then retracts into housing when not in use. Seat belt colors harmonize with interiors. (F)

Litter Basket

Available in red, blue, black or beige to harmonize with car interior. Clings to transmission tunnel, weighted to prevent tipping. Easily removed for emptying. (D)

Chrome Tissue Dispenser

Holds regular size tissue box. Swings out for use, swings back and locks in place when not in use. (D)

Engine Block Water Heater

Electric pre-heater for engine coolant provides fast, effortless engine starts, quick heater action during severe cold. Single unit raises engine coolant overnight from 0°F. to 50°F., dual unit to about 90°F. Operates from standard 110 v house electrical outlet. (D)

Tonneau Cover

Protects convertible interior from rain or hot sun when top is down. Sturdy vinyl snaps off or on in a jiffy. Has zipper opening for single occupancy of driver. (D)

Spare Tire Lock

Prevents theft of spare tire and wheel in trunk. (D)

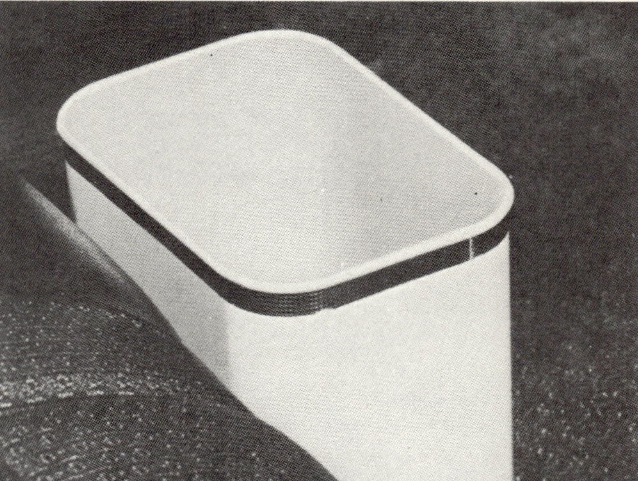

A. Litter Basket ▲

C. Engine Block Water Heater ▼

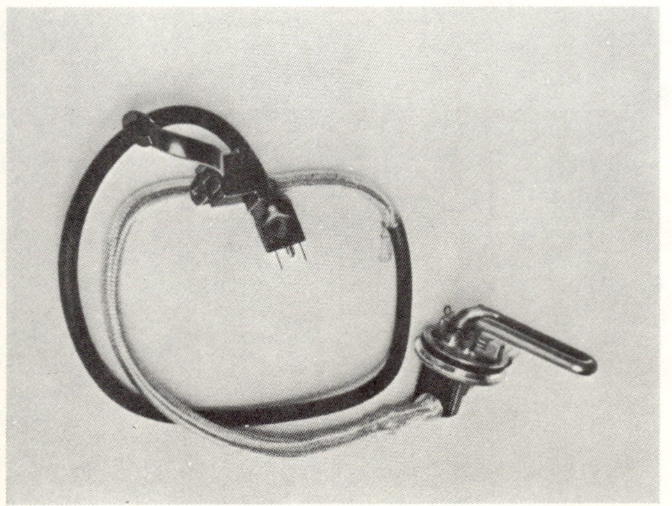

Rally Clock (Code 444)

Features sweep second hand and special built-in automatic self-regulator. Illuminated dial for easy night reading. Not available with Rally Cluster option (Code 448). (F,D)

Rally Cluster (Code 448)

Includes 250° sweep tachometer, speedometer, oil pressure and water temperature gauges—plus fuel indicator and battery tell-tale light. Tachometer not available without Cluster (F). Rally Clock (Code 444) not available with Rally Cluster.

Superlift Shock Absorbers (Code 634)

Help maintain level ride when trunk or trailer-tongue loads are extra heavy. Adjustable air spring is built into shock absorber. Equipped with tire-type air-filler for simple air fill at service stations. (F,D)

Full Transistor Ignition System (Code 671)

The finest of ignition systems. Provides ignition without condenser or mechanical contacts. Combines increased high-speed output with greater ignition stability, is rugged and water-proof. Available as option for premium fuel engines only. (F)

Full Transistor Voltage Regulator (Code 664)

Increases battery life, provides voltage regulation. No moving parts or breaker points. (F)

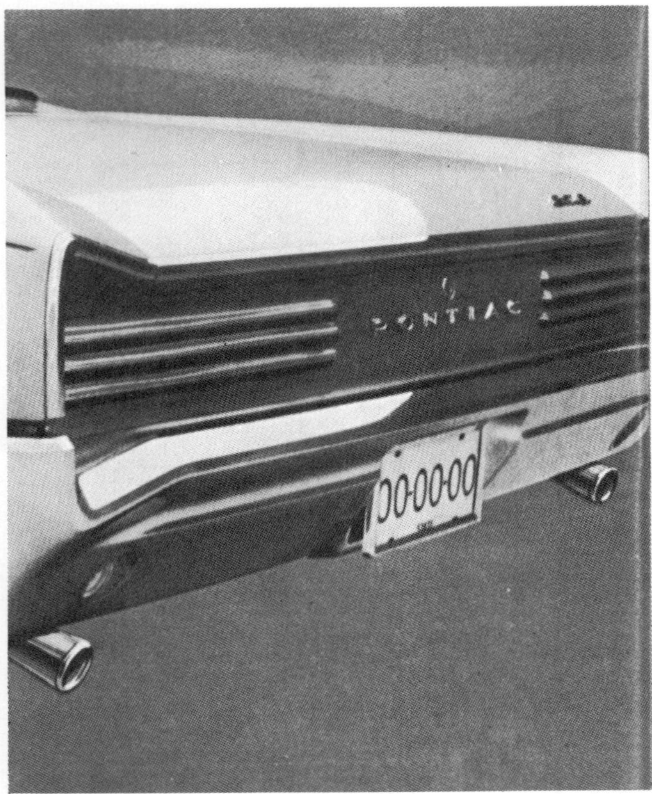

Exhaust Tailpipe Extensions ▲

Custom Wheel Discs ▲

Rally Wheels ▲

Custom Wheel Discs (Code 458)

Made of chrome-flashed stainless steel with handsomely slotted cooling vents. (F,D)

Wire Wheel Discs (Code 452)

For the special flair and sport car look. Gleaming wire spokes handsomely styled and structurally strong. (F,D)

Rally Wheels (Code 454)

With 7.75 x 14 tires only. Functional and sporty. Large openings provide maximum cooling for brakes. Includes stainless steel cap, chrome-plated wheel nuts and stainless steel full trim ring. (F)

Tilt Steering Wheel (Code 504)

Easily adjusts to 7 different positions to meet individual physical requirements. Increases steering comfort, permits easier entry or exit from car. Provides improved over-the-wheel vision. Available with Power Steering only. (N.A. with 3-speed column shift.) (F)

Full-width Floor Mat (Front Only)

Extends over center hump, easily removed for cleaning. Attractively styled in 8 colors that complement interiors. (D)

Floor Mats, Front (Code 631) Rear (Code 632)

Keeps car looking new. Durable and practical. Easily removed for washing. Available in 8 Pontiac colors to harmonize with the interiors. (F,D)

Door Edge Guard (Code 382)

Bright, stainless steel strips help prevent nicks and scratches on door edges. (F,D)

Car Compass

Dependable, with special compensator for car use. Illuminated dial. (D)

Console with 3-Speed or 4-Speed Manual Transmission (Code 472)

Available on Le Mans (except 4-door Hardtop) and GTO Series. Available only with bucket seats. Finished in stylish, ribbed metal. On both 3- and 4-speed transmissions, the shift knob features a shifting diagram. (F)

Console with Automatic Transmission (Code 472)

Available only on Le Mans and GTO models equipped with bucket seats. Finished in stylish, ribbed metal. (F)

Gearshift Knob (Code 524)

Walnut gearshift knob for GTO Series only with 4-speed synchromesh. (F,D)

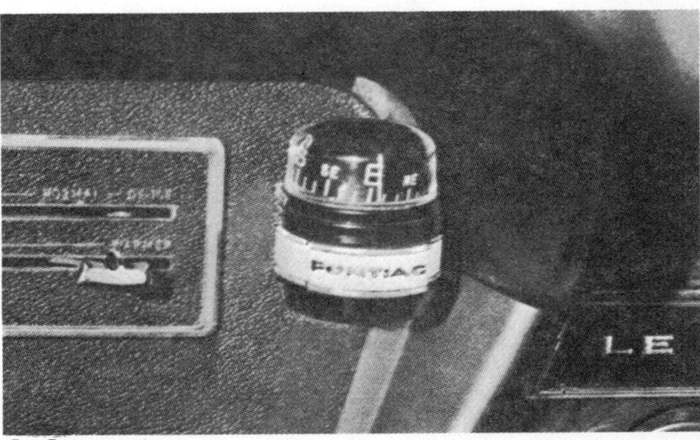

Car Compass ▲

Headrest (Code 571)

Extra protection and comfort. Bolster is covered in handsome, long-wearing Morrokide in complementary colors to the interiors. (F)

Reclining Bucket Seat (Code 574)

Reclines at 45° angle, allows passengers to stretch out and relax. Headrests (Code 571) are included for both passenger and driver's side with Reclining Bucket Seats. (F)

Custom Carpet (Code 572)

Loop pile nylon blend carpet. Handsome and long-wearing. Optional at extra cost on Tempest, standard on Tempest Custom, Le Mans and GTO. (F,D) (Not illustrated)

Console with 3-Speed or 4-Speed Manual Transmission ▼

Gearshift Knob ▼

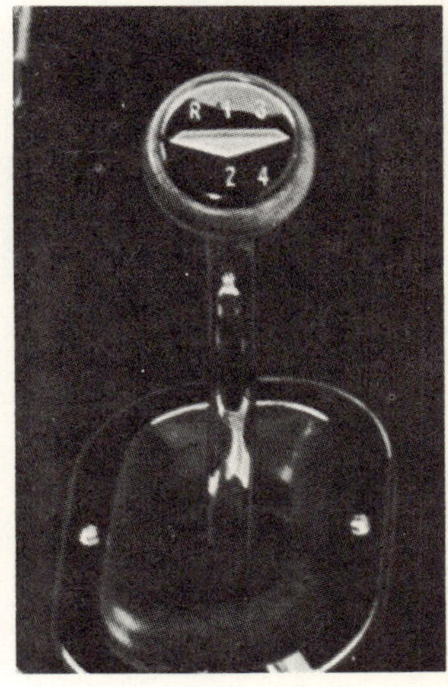

Console with Automatic Transmission ▼

BASIC GROUP (Code 061)

Pushbutton Radio with Manual Antenna

Electric clock (except cars with Rally Gauge Cluster—Code 444)

Dual Stage, Heavy-duty Air Cleaner

MIRROR GROUP (Code 071)

Outside Remote Control Mirror

Visor Vanity Mirror

LAMP GROUP (Code 074)

Luggage Compartment Lamp (except Station Wagons)

Roof Rail Reading Lamp (except Convertibles)

Glove Box Lamp

Ash Tray and Lighter Lamp

Courtesy Lamp (standard on Convertibles)

Underhood Lamp

Ignition and Starter Switch Lamp

PROTECTION GROUP (Code 062)

Door Edge Guards

Floor Mats, Front and Rear

Rear Window Defogger (except Station Wagons and Convertibles)

Custom Seat Belts, Front and Rear.

B. CUSTOM AIR CONDITIONER (Code 582)
It's combined with Circ-L-Aire heater to give full range comfort control. It heats and cools air, controls humidity, limits window fogging and filters the air. Lets you ride in cool or warm, clean, noise-free comfort. (F,D)

Custom Air Conditioner ▲

C. SOFT-RAY GLASS (Code 531)
Reduce glare and enjoy more comfortable driving with fully tinted windows. The upper area of the windshield is shaded for added glare reduction. Recommended with air conditioning. Also available on windshield only. (Code 532). (F)

D. REAR WINDOW DEFOGGER (Code 374)
A blower under the rear package shelf channels air through a grille to the rear window. Result—helps give you a clear view all the time. Not available on Station Wagons or Convertibles. (F,D)

E. ROOF OR DECK LID SKI AND LUGGAGE CARRIER
Can be installed or removed in minutes. Available on all models. Carries up to six pairs of skis or 100 lbs. of luggage. Has a key lock. Made of bright chrome and stainless steel. (D)

F. REMOVABLE LUGGAGE CARRIER—KARPAK
Lightweight, easily removed, quickly installed on roof or deck lid. All models except Station Wagons with luggage carrier. (D)

G. VENTILATED CUSHION
Make summer driving more comfortable. Special coil spring construction allows air to circulate between passenger and seat. (D)

Cruise Control ▲

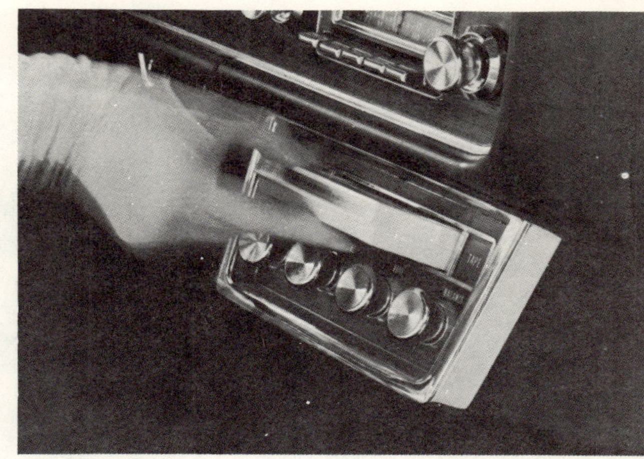
A. Delco Stereo Tape Player ▲

B. Pushbutton AM-FM Radio ▾

C. Pushbutton Radio ▾

A. POWER STEERING (Code 501)
One or two pounds of effort is all you need for the easiest steering you'll ever experience. Makes driving, turning and parking a breeze. (F,D)

B. POWER BRAKES (Code 502)
Just a light touch of the toe gives adequate braking pressure. Includes bright metal trim plate on brake pedal when factory-installed. (F,D)

C. REAR DECK LID RELEASE (Code 492)
Here's real convenience. You can release the trunk lock electrically from the driver's seat. The pushbutton control is located inside the glove box. The trunk also may be unlocked with a key. All models except Station Wagons. (F,D)

D. CRUISE CONTROL (Code 441)
Maintain a preselected speed automatically by depressing a button located at the end of your turn signal indicator lever. Cruise control releases to accelerator control with slightest brake pressure. Great for turnpike driving. Available only with Turbo Hydra-Matic or automatic transmissions, V-8 engines. (F,D)

F. POWER BUCKET SEAT (L.H. only) (Code 564)
Moves seat forward and backward; raises and lowers seat to many positions for driving comfort. (F)

H. TILT STEERING WHEEL (Code 504)
Adjusts to seven different positions for individual driving comfort. Permits easier entry and exit, better visibility for shorter people. Available with Power Steering only. Not with 3-speed column shift. (F)

I. POWER WINDOWS (Code 551)
Gives the driver fingertip control of all vertical side windows from a single control panel at his side. Each window has its own control button, too. Inoperable when ignition is off. (F)

A. DELCO STEREO TAPE PLAYER (Code 354)
Mounted under the instrument panel with or without console. The Delco Stereo Tape Player comes with one rear speaker, plus the standard front speaker. It's available only with any of the several radio options. It has its own built-in amplifiers and plays the new 8-track Stereo Tape Cartridges. It has a "Balance" control that lets you vary the volume between the front and rear speakers. It also has a track selector and tone and volume controls. Not available with heaterless cars. (F,D)

B. PUSHBUTTON AM-FM RADIO WITH MANUAL ANTENNA (Code 344)
Offers dual listening enjoyment on either AM or FM frequencies. Completely transistorized. Pushbuttons can be set to either AM or FM or combinations of both. Unusually fine quality and fidelity. (F,D)

C. PUSHBUTTON RADIO AND MANUAL ANTENNA (Code 342)
Superior tone and fidelity. Completely transistorized. Wide dial provides space for precise turning. (F,D)

D. MANUAL CONTROL RADIO AND MANUAL ANTENNA (Code 348)
Completely transistorized. Excellent tone quality and fidelity. Wide dial for precise tuning. (F,D)

E. REAR SPEAKER (Code 351)
Brilliant tone and depth control. 3-step switch lets you play front, rear or both speakers. Not available with Delco Stereo Tape Player. (F,D)

F. VERBRA-PHONIC REAR SPEAKER (Code 352)
Brilliant tone simulates acoustics in an auditorium when both speakers are playing. 3-step switch lets you play through front, rear or both speakers. All models except Station Wagons and cars with Delco Stereo Tape Player. (F,D)

G. ELECTRIC POWER ANTENNA (Code 341)
Available with all radios. Raises and lowers the antenna by a switch on the instrument panel. Antenna is mounted on right rear fender on all models. Not available on Station Wagons. (F,D)

B. SIDE ROOF RAIL AND READING LAMPS (Code 404)
Mounted on interior side of roof rails. One lamp on each side. They light up when the door is opened, each lamp has an individual switch. Not available on Convertibles. (F)

L. Highway Emergency Kit

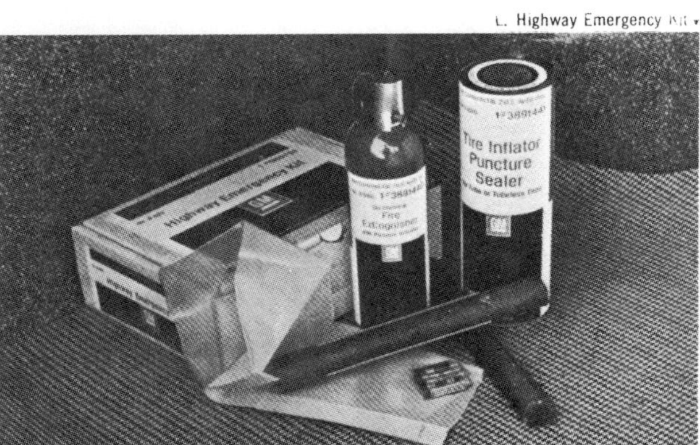

F. Anti-Theft Barrier

H. Vacuum Gauge

E. UNDERHOOD LAMP (Code 421)
Unit similar to Luggage Lamp, but located under engine hood. Available on all models (F,D) (not illustrated)

F. ANTI-THEFT BARRIER
A heavy-gauge, steel wire mesh screen fits between the rear seat and the trunk compartment. Gives extra protection; it's bolted from the trunk side; cannot be dismantled from the passenger side. Available on Convertibles only. Note: Spare tire wheel cover is available only through your dealer while supply lasts. (D)

G. RED FENDER LINERS (Code 522)
Red heavy-duty plastic liners for the front fender skirts and rear wheelhouse areas give every Tempest added dash and flair. Not available on Station Wagons. (F,D)

H. VACUUM GAUGE
Available with console only. Vacuum gauge measures manifold vacuum—lets you know when you're driving in the most economical fuel range. (D)

I. IGNITION AND STARTER SWITCH LAMP (Code 422)
Turn on your parking lights and a special light makes the ignition switch immediately visible. No more fumbling to find the keyhole. (F)

J. SAFEGUARD SPEEDOMETER (Code 442)
Warns of excess speed. Control knob lets you select desired speed limit. Buzzer signals when car exceeds this speed. Not available with Rally Cluster. (F)

L. HIGHWAY EMERGENCY KIT
Includes antenna emergency flag, fire extinguisher, tire inflator and warning flares and extra fuses. (D)

REMOTE-CONTROL OUTSIDE MIRROR (Code 394)
Mounts on left-hand door. Convenient and easy to adjust from inside car. (F,D)

FRONT SEAT SHOULDER STRAPS (Code 434)
Give extra security by keeping the torso erect in case of sudden stops. Available with all seat belts for driver and front seat passenger. One end is anchored to the floor, the other end is anchored at the roof rail above the driver or passenger on all models except Convertibles where it anchors at the rear inner quarter panel. The shoulder strap is worn diagonally across the torso in conjunction with your seat belt. It has a pushbutton buckle release. (F,D)

SEAT BELT RETRACTORS FOR STANDARD REAR SEAT BELTS
Not recommended for buckle half of the seat belt. The retractors hold belts snugly against the rear seat when they're not in use. (D)

CUSTOM FRONT AND REAR SEAT BELTS WITH RETRACTORS (Code 701)
On 4-door models Custom Seat Belts with retractors in both front and rear seats. On 2-door models Custom Seat Belts with retractors in front seat; Custom Seat Belts less retractors in rear seat. On Station Wagons, Custom Seat Belts with retractors in both front and rear seats. Pushbutton on buckle releases belt which then retracts when not in use. Seat belt colors harmonize with interiors. (F)

CENTER REAR SEAT BELTS (Code 432)
Add a third seat belt to your rear seat for the passenger who rides in the center. Select Custom or Standard Belts.

CUSTOM SPORTS STEERING WHEEL (Code 471)
Handsome "just like wood" appearance. Has three equally spaced, brushed stainless steel spokes. Horn button in center. (F)

HOOD RETAINERS
Enthusiasts will recognize them immediately. Double locking protection at all times with dual stainless steel posts to keep the hood secured. Chrome finished. (D)

RALLY STRIPE PACKAGE
Get the Sports Car appearance. Rally stripe goes from the front of the hood, over the top to the rear edge of the deck. Available in Red, Black, White and Blue. (D)

DUAL STAGE, HEAVY-DUTY AIR CLEANER (Code 361)
Dual filter design consists of wetted paper inner filter surrounded by a special polyglycol wetted polyurethane foam outer filter. These two filters give finer filtration, extended service. Not available on the 4 barrel OHC 6 cylinder engine or GTO with 4 barrel engine. (F,D)

TACHOMETER
New hood-mounted design, installed outside the car in front of the windshield, in line with the driver. Offers easy, instant reading—minimum of distraction. (D)

LITTER BASKET
Clings to transmission tunnel. Weighted to prevent tipping, empties easily. Available in red, blue, black, beige. (D)

TONNEAU COVER
Protect your Convertible interior from hot sun when the top is down. Made of sturdy vinyl, it snaps on and off in a jiffy. Can be left on when driver is alone in the car. (D)

VISOR VANITY MIRROR (Code 391)
Mounts on back of visor. Out of sight when not in use. Ideal for checking makeup, combing hair, etc. (F,D)

CHROME TISSUE DISPENSER
Holds a regular-size box of tissues. Swings back under the center of the control panel when not in use. Locks in place. Not available on cars equipped with air conditioning. (D)

ENGINE BLOCK WATER HEATER
Electric pre-heater for engine coolant provides fast, effortless starts, quick heater action during severe cold. Single unit raises engine coolant overnight from 0° F to 50° F, dual unit to about 90° F. Operates from standard house electrical outlet. (D)

SPARE TIRE LOCK
Prevents theft of spare tire and wheel in trunk. (D)

Hood Retainers ▲

Rally Stripe Package ▼

Tachometer ▼

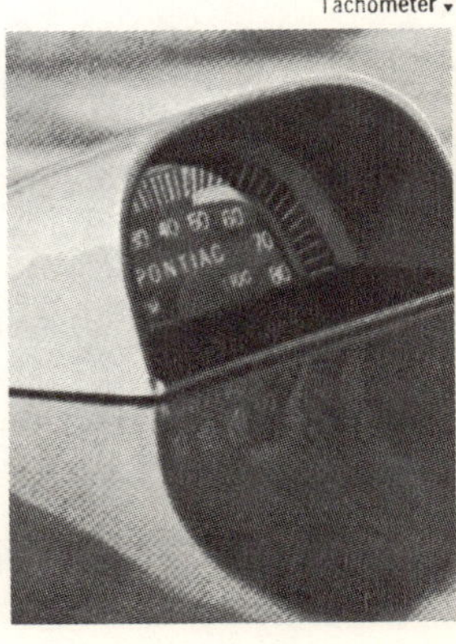

B. CAR COMPASS
Dependable with special compensator for in-car use. Illuminated dial. (D)

C. FIRE EXTINGUISHER
A 5-lb., dry chemical fire extinguisher for all types of fires, including grease, oil, gasoline and electrical. It's rechargeable. (D)

D. DOOR EDGE GUARDS (Code 382)
These bright, stainless steel strips help prevent nicks and scratches on door edges. (F,D)

E. HEAVY-DUTY BATTERY (Code 678)
This 61 amp. hr. battery provides longer life, greater power and increased cranking ability. Its "thru the partition" cell connection structure adds wattage. Keeps your power accessories operating efficiently. (F,D)

F. TRUNK AUXILIARY FLOOR MAT (Code 362)
A heavy-duty, rugged, solid vinyl floor mat gives extra protection for trunk compartment as well as for cargo. Not available on Station Wagons. (F,D)

G. FULL-WIDTH FLOOR MAT (Front only)
Long-lasting, easily removed for cleaning. Extends over center tunnel, protects whole floor. Available in six Pontiac colors. (D)

I. REAR DOOR LOCK GUARDS (4 Door Models Only)
Prevents children from unlocking and opening rear doors. When buttons are down and lock guards are pushed in, rear doors can't be opened without inserting key into lock button. 1.—Unlocked position. 2.—Regular locked position. 3.—Guard Lock position. Any one of your car keys may be used to unlock the Lock Guards. (D)

J. FLOOR MATS, FRONT (Code 631)
REAR (Code 632)
Keep car looking new. Easily removed for washing. Available in six Pontiac colors to harmonize with interiors. (F,D)

A. SAFE-T-TRACK DIFFERENTIAL (Code 731)
Minimizes the hazard of getting stuck. Power is directed from one driving wheel to the other, always the one with the best grip on the road surface. Sure handling through rutted roads, on sand or gravel, over bumps or chuck holes, through heavy snow, on wet or icy roads. (F)

B. EXHAUST TAILPIPE EXTENSIONS (Code 482)
Two gleaming extension pipes for dual exhaust systems; one extension for OHC L-6 4-bbl engine. (F,D)

C. FRONT WHEEL DISC BRAKES (Code 521)
Includes Power Brakes. Available on Tempest, Tempest Custom, Tempest Safari, Le Mans and GTO. (F,D)

D. RALLY CLOCK (Code 474)
Features sweep second hand and special built-in automatic self regulator. Illuminated dial for easy night reading. Not available with Rally Cluster Option (code 444). (F,D)

E. RALLY GAUGE, CLUSTER, AND TACHOMETER (Code 444)
Includes 250° sweep tachometer, speedometer, oil pressure and water temperature gauges—plus fuel indicator and battery tell-tale light. (F).

F. TRANSISTORIZED VOLTAGE REGULATOR (Code 664)
Increases battery life, provides voltage regulation. No moving parts or breaker points. Especially valuable in cold-weather areas and on cars requiring heavy electrical loads. (F)

G. SUPERLIFT SHOCK ABSORBERS, REAR (Code 634)
Help maintain a level ride when trunk or trailer-tongue loads are extra heavy. Adjustable air spring is built into rear shock absorber. Equipped with tire-type air filler valve for simple air fill at filling stations. (F,D)

H. CAPACITOR DISCHARGE IGNITION SYSTEM (Code 671)
The finest of ignition systems. Gives ignition without condenser or mechanical contacts. Combines increased high-speed output with greater ignition stability. Lengthens spark plug life, is rugged and waterproof. Available as option for premium fuel engines only. Not available on cars with AM-FM radio. (F)

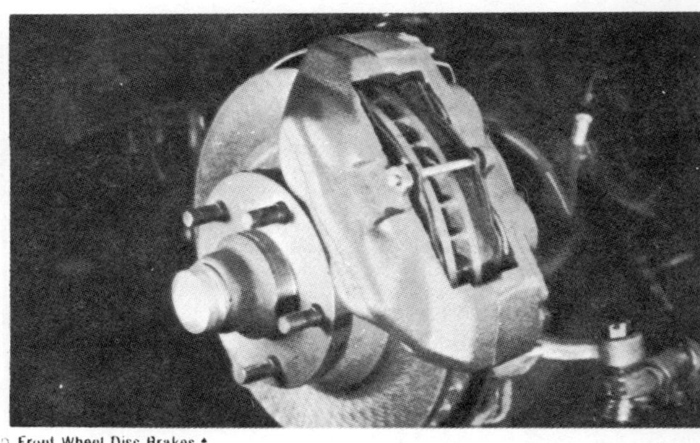
D. Front Wheel Disc Brakes ▲

1
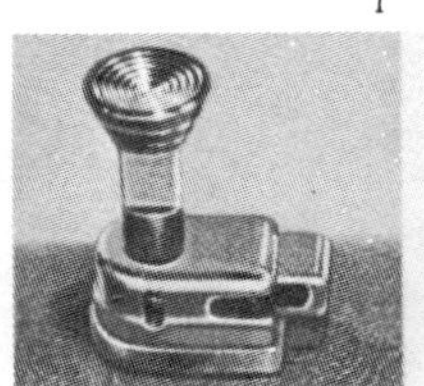
2

3

I. Rear Door Lock Guard ▲

C. Fire Extinguisher ▼

F. Trunk Auxiliary Floor Mat ▼
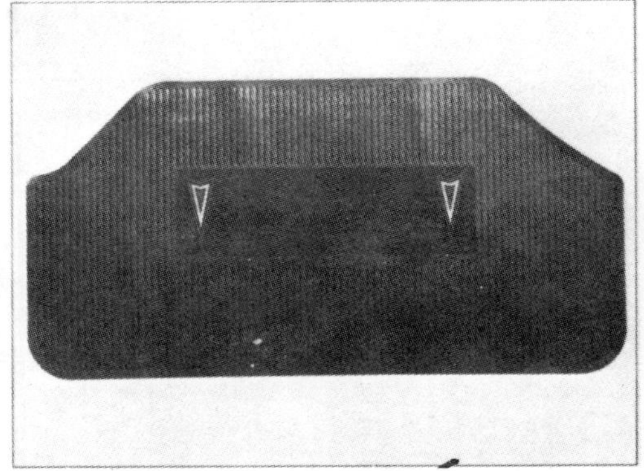

A. CUSTOM WHEEL DISCS (Code 458)
Made of chrome-flashed stainless steel with gray matte finish; black matte panels are surrounded with gleaming chrome. A three-pronged spinner adds a look of ruggedness. The center of the spinner is black plastic insert with red "PMD" letters framed in chrome. (F,D)

B. WIRE WHEEL DISCS (Code 452)
For that special flair and sports-car look. Gleaming wire spokes handsomely styled and structurally strong. (F,D)

C. RALLY I WHEELS (Code 454)
Functional and sporty. Large openings provide maximum cooling for brakes. Includes stainless steel cap, chrome-plated wheel nuts and stainless steel full trim ring. (F)

D. RALLY II WHEELS (Code 453)
These are specially styled, 14-inch steel wheels with a new center emblem. They have a stainless steel trim ring and chrome wheel nuts. Available with Front Wheel Disc Brakes. Available on all Tempest Series. (F)

E. DELUXE WHEEL DISCS (Code 461)
Made of chrome-flashed stainless steel with polished ribs and alternating cutouts and gray matte panels. A black plastic insert forms the center hub ornament with red "PMD" letters framed in chrome. (F,D)

F. CONSOLE WITH 3-SPEED OR 4-SPEED MANUAL TRANSMISSION (Code 472)
Available on Le Mans with bucket seats (except 4-Door Hardtop) and GTO series. Finished with wood grain appearance. On both 3- and 4-speed transmission, the standard shift knob features a shifting diagram. (F)

G. CONSOLE WITH AUTOMATIC TRANSMISSION (Code 472)
Available only on Le Mans with bucket seats (except 4-Door Hardtop). Finished with wood grain appearance. (F)

A. Custom Wheel Discs ▴

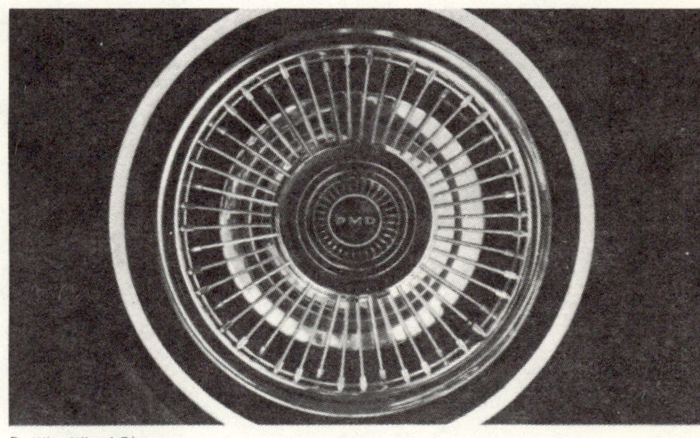
B. Wire Wheel Discs ▴

D. Rally II Wheels ▴

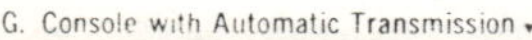
G. Console with Automatic Transmission ▾

H. Console for Turbo Hydra-Matic Transmission ▾

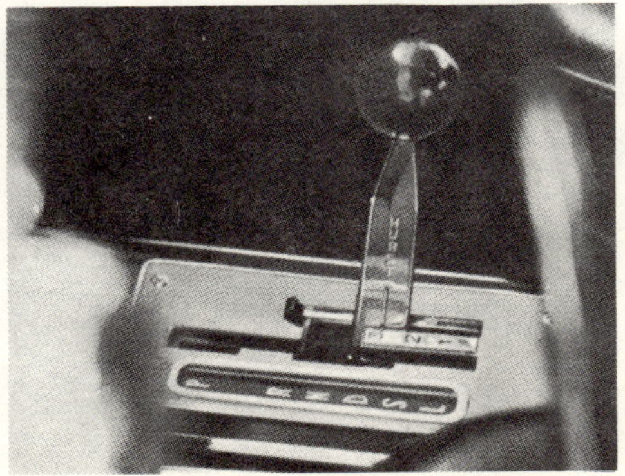

F. Console with 3-Speed or 4-Speed Manual Transmission ▾

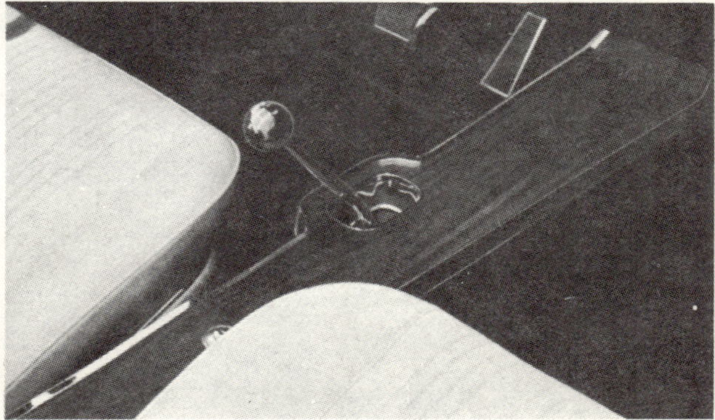

H. CONSOLE FOR TURBO HYDRA-MATIC TRANSMISSION (Code 472)

Available on GTO only. Finished with wood grain appearance. (F)

I. CUSTOM GEARSHIFT KNOB (Code 524)

Walnut-appearing Gearshift Knob for 3- and 4-speed manual floor shift. Has ebony-appearing Pontiac Crest with shift position designations. Available on all models. (F,D)

J. HEADREST (Code 572)

Provides extra protection and comfort. Bolster is covered in handsome, long wearing Morrokide in colors complementary to the interiors. Available with bench seat (code 572) or bucket seats (code 571). (F)

K. RECLINING BUCKET SEAT—PASSENGER SIDE ONLY (Code 578)

Reclines at 45° angle, allows passenger to stretch out and relax. Headrests (code 571) are included for both passenger and driver with Reclining Bucket Seat. (F)

L. CUSTOM CARPET (Code 511)

Loop pile, nylon blend carpet. Handsome and long-wearing. Optional at extra cost on Tempest. Standard on all other Tempest series. (F,D) (Not illustrated)

J. Headrest ▲

BASIC GROUP (Code 321)

Pushbutton Radio and Manual Antenna (Available all Pontiac models).

Heavy-duty Air Cleaner (Available all Pontiac models).

Electric Clock (Available all Firebirds, Tempest, Tempest Custom, LeMans, Tempest Safari, GTO and Catalina models).

LAMP GROUP (Code 332)

Ignition Switch Lamp (Available on Firebird, Tempest, Tempest Custom, LeMans, Tempest Safari, GTO models. Standard on all other Pontiac models).

Roof Rail and Reading Lamps (Available on all Pontiacs except Firebird and convertible models).

PROTECTION GROUP (Code 322)

Door-edge Guards—all Pontiac models.

Custom Seat Belts—all Pontiac models.

Floor Mats, Front and Rear—all Pontiac models.

Spare Tire Cover—all Pontiac models except with "Space-Saver Spare" or station wagons. (Standard with Brougham option.)

Rear-window Defogger—all Pontiac models except convertibles (other than Firebird) and station wagons.

MIRROR GROUP (Code 331)

Luggage Lamp (Available on all Firebirds, Tempest, Tempest Custom, LeMans, GTO, except Tempest Custom Station Wagon. Standard on all other Pontiac models except station wagons).

Visor Vanity Mirror, RH and LH—all Pontiac models.

Outside Remote-control Mirror—all Pontiac models.

Transmission Consoles (Code 472)

Available on all Pontiac models with bucket seats. Standard on Grand Prix with bucket seats. Not available with OHC 6, 3-speed manual transmission or Tempest, Tempest Custom, Tempest Safari models.

Console for 3-speed Manual Transmission.

Console for Automatic or Turbo Hydra-Matic Transmission.

Console for 4-Speed Manual Transmission.

Console for "Dual-Gate" Turbo Hydra-Matic Transmission. Available only on GTO.

Power Options

Power Brakes (Code 502). Just a light touch of the foot gives adequate braking pressure. Available on all models. (F, D)

Power Steering (Code 501). One or two pounds effort is all you need for the easiest steering you'll ever experience. Available on all models. (F, D)

Deck-lid Release (Code 492). You can unlock the trunk while you sit in the car by pressing the button control, located inside of the glove compartment. Trunk may also be unlocked with the key. Available on all models except station wagons and Firebirds. (F, D)

Power Bucket Seat (Code 564). Moves left-hand bucket seat forward and backward and up and down to any desired position for comfort. Available on all models with bucket seats except Firebirds. (F)

Cruise Control (Code 441). Maintain a preselected car speed automatically. Disengages with slight touch of the foot on the brake pedal. Available on all models with V-8 engines and automatic transmissions only. (F, D)

Power Window Lifts (Code 551). Gives driver fingertip control of all vertical side windows from a single control panel on his door. Each window has its individual control switch, too. Not operable with ignition key off. Standard with Brougham Option. Available on all models. (F)

Radio and Stereo

Pushbutton AM-FM Stereo-Multiplex Radio and Manual Antenna (Code 388). The most complete radio system you can equip your Pontiac with. You can listen to AM or FM frequencies and enjoy true stereophonic sound when the program is being broadcast in stereo. Includes two special stereo rear speakers and one front speaker with a special balance control to vary front and rear speaker volume. (Only one rear speaker in station wagons, convertibles and all Tempest models.) (F, D) Available all models except Firebirds. Firebird has Stereo-Multiplex Adapter package, dealer-installed with AM-FM radio.

Pushbutton Radio and Manual Antenna (Code 382). Enjoy completely transistorized listening pleasure. Superior tone and fidelity. Wide dial permits precise tuning. Antenna has air-foil-shaped tube for minimum wind resistance. Available all models. (F, D)

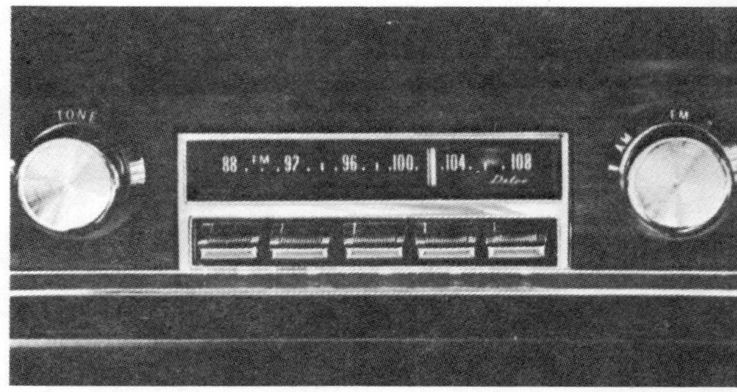

Pushbutton AM-FM Radio and Manual Antenna (Code 384). Dual listening pleasure with either AM or FM frequencies by rotating the frequency dial. Completely transistorized. Pushbuttons set for either AM or FM stations, or both. Unusually fine quality and fidelity. Available all models. (F, D)

Note: Due to technical limitations of stereo broadcasting and reception, owners may occasionally experience limited range FM and stereo reception and/or stereo distortion and flutter in certain localities.

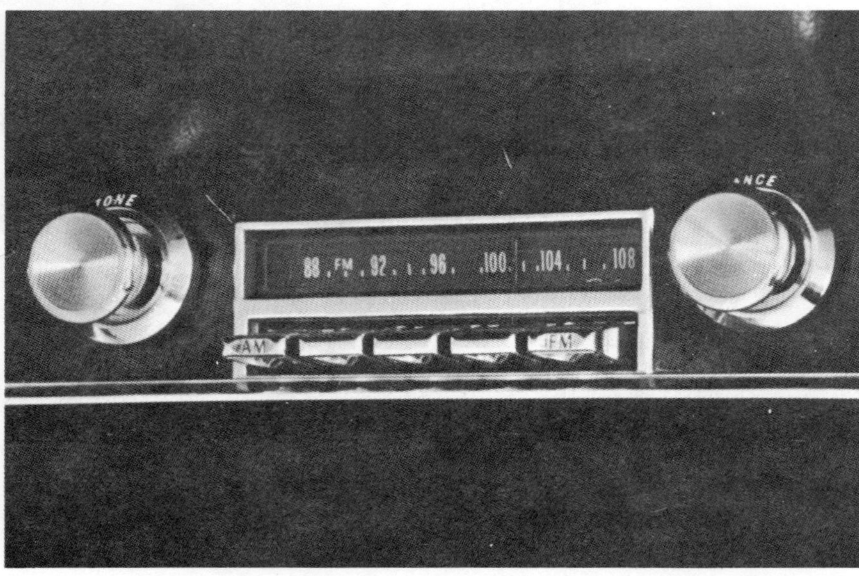

Stereo Tape Player (Code 394). Mounted under the instrument panel or on the transmission console, the stereo tape player comes with two special stereo rear speakers. Available only with any of the radio options. It has its own built-in amplifiers and plays the popular 8-track tape cartridges. It has a track selection control, its own volume and tone controls and a balance control for varying the volume between front and rear speakers. Available for all models except those equipped with floor-mounted manual transmissions. Not available on Firebird with electric clock. (F, D)

Rear Speaker (Code 391). Fader switch lets you vary front to rear speaker volume for brilliant, surrounding sound. Available all models except those equipped with Stereo-Multiplex Radio (Code 388) or Stereo Tape Player (Code 394.) (F, D)

Verbra-Phonic Rear Speaker System (Code 392). Brilliant "in-depth" tone simulates concert hall acoustics when both front and rear speakers are playing. Available all models except Firebirds and those equipped with Stereo-Multiplex Radios (Code 388) or Stereo Tape Player (Code 394). (F, D)

Electric Power Antenna (Code 381). Available with all radios on all models except Firebirds. Raises and lowers antenna by a switch on the instrument panel. Antenna is mounted on the right rear fender. (F, D)

Wheel Covers

Wire Wheel Discs (Code 452). For a special flair and sports look. Gleaming, chrome-plated wire spokes with a bright red, medallion hub insert. Available for all models except Catalina, Executive, Bonneville and Grand Prix models equipped with disc brakes or 15" wheels. (F, D)

Rally I Wheels (Code 454). Functional and sporty. Large openings provide maximum cooling for brakes. Includes stainless steel hub caps, wheel nuts and stainless steel full trim ring. Available for all Tempest, Tempest Custom, LeMans, Tempest Safari and GTO models. (F)

Rally II Wheels (Code 453). Specially styled, 14-inch steel wheels for the ultimate in sports wheel styling. They have a stainless steel wheel trim ring and chrome-plated wheel nuts. Available on all models except station wagons. Not available with disc brakes or 15-inch wheels on Catalina, Executive, Bonneville and Grand Prix models. (F)

Deluxe Wheel Discs (Code 461). Chrome-flashed stainless steel with a deep center section. Available all models. Part of Firebird Custom Option and Tempest, Tempest Custom, LeMans, Tempest Safari, GTO and Catalina Decor Group Option. Standard on all Executive, Bonneville and Grand Prix models. (F, D)

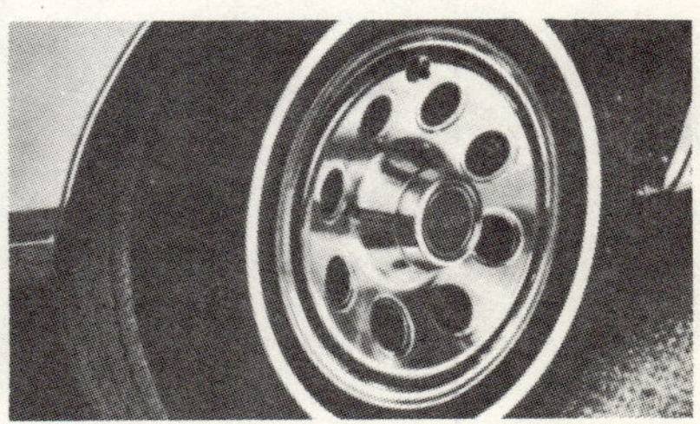

Custom Wheel Discs (Code 458). Available for all Firebird, Tempest, Tempest Custom, LeMans, Tempest Safari and GTO models. Smart, gleaming stainless steel discs with a real sports appearance for that extra-dressy touch. (F, D)

Miscellaneous Accessories

Custom Seat Belts (Code 431). On all 4-door models except station wagons. 3 custom seat belts with retractors on two outside belts in front seat. 3 custom seat belts with retractors on two outside belts in rear seat. Same on station wagons with the addition of 2 custom seat belts, less retractors in third seat. On 2-door models, 3 custom seat belts with retractors on two outside belts in front seat, except models with bucket seats which have belts with retractors for each bucket seat. Rear seats have 3 custom seat belts, no retractors. Seat belt colors harmonize with interiors and belts have a rich, heavy brushed-chrome buckle. (F)

Front Shoulder Belts (Code 754), Custom Front Shoulder Belts (Code 754 with Code 431). For driver and right, front-seat passenger only. Custom Front Shoulder Belts feature smart-looking brushed-chrome buckle, and belt color-keyed to interior. Available all Pontiac models. (F)

Head Restraints (Code 571) for Bucket Seats; (Code 572) for Bench Seats. Available with any type front seat—for passenger and driver. Matches seat trim. Provides an extra measure of protection. Included in reclining seat option —Code 578. (F)

Electric Clock (Code 474). It has a sweep second hand and built-in automatic self-regulator. Dial is illuminated for easy night reading. Standard on Executive, Bonneville and Grand Prix—included with Custom Gauge Cluster (Code 444). (F, D)

Rally Clock (Code 474). Available on Tempest, Tempest Custom, Le Mans and GTO models only—except those equipped with Code 444, Rally Gauge Cluster. Features sweep second hand and automatic self-regulator. (F, D)

Remote-control Outside Mirror (Code 424). Mounts on left-hand door. Control conveniently adjusts mirror from inside the car. Available all models. No dealer package for Firebird. (F, D)

Reclining Seat, Passenger Side (Code 578). Available for Bonneville Brougham and Grand Prix models with either Strato-bucket or Strato-bench seat. Le Mans, GTO, Catalina and Bonneville models with Strato-bucket seats. Passenger side seat reclines at a 45° angle. Includes head restraints for both passenger and driver. (F)

Visor Vanity Mirror (Code 421); Right- and left-hand Visor Mirrors (Code 422). Mounts on back of visor. Out of sight when not in use. Ideal for checking make-up, combing hair, etc. Available for right-hand visor only or both visors on all models. (F, D)

Tilt Steering Wheel (Code 504). Adjusts to seven different positions for individual driving comfort. Permits easy exit and entry. Provides ample lap room for stouter people. Available on all models with power steering only. Not available with 3-speed manual column shift transmission. (F)

Rear-window Defogger (Code 404). A blower under the package shelf channels air through a directional grille out the rear window. Helps give you a clear view when inside windows have tendency to fog up. Available on all models except station wagons and convertibles other than Firebirds. (F, D)

Soft-Ray Glass (Code 531). All windows. Recommended with air conditioning. (Convertible rear windows on Tempest Custom, Le Mans, GTO and Firebirds not tinted.) Upper area of windshield is shaded for added brightness reduction. Tinted windshield only is available on all models. (Code 532). (F)

Custom Sports Steering Wheel (Code 471). Smart, "just-like-wood" appearance. Has three equally spaced, brushed stainless steel spokes. Horn button in center. Available all models. (F)

Rear-door Child Lock Guards (4-Door Models Only). Prevents children from unlocking and opening rear doors. When buttons are down and Lock Guards are pushed in, rear doors can't be opened without inserting key into lock button. 1—Unlock position. 2—Regular locked position. 3—Lock Guard position. Any of your regular car keys may be used to release the Lock Guards. (D)

Custom Gearshift Knob (Code 524). Walnut-appearing gearshift knob for 3- or 4-speed, floor-mounted transmission shift levers. Has shift position indicated on 4-speed knob. Has Pontiac "Vee" Crest on 3-speed knob. Available all models with floor-mounted transmission. (F, D)

Tachometer (Code 434). New Pontiac design. Hood-mounted unit, installed outside the car in front of the windshield, in line with the driver's vision. Offers easy, instant reading. Available all models. (F, D)

Rally Gauge Cluster and Rally Clock (Code 484). Available on Tempest, Tempest Custom, Le Mans and GTO models only. Includes sweep second hand and automatic self-regulator clock, speedometer, oil-pressure and water-temperature gauges—plus fuel indicator and battery telltale light. (F) Also available is **Rally Gauge Cluster and Instrument Panel Mounted Tachometer (Code 444).** (F)

Safeguard Speedometer (Code 442). Warns of excessive speed. Control knob lets you select desired speed limit. Buzzer signals when car exceeds this speed. Not available with Rally Cluster on Tempest, Tempest Custom, Le Mans and GTO models. (F)

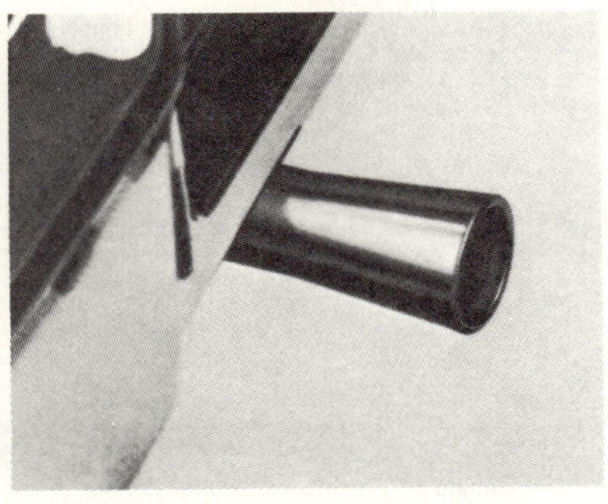

Exhaust Tailpipe Extensions (Code 482). Available on all Firebird, Tempest, Tempest Custom, Le Mans, GTO models except station wagons. Two gleaming extension pipes for dual exhaust system; one extension for OHC 6 4-BBL engine. (F, D)

Concealed Headlamps—GTO (Code 414). Available only on GTO models. Provides a distinctively clean appearance to the front end. Sections of the grille swing down and out of the way when headlamps are in use. Headlamp switch automatically controls position of headlamp doors. (F)

Safe-T-Track Differential (Code 361). Power is directed to the rear driving wheel that has the most traction. Surer handling through rutted roads, sand, gravel, bumps, chuck holes, heavy snow or on wet and slippery roads. Minimizes the hazard of getting stuck. Available all models. (F)

Front-wheel Disc Brakes (Code 521). Power brakes required on Tempest Custom and Tempest Safari Station Wagons. Power brakes, 8.45 x 15 tires and 15-inch wheels included on all Catalina, Executive, Bonneville and Grand Prix models. (Power brakes not included on all other models.) (F)

Space-Saver Spare Tire (Code 702). Adds up to 3 cubic feet of usable luggage capacity. Easily inflated with handy pressure can and affords approximately 2,000 miles of spare tire driving. Available on all models. Standard on Firebird series. (F). New Space-Saver Tire inflators for replacement are available at your dealer. (D)

Door-edge Guards (Code 412). The bright, stainless steel strips help prevent nicks and scratches on door edges. (F, D)

Hood Retainers. Enthusiasts will recognize them immediately. Double locking protection at all times with dual stainless steel posts to keep the hood secure. Chrome finished. (D)

Superlift Shock Absorbers (Code 634). Available all models except Firebirds. Help maintain a level ride when trunk or trailer tongue loads are extra heavy. Adjustable air spring is built into rear shock absorber. Equipped with tire-type air filler valve for simple air fill at filling stations. (F, D)

Heavy-duty Battery (Code 701). This high 55 amp. hr. battery provides longer life, greater power and increased cranking ability. Its "thru-the-partition", cell-connection structure adds wattage. Keeps your power accessories operating efficiently. (F)

Dual Stage, Heavy-duty Air Cleaner (Code 731). Dual-filter design consists of wetted paper in filter, surrounded by polyglycol wetted polyurethane foam outer filter. Fine filtration, extended surface. Available all models except those equipped with 428 H.O. engines. (F, D)

Instrument Panel Courtesy Lamp (Code 661). Lights when front door is opened. Also manually operated by switch. Available and is part of Lamp Group—Code 332—for all models except convertibles, Firebird, Catalina, Executive, Bonneville and Grand Prix—where it is standard equipment. (F, D)

Glove Compartment Lamp (Code 664). Lights automatically when glove compartment door is opened. Available and is part of Lamp Group —Code 332—for all models except Firebird, Catalina, Executive, Bonneville and Grand Prix—where it is standard equipment. (F, D)

Luggage Compartment Lamp (Code 652). Lights automatically when trunk lid is lifted. Available and is part of Lamp Group—Code 332—for all models (except station wagons) other than Catalina, Executive, Bonneville, Grand Prix where it is standard equipment. (F, D)

Ignition Switch Lamp (Code 672). Turn on parking or headlamps, and ignition key switch is illuminated. Available and part of the Lamp Group—Code 332—for all models except Catalina, Executive, Bonneville and Grand Prix where it is standard equipment. (F)

Child Safety Seat. Especially designed to give additional protection for small child passenger. Utilizes standard seat belt. Heavily padded, sturdily constructed with special chest retainer strap to restrict forward movement during quick stops. Ivory color. (F, D)

Removable Luggage Carrier—Karpak. Lightweight, easily removed, quickly installed on roof or deck lid. Water- and dust-resistant to protect luggage. All models except station wagons with luggage carrier. (D)

Ventilated Cushions. Helps make driving more comfortable, especially in hot, sticky weather. Special, coil-spring construction allows air to circulate between passenger and seat. (D)

Ashtray and Lighter Lamps (Code 662). They illuminate automatically when parking lamps or headlamps are switched on. Available and are part of Lamp Group—Code 332—for all models except Firebird, Catalina, Executive, Bonneville and Grand Prix—where they are standard equipment. (F, D)

Underhood Lamp (Code 671). Lights automatically when hood is raised. Available and is part of Lamp Group—Code 332—for all models except Catalina, Executive, Bonneville and Grand Prix—where it is standard equipment. (F, D)

New Tissue Dispenser. Holds a junior-sized box of tissues. Smart-looking new design which attaches to underside of instrument panel—easy to use, less bulky. (D)

Gas-cap Lock. Prevents fuel theft. Separate key. Available on all models. (D)

Side Roof Rail Courtesy and Reading Lamps (Code 654). Available all models except convertibles and Firebirds. One lamp on each side, mounted on interior side roof rails. Provides more light for map reading, etc. Reading lamp on each side has individual switch. (Standard with Lamp Group—Code 332.) (F)

Underhood Utility Lamp. Ideal for emergency repairs or tire changes after dark. It has 17 feet of self-storing extension cord. Available on all models except Firebird. (D)

Spare Tire Lock. Prevents theft of spare tire and wheel in trunk. (D)

Car Compass. Dependable with special compensator for in-car use. Illuminated dial for all models. (D)

Litter Basket. Clings to transmission tunnel. Weighted to prevent tipping, and empties easily. Available in red, blue, black or beige. (D)

Fire Extinguisher. A 2½-lb. dry chemical fire extinguisher for all types of fires, including grease, oil, gasoline and electrical. It's rechargeable. (D)

Highway Emergency Kit. Includes antenna emergency flag, fire extinguisher, tire inflator and warning flares with extra fuses. (D)

Engine Block Water Heater. Electric preheater for engine coolant provides fast, effortless starts, quick heater action during severe cold. Single unit raises engine coolant overnight from 0°F to 50°F, dual unit to about 90°F. Operates from standard house electrical outlet. (D)

Spare Tire Cover (Code 402). Protects trunk contents and tire. Slips on/off easily. Dresses up luggage compartment. Available all models except station wagons and models using Space-Saver Spare tire. (F, D)

Luggage Compartment Floor Mat (Code 732). A heavy-duty, rugged, solid Gray vinyl floor mat gives extra protection for trunk compartment as well as for cargo. Not available on station wagons. (F, D). Rear compartment covering available for Firebird models, factory-installed only.

Full-width Floor Mat (Front Only). Long-lasting, easily removed for cleaning. Extends over center tunnel, protects whole floor. Available in seven Pontiac colors. Available all Pontiac series except Firebird. (D)

Floor Mats, Front (Code 631); Rear (Code 632). Keeps car looking new. Easily removed for washing. Available in seven Pontiac colors to harmonize with interiors for all Pontiac series. (F, D)

GROUPS

Some of Pontiac's more popular accessories have been combined into convenient ordering Groups. These Groups, listed below, are installed at the factory, saving you installation costs and delivery delays.

BASIC GROUP (Code 321—UPC Y88)

- Pushbutton Radio and Manual Antenna (available all models-windshield antenna standard on Grand Prix).
- Visor Vanity Mirror, Right-hand (all models).
- Outside Remote-control Mirror (all models).
- Deck Lid Release (available all models except Station Wagons).
- Dual-stage, Heavy-duty Air Cleaner (all models).
- Electric Clock (available all Firebird, Tempest, Custom S, LeMans, LeMans Safari, GTO and Catalina models).
- Custom Foam Front-seat Cushion (available Tempest, Custom S, LeMans Safari, Catalina, Executive and Bonneville models).

LAMP GROUP (Code 322—UPC Y92)

- Cornering Lamps (all models except Firebird).
- Underhood Utility Lamp (Catalina, Executive and Bonneville only).
- Underhood Lamp (Tempest, Custom S, LeMans, LeMans Safari, GTO and Grand Prix only).
- Luggage Lamp (Tempest, Custom S, LeMans and GTO only).
- Warning Lamps (Catalina, Executive and Bonneville only).
- Instrument Panel Courtesy Lamp (Tempest and Custom S only).
- Ashtray Lamp (Tempest and Custom S only).
- Glove Box Lamp (Tempest and Custom S only).

POWER ASSIST GROUP (Code 331—UPC WS6)

- Turbo Hydra-Matic (all models).
- Regular Power Steering (all Tempests and GTO's).
- Variable-ratio Power Steering (available Firebird, Catalina, Executive, Bonneville and Grand Prix models).
- Power Disc Brakes, Front (all models).

TURNPIKE CRUISE GROUP (Code 322—UPC WS5)

- Cruise Control (available all models with V-8 engines and automatic transmissions).
- Tilt Steering Wheel (available all models with Power Steering, except with manual transmission—column shift).
- Power Bench Seat (4-way, available Tempest, Custom S, LeMans, LeMans Safari; 6-way: Catalina, Executive, Bonneville and Grand Prix).
- Power Bucket Seat, Driver (all models with bucket seats).

RALLY GROUP (Code 334—UPC WS8) available Firebird, Tempest, Custom S, LeMans, LeMans Safari and GTO models only.

- Rally II Wheels.
- Custom Sports Steering Wheel.
- Rally Gauge Cluster and Clock.
- Hood Ram Air Induction (Firebird 400 and GTO only).
- Ride and Handling Springs and Shocks.

CUSTOM AIR CONDITIONING (Code 582—UPC C60)
Available all models except Firebird Sprint and Ram Air IV, where air conditioning is not available.

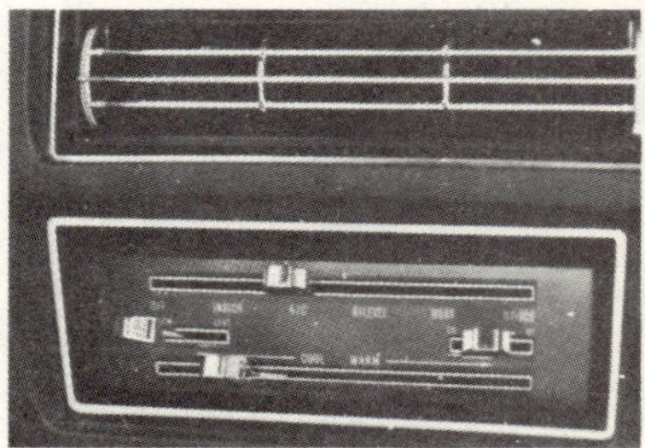

Custom Air Conditioning Controls for Tempest, Custom S, LeMans, LeMans Safari or GTO.

TRANSMISSION CONSOLES (Code 472—UPC D55) (F)

Available for Firebird, LeMans and GTO models with bucket seats. Not available with OHC 6, 1-bbl. and 3-speed manual transmission, except with floor shift.

Console for 3- or 4-speed Manual Transmissions with Floor Shift. Available at extra cost on LeMans (except 4-door Hardtop) and GTO models equipped with either of these transmissions. Padded, vinyl-coated fabric trim is color-keyed to match interiors.

Console for 2-speed Automatic and Turbo Hydra-Matic. The console for the 2-speed automatic is extra-cost on LeMans (except 4-door Hardtop). Both consoles feature dark walnut wood grain appearance insert and padded top panel. The console for Turbo Hydra-Matic on GTO features a "Rally Sports" speed shift unit that permits fully automatic or manual shifting.

PERFORMANCE OPTIONS

Hood-mounted Tachometer (Code 471—UPC UB5). Front-of-the-windshield installation lines it up for easy, instant readout by driver. Available Firebird, Tempest, Custom S, LeMans and GTO models. (F,D)

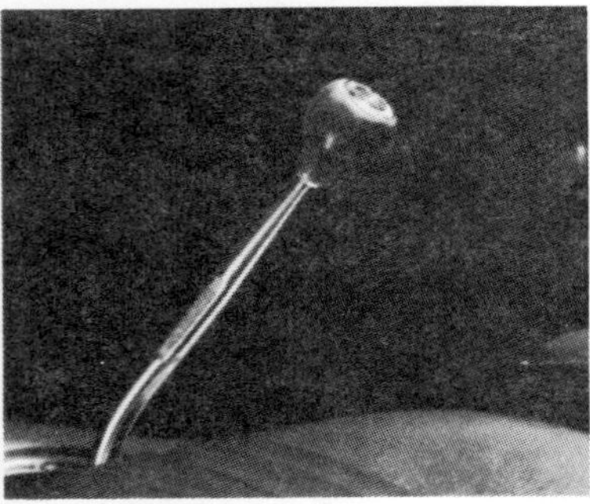

Custom Gearshift Knob (Code 534—UPC M09). Available on all models with floor-mounted transmission (standard on Grand Prix). Simulated walnut gearshift knob for 3- or 4-speed, floor-mounted transmission shift levers. Has Pontiac emblem on 3-speed knob. (F,D)

Heavy-duty Battery (Code 672—UPC UA1). A 61-amp.-hr. battery for longer life, better cranking ability, more power for accessories. Available for all models. (F)

Power Disc Brakes, Front (Code 511—UPC JL2). New single-piston, floating-caliper design provides same braking area as 4-piston type. Power assist standard with disc brake. Available all models. (F)

Power-Flex, Variable-pitch Fan (Code 692—UPC KB2). Automatically varies fan pitch under acceleration to provide greater cooling performance. Operates much more quietly and requires a minimum of horsepower at higher engine speeds. Available for all models. (F)

Rally Gauge Cluster & Rally Clock (Code 484—UPC W63). Integrates speedometer, oil-water-fuel-battery monitors and sweep second hand rally clock. Or rally clock can be replaced with Instrument Panel Tachometer (Code 444—UPC U30). Either option available for Firebird, Tempest, Custom S, LeMans, GTO and Grand Prix models. Illustrated is Rally Gauge Cluster and Rally Clock on Firebird model. (F)

Custom Sports Steering Wheel (Code 462—UPC N34). One style available for all models. New shallow design and new molded vinyl hub with center horn button ornament. It has a smart, simulated wood appearance and three, equally spaced, bright steel spokes. (F)

Dual-stage, Heavy-duty Air Cleaner (Code 731—UPC K45). Dual-filter design consists of wetted paper in filter, surrounded by polyglycol wetted polyurethane foam outer filter. Fine filtration, extended surface. Available all models except those equipped with 428 H.O. engines. (F)

Heavy-duty Shocks and Springs (Code 622—UPC F40). Maintain proper trim and give better control. Especially helpful when heavy loads are carried in car trunk. Available all models, except Firebird. (F,D)

Heavy-duty Radiator (Code 701—UPC V01). Has greater cooling capacity; standard with air-conditioned cars. Available for all models.

Delcotron Alternator-Regulator (62-Amp. Code 681—UPC K81; 55-Amp. Code 682—UPC K82; Self-regulated 55-Amp. Code 688—UPC K96). Special "solid state" voltage regulator, built into the alternator, provides improved voltage control and added reliability—increases battery life. Available for all series equipped with V-8 engines. Style and amperage determined by engine or equipment. (F)

SUPERLIFT SHOCK ABSORBERS (Code 634—UPC G66) with tire-type air filler valve also available (all models, except Firebird). (F,D)

Hood Retainers. Available all models except Grand Prix. Double locking protection at all times, with dual stainless steel posts to keep the hood secure. Chrome finished. (D)

Safe-T-Track Differential (Code 361—UPC G80). Transfers torque to the rear wheel that has the best traction. Keeps you going with surer handling when your car hits a stretch of slippery road, snow, ice, mud, sand, ruts or chuckholes. Minimizes the getting-stuck hazard. (Available all models.) (F)

Exhaust Tailpipe Extensions (Code 482—UPC N25). Bright metal extension—two for dual exhaust system. (Available all Firebird, Tempest, Custom S, LeMans, GTO models, except station wagons.) (F,D)

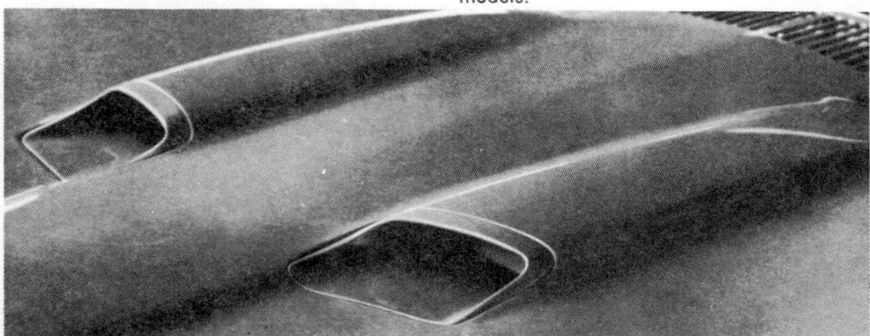

Hood Ram Air Induction (Code 611—UPC T42). New driver-controlled twin hood scoops provide direct air intake to carburetor. Available on GTO and Firebird 400 models.

POWER OPTIONS

Power 4-way Bench Seat Code 561—UPC A41). Whatever direction the control switch is moved, the seats will move—forward, backward, up, down (available only on Tempest, Custom S, LeMans, LeMans Safari and GTO with full-width bench front seats). (F)

Power Left-hand Bucket Seat (Code 564—UPC A46). Left-hand, bucket-seat controls. Seat moves forward, backward, up, down. Extra comfort on long trips (available models with bucket seats). (F)

Regular Power Steering (Code 501—UPC N40). Available for Tempest, Custom S LeMans, LeMans Safari and GTO. (F,D)

Power Window Lifts (Code 551—UPC A31). All vertical side windows can be controlled from a single panel on the driver's door. However, each window also has its individual control switch. Won't operate with ignition off. Standard with Brougham Option (available on all models). (F)

Deck-lid Release (Code 492—UPC A90). No need to get outside the car to unlock the trunk. Just press the button inside the glove compartment. Trunk can also be locked and unlocked with a key (available on all models except station wagons). (F,D)

Cruise Control (Code 441—UPC K30). Select your speed, and it will stay there until you disengage by lightly touching the brake pedal (available on all models with V-8 engines and automatic transmissions only). (F,D)

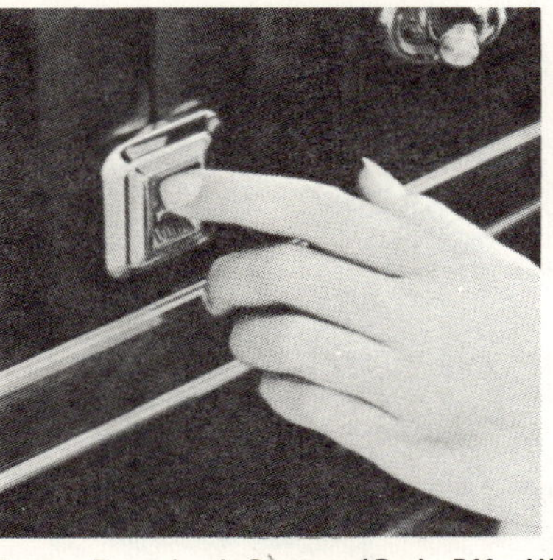

Power Door Lock System (Code 541—UPC A93). All doors are locked or unlocked at the same time by a master control lever on the inside door panel on the driver's side. Excellent convenience and security accessory (available all models except Firebird). (F)

Power-flow Ventilation System (Code 588—UPC C57). Helps improve air circulation on models with upper-level ventilation system, especially while stopped at traffic lights. Features a blower fan ahead of each outlet (available all models with upper-level ventilation system). (F,D)

RADIO AND STEREO

Pushbutton AM/FM Stereo Radio and Manual Antenna (Code 388—UPC U58). Complete listening pleasure. Tune in on either AM or FM stations. Enjoy true stereophonic sound when FM program is being broadcast in stereo. Includes two rear speakers and one front speaker with a special balance control to vary front and rear speaker volume. (Only one rear speaker in station wagons, convertibles and all Tempest models. Two front and two rear speakers on Firebird.) (F,D)

Note: Due to technical limitations of stereo broadcasting and reception, owners may occasionally experience limited range FM and stereo reception and/or stereo distortion and flutter in certain localities.

Pushbutton AM/FM Radio and Manual Antenna (Code 384—UPC U69). Listen to either AM or FM. Doubles the listening pleasure. Pushbuttons can be set for either AM or FM stations, or both. Completely transistorized. Excellent quality and fidelity (available all models). Grand Prix has windshield antenna. (F,D)

Pushbutton Radio and Manual Antenna (Code 382—UPC U63). Fine tone and fidelity. Radio is completely transistorized. Roomy dial for easy fine-tuning. Antenna streamlined for minimum wind resistance (available all models except Grand Prix, which has windshield antenna as standard). (F,D)

Rear Speaker Convertible, shown on Catalina.

Rear Speaker (Code 391—UPC U80). Available all Pontiac models, except those equipped with Stereo AM/FM Radio (Code 388) or Stereo Tape Player (Code 394). New control is escutcheon behind the radio station selector knob. You can have sound come from back seat only, or turn both speakers on for an enveloping effect. (Rear speaker for station wagons, see Page 18.) (F,D)

(F) Factory-installed. (D) Can be installed by dealer.
(F,D) Can be either factory- or dealer-installed.

WHEELS AND WHEEL COVERS

Custom Wheel Covers (Code 452—UPC P02). Gleaming bright chrome, 14-inch wheel size covers featuring new sports appearance (extra cost on Firebird, Tempest, Custom S, LeMans, LeMans Safari and GTO). (F,D)

Rally II Wheels (Code 454—UPC N98). Available on all models. New and larger. 15" diameter for Catalina, Executive and Bonneville. 14" diameter on Firebird, Tempest, Custom S, LeMans, LeMans Safari, GTO and Grand Prix. Stamped steel gives appearance of magnesium. Chrome plated wheel nuts. (Conventional spare wheel provided with space saver tire.) (F)

Deluxe Wheel Covers (Code 451—UPC P01). Newly styled, 14-inch wheel size covers featuring chrome-flashed stainless steel with deep center section. Extra cost on Firebird, Tempest, Custom S, LeMans, LeMans Safari and GTO. (F,D)

Wire Wheel Covers (Code 453—UPC N95). Add a special flair and sportier look to wheels. Chrome-plated wire spokes and bright red, medallion hub insert. (Available all models, with 14- or 15-inch wheels, including models equipped with front disc brakes.) (F,D)

Stereo Tape Player (Code 394—UPC U57). Amazing, lifelike sound from two special stereo rear speakers. Equipped with built-in amplifiers and volume and tone controls, a track selection control, and a control for balancing the volume between front and rear speakers. Plays the popular 8-track tape cartridges. Available only with radio. (Not available on Grand Prix or cars not equipped with heater.) (F,D)

Electric Power Antenna (Code 381—UPC U75). Available with all radios on all models except Custom S Station Wagon, LeMans Safari and Grand Prix. Raises and lowers antenna by a switch on the instrument panel. Antenna is mounted on the right rear fender. (F)

Verbra-Phonic (Reverberating) Rear Speaker System (Code 392—UPC U84). Available all models except Firebirds and those equipped with Stereo AM/FM Radios (Code 388), Stereo Tape Player (Code 394) or power ventilation (Code 588). When both front and rear speakers are playing, an "in-depth" tone is created that resembles the acoustics of a concert hall. (F,D)

(F) Factory-installed. (D) Can be installed by dealer.
(F,D) Can be either factory- or dealer-installed.

MISCELLANEOUS ACCESSORIES

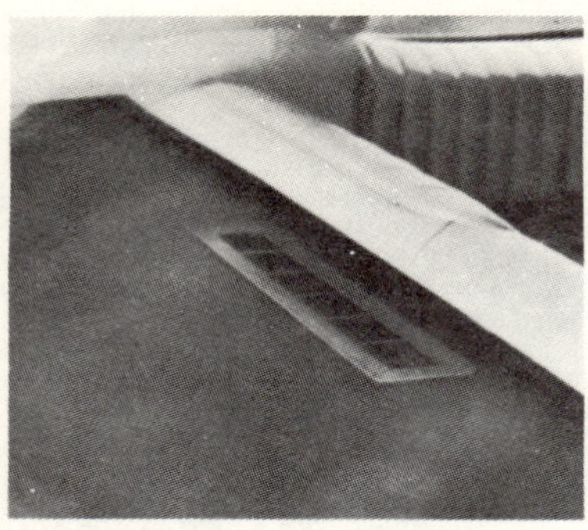

Rear-window De-fogger (Code 404—UPC C50). Air is directed to the rear window through a directional grille in the rear shelf. A blower underneath forces the air. Helps give you a clear view out the rear window (available all models except Grand Prix and station wagons and convertibles). (F,D)

Remote-control Outside LH Mirror (Code 424—UPC D33). Mounts on left-hand door. Adjusted from convenient controls inside car. Available all models. (F,D)

Reclining Bucket Seat, Passenger Side (Code 578—UPC A70). Available LeMans, GTO, Catalina, Bonneville and Grand Prix models with Strato-bucket seats. Passenger side reclines to 45° angle. (F)

Tilt Steering Wheel (Code 504—UPC N33). Set at any one of seven different positions. Makes exit and entrance easier. Provides more lap room and can be changed from one position to another for more relaxed driving. (Available for all models with power steering. Not available with manual transmission column shift.) (F)

Soft-Ray Glass (Code 531—UPC A01). For all windows. Recommended with air conditioning. Windows are fully tinted. The upper area of the windshield is shaded to reduce glare. (Also available on windshield only.) (Code 532—UPC A02.) (F)

RH Visor Vanity Mirror (Code 421—UPC D34). Left-hand Visor Mirror. (Code 422—UPC DH5). Mounts on back of visor. When not being used, it's out of sight. (Available for right and/or left visors, all models.) (F,D)

Custom Seat Belts and Front Shoulder Belts (Code 431—UPC WS1). Features new, compact, press-to-release pushbutton buckle on a fixed-length belt for driver and outboard passenger. Belt adjustment is made after belt hook-up by moving belt toward outboard retractor. This permits the automatic locking retractor to take up slack and provide desired tension. New twist button on retractor housing releases belt tension to permit wearer to move away from position without disconnecting buckle. All belts, front and rear, available in seven harmonizing colors. Available for all models except Firebird. Also available are Custom Seat Belts and *Front* and *Rear* Shoulder Belts (Code 432—UPC WS2). (F)

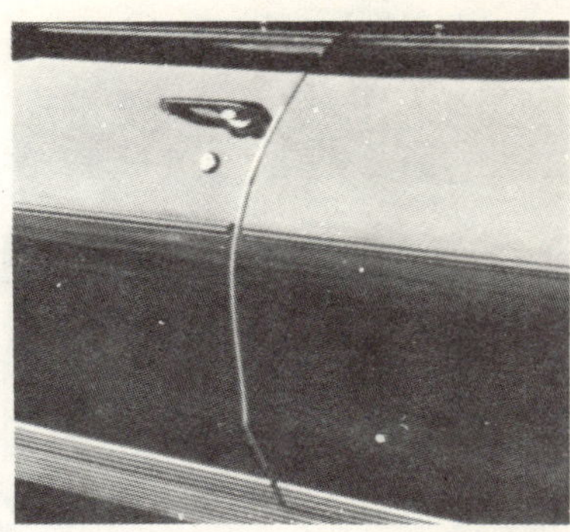

Door-edge Guards (Code 412—UPC B93). Bright, stainless steel strips help prevent nicks and scratches on door edges. (Available all models.) (F,D)

Safeguard Speedometer (Code 442—UPC U15). Available all Pontiac models. Not available with Rally Cluster. You set the speed limit with a control knob. Then a buzzer signals if your car exceeds this speed. (F)

Child Safety Seat. Available all models. Provides extra protection for small child. Utilizes standard seat belt. Sturdily constructed with special chest retainer strap to restrict forward movement during quick stops. Ivory color only. (D)

Electric Clock (Code 474—UPC U35). Features sweep second hand and built-in automatic/self-regulator. Illuminated dial for easy night reading. (1) Catalina series only (standard —Executive, Bonne-

Concealed Headlamps (Code 414—UPC T83). Available only for GTO models. Give a clean, unbroken appearance to the front end. Sections of the grille swing down and out of the way when headlamps are in use. Headlamp switch automatically controls position of headlamp doors. (F)

License Plate Frames. Available individually for front and rear. Stainless steel to enhance and protect license plates. Clip on easily. Rear frame has finger-pull for ready access to fuel filler cap. (D)

Cornering Lamps (Code 651—UPC T87). Available for all models except Firebird. Part of Lamp Group (Code 332). Lights up blind spots when turning. Goes on when headlamps are on and turn signal is activated. Mounted on forward side of front fender. (F)

(F) Factory-installed. (D) Can be installed by dealer.
(F,D) Can be either factory- or dealer-installed.

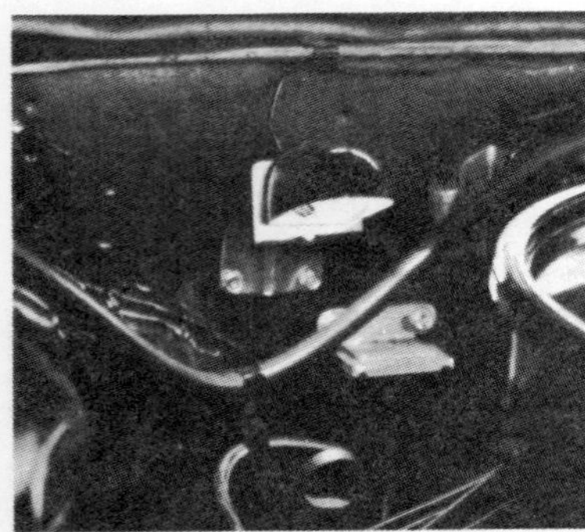

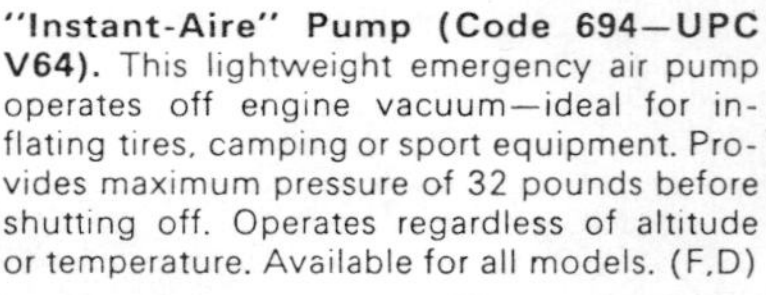

"Instant-Aire" Pump (Code 694—UPC V64). This lightweight emergency air pump operates off engine vacuum—ideal for inflating tires, camping or sport equipment. Provides maximum pressure of 32 pounds before shutting off. Operates regardless of altitude or temperature. Available for all models. (F,D)

"Space-Saver Spare" Tire (Code 704—UPC N65). Available for all Tempest and Grand Prix models—standard on Firebird. Adds approximately 3 cubic feet of usable luggage capacity. Easily inflated with handy pressure can and provides many miles of spare tire driving. (F) New "Space-Saver Spare" Tire Inflators for replacement available from dealer. (D) Also, see "Instant-Aire" Pump—this page.

Underhood Lamp (Code 671—UPC U26). Available for all models, all series—included in Lamp Group (Code 322). Light floods entire engine compartment. Activated by the hood spring, it lights automatically when hood is raised. (F,D)

Luggage Compartment Lamp (Code 652—UPC U25). Available for Firebird, Tempest, Custom S, LeMans and GTO only—included in Lamp Group (Code 322). (Not available for station wagons.) Lights automatically when trunk lid is lifted. (F,D)

Spare Tire Cover (Code 402—UPC P17). Available for all models except station wagons and models equipped with "Space-Saver Spare" Tire—standard on Bonneville. Protects trunk contents. Slips on, off easily. Dresses up luggage compartment. (F,D)

Floor Mats, Front (Code 631—UPC B32); Rear (Code 632—UPC B33). Available for all series. Keep car looking new and clean. Easily removed for washing. Available in Black, Blue, Gold, Red Green and Ivory to harmonize with interiors. (F,D)

Full-width Floor Mat (front only). Durable, long-wearing. Easily removed for cleaning. Available in Black, Gold, Green, Blue, Ivory and Red. (Not available for Firebird or Grand Prix.) (D)

Luggage Compartment Floor Mat (Code 732—UPC B36). Heavy-duty, rugged, solid Gray vinyl floor mat gives extra protection for trunk compartment as well as cargo. Not available for station wagon models. (F,D)

Fire Extinguisher. A 2¾-lb. dry chemical fire extinguisher for all kinds of fires including grease, oil, gasoline and electrical. Rechargeable. (D)

Gas-cap Lock. Helps prevent fuel theft. Separate key. Available for all models. (D)

Car Compass. Dependable with special compensator to assure correct directional indication. Illuminated dial. (D)

Highway Emergency Kit. Includes antenna emergency flag, fire extinguisher, tire inflator, extra fuses and warning flares. (D)

Litter Basket. Clings to transmission tunnel. Weighted to prevent tipping. Available in Red, Blue, Black or Beige. (D)

New Tissue Dispenser. Holds junior-size box of tissues. Smart design. Easy to use. Attaches to underside of instrument panel. (D)

(F) Factory-installed. (D) Can be installed by dealer.
(F,D) Can be either factory- or dealer-installed.

A PONTIAC EXCLUSIVE

NOW! A jacket designed for performance and safety behind the wheel, roadside, trackside, and in the pits.

"Wring out" these performance and safety features.

- Vertically offset crossover entry pockets allow non-acrobatic entry—even with shoulder harness.
- Sleeve stripes of Retro-Reflective safety tape—roadside, trackside or in the pits—make you visible to night drivers.
- Racing-styled collar, cuffs and drawstring waist.
- Raglan sleeves for greater freedom.
- Convenient sleeve pocket.
- Heavy water-repellent, stain-resistant oxford nylon.
- "GTO", "Firebird" or "The Judge" emblem.

This jacket, inspired by "GTO", "Firebird", and "The Judge" (a special GTO by Pontiac) is designed to function. The drivers who wear them don't want it any other way. No other jacket has all these features, and it's only available from Pontiac. Order yours today.

Check the emblem you choose, then indicate style, size and quantity. (If you are ordering a number of jackets with different emblems, please indicate a "J", "G" or "F" for each jacket desired in the quantity block under the appropriate size and style.)

- ☐ "The Judge"
- ☐ "GTO"
- ☐ "Firebird"

MEN'S @ $9.75	Size	X-Small 32-34	Small 36-38	Medium 40-42	Large 44-46	X-Large 48-50	XX-Large 52
	Quantity						
WOMAN'S @ $9.75	Size Blouse Dress		Small 30-32 8-10	Medium 34-36 12-14	Large 38-40 16-18		
	Quantity						
BOY'S @ $9.45	Size (Age group)		Small (6-8)	Medium (10-12)	Large (14-16)		
	Quantity						

Print or type

NAME ____________________

ADDRESS ____________________

CITY & STATE ____________________ ZIP ________

Mail remittance and coupon to MacManus, John & Adams, Inc. Order Processing Section, Bloomfield Hills, Michigan 48013.

- Write check or money order to MacManus, John & Adams, Inc. • ADD state & local taxes where applicable. (Michigan residents 4%)
- Your remittance must accompany order. Amount $__________.

SP 3086 Litho in U.S.A

GROUPS

For your convenience in ordering, some of Pontiac's more popular accessories are combined in groups, as shown below. These accessory groups are factory-installed, thereby saving you both time and installation costs.

BASIC GROUP (Code 321—UPC Y88)

- Pushbutton AM Radio with Windshield Antenna.
- Visor Vanity Mirror, Right-hand (all models).
- Outside Remote-control Mirror (all models).
- Deck-lid Release (available all models except station wagons).
- Dual-stage, Heavy-duty Air Cleaner (all models).
- Electric Clock (available all Tempest, LeMans, LeMans Sport, GTO and Catalina models).

LAMP GROUP (Code 322—UPC Y92)

- Underhood Lamp (Tempest, LeMans, LeMans Sport and GTO only).
- Dome Reading Lamp (all models except convertibles).

POWER ASSIST GROUP (Code 331—UPC WS6) available all models.

- Turbo Hydra-matic Transmission.
- Variable-ratio Power Steering.
- Power Front Disc Brakes (standard on Grand Prix).

RALLY GROUP (Code 334—UPC WS8) available Tempest, LeMans, LeMans Sport and GTO models only.

- Rally II Wheels.
- Custom Sports Steering Wheel.
- Rally Gauge Cluster and Clock.
- Ride and Handling Springs and Shocks.

DECOR GROUP (Code 324—UPC Y86)

Hardtop Coupe: Exterior decor trim features dual horns on LeMans; wheel opening moldings and deluxe wheel covers on LeMans and GTO.

Convertibles: Exterior decor trim features deluxe wheel covers and wheel opening moldings. (F)

AIR CONDITIONING

CUSTOM AIR CONDITIONING (Code 582—UPC C60). Available all models except Ram Air IV or 6-cylinder with 2-speed automatic transmission.

Combines heating and cooling units in a single system for balanced all-season comfort. Easy-to-operate, manual sliding-lever controls permit selection of inside air, outside air, bi-level combination (upper-level air cooling and lower-level air heating), heating or de-fogging/de-icing. When outside temperature is below freezing or switch is in OFF position or lever is set at VENT, the compressor is off. Otherwise, it remains in operation to reduce inside humidity and prevent windshield fogging. (The fan operates in all but the OFF position.) Air outlets are adjustable for directing air flow. (F)

Custom Air Conditioning Controls for Tempest, LeMans, LeMans Sport or GTO.

PERFORMANCE OPTIONS

Hood-mounted Tachometer (Code 491—UPC UB5). Front-of-the-windshield installation lines it up for easy, instant readout by driver. Available Tempest, LeMans, LeMans Sport and GTO models. Not available with 6-cylinder engines. Dealer-installed on Grand Prix. (F,D)

Rally Gauges with Clock (Code 488—UPC W63). Integrates oil, water and fuel gauges with alternator telltale on Tempest, LeMans, LeMans Sport, GTO and Grand Prix. Also includes clock, where not already standard. **Rally Gauges with Instrument Panel Tachometer (Code 484—UPC U30).** Same as above, but with tachometer substituted for clock. Illustrated on LeMans model. (F)

Formula Steering Wheel (Code 464—UPC NK1). New and available all models with power steering. 14-inch diameter aluminum wheel. Soft, molded, urethane foam rim gives look and feel of heavily padded leather. (F)

Custom Gearshift Knob (Code 614—UPC M09). Available all models with floor-mounted manual transmission (standard on Grand Prix). Simulated walnut gearshift knob for 3- or 4-speed, floor-mounted transmission shift levers. Has Pontiac emblem on 3-speed knob. (F,D)

Hood Ram Air (Code 601—UPC T42). Handy cable control allows driver to open ducts on hood air scoops, so as to admit cooler, denser outside air for better engine performance. Includes Ram Air decals on hood scoops. Available on GTO with 455-cu.-in., V-8 engine (standard with Ram Air and Ram Air IV engines). (F)

Note: All Group Accessories may be purchased individually, if desired.

Custom Sports Steering Wheel (Code 462—UPC N34). One style available for all models. New shallow-dish and new molded-vinyl hub with center horn button ornament. Smart, simulated wood appearance and three, equally spaced, dull chrome spokes. (F)

"The Judge" Performance Option (Code 332—UPC WT1). Available GTO only. Includes such features as: 400-cu.-in. Ram Air V-8 engine; functional, driver-controlled, air-intake hood scoops; Quadra-jet carburetor; chromed rocker arm covers, oil filler cap and air cleaner cover; 3-speed heavy-duty floor shift transmission with Hurst "T" handle; rear-deck airfoil; heavy-duty springs and shocks; fender striping; G70—14 wide-tread fiberglass-belted, black tires; and dechromed Safety Rim Rally II Wheels. Plus Ram Air decal on hood scoops; "The Judge" nameplate on front fenders, reardeck and instrument panel. (F)

Ride & Handling Package (Code 621—UPC Y96). For excellent cornering and handling—extra-firm front and rear springs and shocks, for all Pontiac models. Heavier stabilizer bar for Tempest and Pontiac series only. (F)

Safe-T-Track Differential (Code 361—UPC G80). Transfers torque to rear wheel that has best traction. Keeps you going with surer handling when your car hits a stretch of slippery road, snow, ice, water, mud, sand, ruts or chuck-holes. Available all models. (F)

Power Disc Brakes, Front (Code 502—UPC JL2). Single-piston, floating-caliper design provides powerful braking and is easy to apply in emergencies without locking wheels. Available all models. (Standard on Grand Prix.) (F)

Delcotron Alternator-Regulator (62-Amp. Code 681—UPC K81). Special "solid-state" voltage regulator, built into alternator, provides improved voltage control and added reliability—increases battery life. Available all series equipped with V-8 engines. Style and amperage determined by engine or equipment. (F)

(F) Factory-installed. (D) Can be installed by dealer. (F, D) Can be either factory- or dealer-installed.

Dual-stage, Heavy-duty Air Cleaner (Code 724—UPC K45). Dual-filter design consists of wetted paper in filter, surrounded by polyglycol-wetted, polyurethane-foam outer filter. Fine filtration, extended surface. Available all models. (F)

Heavy-duty Battery (Code 692—UPC UA1). 61-amp.-hr. battery for longer life, better cranking ability, more power for accessories. Available all models. (Included with air conditioning.)

Hood Retainers. Available all models except Grand Prix. Double-locking protection at all times, with dual stainless steel posts to keep hood secure. Chrome finished. (D)

Heavy-duty Shocks and Springs (Code 622—UPC F40). Maintain proper trim and give excellent control. Especially helpful when heavy loads are carried in car trunk. Available all models. (F,D)

POWER OPTIONS

Cruise Control (Code 481—UPC K30). Select speed, and it will stay there until you disengage by lightly touching brake pedal. Available all models with V-8 engines and automatic transmissions only. (F,D)

4-way Power Bench Seat (Code 561—UPC A41). Whatever direction control switch is moved, the seats will move—forward, backward, up, down. Available only Tempest, LeMans, LeMans Sport, GTO and Grand Prix with full-width bench front seats. (F)

Variable-ratio Power Steering (Code 501—UPC N41). Permits fast steering response. Requires fewer turns in slow-speed maneuvering, such as parking. Available all models. (F)

Left-side Power Bucket Front Seat (Code 564—UPC A46). Left-hand, bucket seat controls. Seat moves forward and backward, and tilts by moving up and down at the rear only. Extra comfort on long trips. Available models with bucket front seats. (F)

Electric Door Locks (Code 552—UPC AU3). New and available all models. Respond faster than vacuum system, eliminate vacuum runout. Include electric seat back locks on 2-door models. Front seat backs automatically unlock when doors are opened and automatically lock when doors are closed. Manual unlocking device still present. (F)

Deck-lid Release (Code 554—UPC A90). No need to get outside car to unlock trunk. Just press button inside glove compartment or console. Trunk can also be locked and unlocked in conventional manner. Available on all models except station wagons. (F,D)

Power Windows (Code 551—UPC A31). All side windows controlled from single panel on driver's door. Each window also has its individual control switch. Won't operate with ignition off. Standard with Brougham Option—available all other models. (F)

Power-flow Ventilation System (Code 588—UPC C57). Helps improve air circulation, especially while stopped at traffic lights. Features blower fan ahead of each outlet to provide air flow equivalent to car speed of about 40 mph. (F,D)

RADIO AND STEREO

Pushbutton AM/FM Stereo Radio and Windshield Antenna (Code 404—UPC U58). Complete listening pleasure on either AM or FM stations. True stereophonic sound when FM program is being broadcast in stereo. Includes two rear speakers and one front speaker with special balance control to vary front and rear speaker volume. Antenna hidden in windshield for cleaner exterior appearance and to eliminate bent or broken antennas. (Only one rear speaker in station wagons, convertibles and all Tempest models.) (F,D)

Note: Due to technical limitations of stereo broadcasting and reception, owners may occasionally experience limited range FM and stereo reception and/or stereo distortion and flutter in certain localities.

Pushbutton AM/FM Radio and Windshield Antenna (Code 402—UPC U69). Listen to either AM or FM. Doubles the listening pleasure. Pushbuttons can be set for either AM or FM stations, or both. Completely transistorized. Excellent quality and fidelity. Available all models. (F,D)

Pushbutton AM Radio and Windshield Antenna (Code 401—UPC U63). Fine tone and fidelity. Radio is completely transistorized. Roomy dial for easy fine-tuning. (F,D)

Rear Speaker (Code 411—UPC U80). Available all Pontiac models, except those equipped with Stereo AM/FM Radio (Code 404) or Stereo Tape Player (Code 412). New control is escutcheon behind radio station selector knob. You can have sound come from back seat only, or turn both speakers on for an enveloping effect.

Stereo Tape Player (Code 412—UPC U57). Amazing, lifelike sound from two special stereo rear speakers (except Tempest models, station wagons and convertibles). Equipped with built-in amplifiers and volume and tone controls, track selection control and control for balancing volume between front and rear speakers. Plays popular 8-track stereo tape cartridges. On Grand Prix equipped with bucket seats, player mounts on drive tunnel behind console and faces forward. Available only with radio. (F,D)

TRANSMISSION CONSOLES (Code 494—UPC D55) (F)

Console for Turbo Hydra-matic. Console features dark walnut wood grain appearance insert and padded top panel. Includes "Rally Sport" speed shift unit that permits fully automatic or manual shifting.

Console for 3- or 4-speed Manual Transmissions with Floor Shift. Available on LeMans Sport (except 4-door Hardtop and Safari) and GTO models equipped with either of these transmissions. Padded, vinyl-coated, fabric trim, color-keyed to match interiors.

WHEELS AND WHEEL COVERS

Deluxe Wheel Covers (Code 471—UPC P01). 14-inch wheel size covers, featuring chrome-flashed stainless steel with deep center section. Available on Tempest, LeMans, LeMans Sport and GTO. (F,D)

Custom Wheel Covers (Code 472—UPC P02). Gleaming bright chrome, 14-inch wheel size covers featuring smart sports appearance. Available on Tempest, LeMans, LeMans Sport and GTO. (F,D)

Rally II Wheels (Code 474—UPC N98). Available all models (except Catalina, Executive and Bonneville Station Wagons). 15-inch diameter for Catalina, Executive and Bonneville. 14-inch diameter on all other models. Stamped steel gives appearance of magnesium. Chrome-plated wheel nuts. (Conventional spare wheel provided with "Space-Saver Spare" Tire.) (F)

Wire Wheel Covers (Code 473—UPC N95). Add special flair and sportier look to wheels. Chrome-plated wire spokes and bright red, medallion hub insert. Available all models, with 14- or 15-inch wheels, including models equipped with power front disc brakes. (F,D)

MISCELLANEOUS ACCESSORIES

Electrically Heated Rear-window Defroster (Code 534—UPC C49). Keeps rear window clear of steam, snow and ice. Current flows through small electrical conductors on inside glass surface. Improved 1970 design heats faster. Available all models except station wagons and convertibles. (F)

Child Safety Seat. Available all models. Provides extra protection for small child. Utilizes standard seat belt. Sturdily constructed with special chest retainer strap to restrict forward movement during quick stops. Ivory color in standard and deluxe models. (D)

Custom Seat Belts and Front Shoulder Belts (Code 451—UPC AK1). Features compact, press-to-release pushbutton buckle on fixed-length belt for driver and outboard passenger. Front outboard belt adjustment is made automatically after belt hookup by outboard retractor which takes up slack and provides desired tension. All other belts adjust in the conventional manner. All belts, front and rear, available in seven harmonizing colors. Available all models. **Also available are Custom Seat Belts and Front and Rear Shoulder Belts** (Code 452—UPC AK2). (F)

License Plate Frame. Available for front and rear. Stainless steel to enhance and protect license plate. Clips on easily. Has finger pull for ready access to fuel filler cap. (D)

Rear-window De-fogger (Code 541—UPC C50). Blower directs air to rear window through directional grille in rear shelf. Helps give clear view out rear window. Available all models except station wagons and convertibles. (F,D)

Rear-door Child Lock Guards (4-door models only). Children can't open or unlock rear doors when buttons are down and Lock Guards are in. Yet door can easily be "popped open" with a key. Any of regular car keys can be used. (Illustration 1—Unlocked position; 2—Regular Locked position; 3—Lock Guard position.) (D)

Safeguard Speedometer (Code 482—UPC U15). Available all Pontiac models. Not available with Rally Gauges. You set speed limit with control knob. Buzzer signals if car exceeds this speed. (F)

Infant Safety Carrier. This rear-facing seat is held snugly in place by front or rear seat belt. Built-in chest strap further safeguards baby. Upright section provides support for head and back. Doubles as a handy, sturdy carrier for use outside car. (D)

(F) Factory-installed. (D) Can be installed by dealer.
(F, D) Can be either factory- or dealer-installed.

Door-edge Guards (Code 684—UPC B93). Bright stainless steel strips help protect door edges from nicks and scratches. Available all models. (F,D)

Remote-control Outside LH Mirror (Code 444—UPC D33). Mounts on door. Adjusted by convenient controls inside car. Available all models. (F,D)

Soft-Ray Glass (Code 531—UPC A01). Fully tinted for all windows. Recommended with air conditioning. Upper area of windshield is shaded to reduce glare. Also available for windshield only. (Code 532—UPC A02). (F)

Visor Vanity Mirror (Code 441—UPC D34). Mounts on back of visor. Out of sight when not being used. Available for right and/or left visors, all models. (F,D)

Headlamp Delay (Code 672—UPC T81). New and available all models. Allows you to have lighted path to house by turning off headlight switch *after* ignition is turned off. Headlights automatically stay on for 60 seconds and then go off. (F,D)

"Instant-Aire" Pump (Code 722—UPC V64). Lightweight emergency air pump operating off engine vacuum—ideal for inflating tires, camping or sport equipment. Provides maximum pressure of 32 pounds before shutting off. Available all models except with 6-cylinder, Ram Air or Ram Air IV engines. (F,D)

Litter Basket/Tissue Dispenser. Convenient new combination unit attaches to transmission tunnel. Holds junior-size box of tissues. Has removable plastic tray for litter. Black only. (D)

Maintenance Products. The following quality items are GM-approved and bear the GM name. Glass Cleaner (23-oz. pressure can), Windshield Washer Solvent (pint), Vinyl Protector & Cleaner (9½-oz. pressure can), Wax-treated Polishing Cloth, Permanent Type Anti-freeze/Coolant (quart), Touch-up Paint (in either pressure spray can or tube with built-in brush) for all body colors. Available from your Pontiac dealer. (D)

Dome Reading Lamp (Code 654—UPC C89). Consists of center lamp and two side lamps. Center unit operates as a conventional dome lamp from door jamb switches and headlamp switch knob. Side lamps operate from separate switches on lamp housing and shine over shoulders of front-seat occupants. Available all series. (F)

Electric Clock (Code 492—UPC U35). Features sweep second hand and built-in, automatic, self-regulator. Illuminated dial for easy night reading.

Luggage Compartment Lamp (Code 652—UPC U25). Available Tempest, LeMans, LeMans Sport and GTO only—included in Lamp Group (Code 322). Standard all other series except station wagons. Lights automatically when trunk lid is lifted. (F,D)

Spare Tire Cover (Code 424—UPC P17). Available all models except station wagons and models equipped with "Space-Saver Spare" Tire—standard on Brougham. Protects trunk contents. Slips on, off easily. Dresses up luggage compartment. (F,D)

Gas-cap Lock. Helps prevent fuel theft. Separate key. Available all models. (D)

Car Compass. Dependable with special compensator to assure correct directional indication. Illuminated dial. (D)

Fire Extinguisher. A 2¾-lb., dry-chemical fire extinguisher for all kinds of fires including grease, oil, gasoline and electrical. Rechargeable. (D)

Highway Emergency Kit. Includes emergency flag with 22-foot string for tying around windshield, plus fire extinguisher, tire inflator, extra fuses and warning flares. (D)

Full-width Floor Mat (Front only). Durable, long-wearing. Easily removed for cleaning. Available in Black, White, Dark Green, Dark Brown, Dark Blue, Dark Saddle, Sandalwood and Red. Not available for Grand Prix with bucket seats. (D)

Monitoring System for Rear Lamps. (Code 634—UPC U46). New and available all series. Uses plastic fibers to transmit light from rear lamps to indicator on back window shelf, thus verifying that lamps are working. All models except station wagons and convertibles. (F,D)

Reclining Bucket Seat, Passenger Side (Code 571—UPC A70). Available LeMans Sport, GTO, and Grand Prix models with Strato-bucket seats. Passenger side reclines to 45° angle. (F)

Tilt Steering Wheel (Code 504—UPC N33). Set at any one of seven different positions. Makes exit and entrance easier. Provides more lap room and can be changed from one position to another for more relaxed driving. Available all models with power steering. Not available with manual transmission, column shift. (F)

Underhood Lamp (Code 671—UPC U26). Fixed type. Available Tempest, LeMans, LeMans Sport, LeMans Sport Safari and GTO series—included in Lamp Group (Code 322). Light floods entire engine compartment. It lights automatically when hood is raised. (F,D)

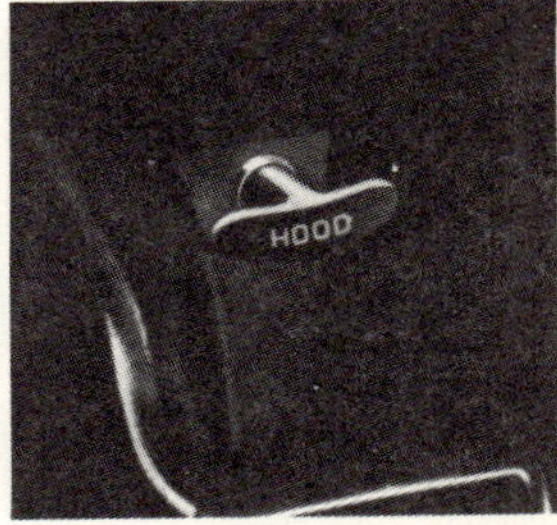

Hood Lock. Cable-controlled device that can be unlocked only from inside car. Locks again automatically when hood is closed. (D)

Floor Mats, Front (Code 521—UPC B32); Rear (Code 522—UPC B33). Available all series and include mats for both sides of car. Keep car looking new and clean. Easily removed for washing. Available in Black, White, Dark Green, Dark Brown, Dark Red, Dark Saddle, Dark Blue, Dark Gold and Sandalwood to harmonize with interiors. (F,D)

Luggage Compartment Floor Mat. Heavy-duty, rugged, solid Gray vinyl floor mat gives extra protection for trunk compartment as well as cargo. Not available station wagon models. (D)

(F) Factory-installed. (D) Can be installed by dealer.
(F, D) Can be either factory- or dealer-installed.

BASIC GROUPS

(Code 321—UPC Y88)—A number of Pontiac's more popular accessories have been combined in a group for your convenience when ordering. By ordering the Basic Group, factory-installed, you save both time and installation costs. Every accessory listed may be purchased individually, if desired.

LeMANS SPORT, GTO BASIC GROUPS

- Turbo Hydra-matic Transmission
- Pushbutton AM Radio
- Power Steering
- Electric Clock
- Power Disc Brakes
- Custom Wheel Covers
- Whitewall Tires (LeMans Sport)
- White Letter Tires (GTO)

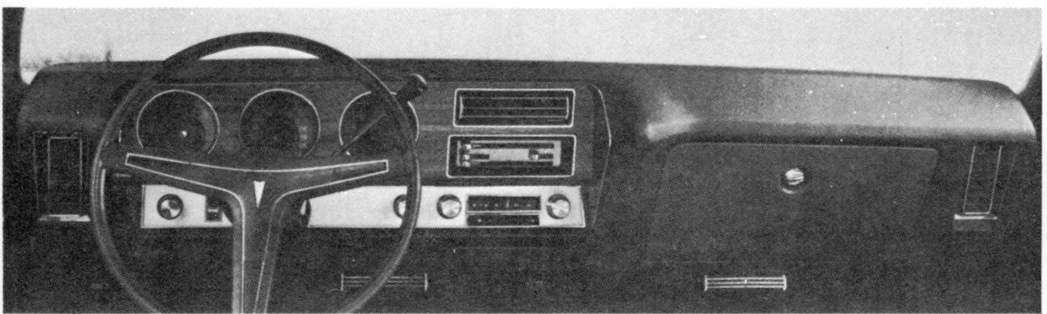

Custom Air Conditioning (Code 582—UPC C60). Available Firebird, Esprit, Formula, Trans Am, T-37, LeMans, LeMans Sport, GTO and Grand Prix. (Not available with 6-cylinder engines on Firebird or with 6-cylinder engine and 2-speed automatic on T-37, LeMans, LeMans Sport and GTO.) Combines heating and cooling units in a single system for balanced, all-season comfort. Easy to operate, manual sliding-level controls permit a wide selection of various conditions: inside air, outside air, combined bi-level cooling and heating together, heating, defogging or deicing. (F)

DECOR AND PROTECTION MOLDINGS...

The beauty of chrome moldings is a personal thing—and now Pontiac for 1971 makes it easier than ever to add the extra touches of chrome that you desire . . . that suit your own particular taste.

Notes:

1. If a molding is not indicated either as standard or available with a model, it is not available on that model.
2. Roof Drip Moldings are included with the Cordova Top.
3. The Roof Drip Molding also serves as a roof gutter on the Firebird, Formula, Trans Am and Catalina pillar models. If Roof Drip Moldings are not obtained (either separately or with a Cordova Top), these cars will not have roof gutters.
4. Body Side Moldings are available in black only. They are not available with Wood Grain Safari Option, the GT-37, the Judge or with D98 Stripes on T-37, LeMans Sport and GTO models.
5. Belt Reveal Moldings also include Hood Rear-edge Moldings on Firebirds. These Hood Rear-edge Moldings are standard on all other cars except the T-37 series.

A. Bright Metal Roof Drip Molding (Code 481—UPC B80)

D. Rocker Panel Molding (Code 728—UPC B83)

E. Body Side Molding (Code 494—UPC B84)

F. Door Edge Guards (Code 492—UPC B93)

G. Wheel Opening Molding (Code 491—UPC B96)

MODEL	STANDARD	AVAILABLE
GTO		
HARDTOP COUPE	A, D	E, F, G
CONVERTIBLE	D	E, F, G

(F) Factory-installed. (D) Can be installed by dealer.
(F, D) Can be either factory- or dealer-installed.

APPEARANCE ACCESSORIES

Wheels and Wheel Covers

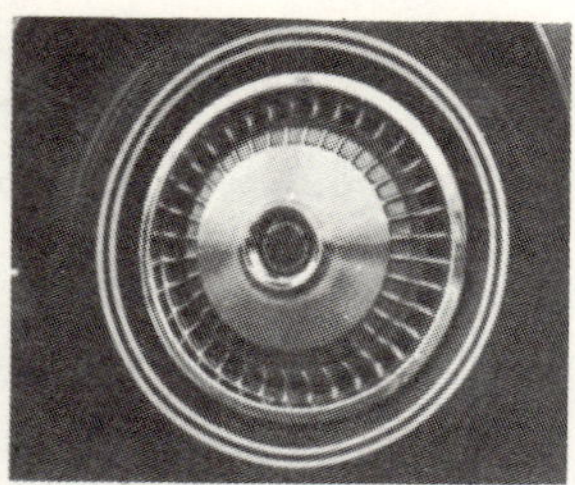

Custom Wheel Covers (Code 472—UPC P02). 14-inch wheel size, featuring brushed stainless steel center hub surrounded by simulated cooling fins. Available on Firebird, Esprit, Formula, T-37, LeMans, LeMans Sport and GTO. (F,D)

Wire Wheel Covers (Code 473—UPC N95). 14-inch wheel size, featuring bright chrome, individual wire spokes and nipples for realistic wire wheel appearance. Available for Firebird, Esprit, Formula, T-37, LeMans, LeMans Sport, GTO and Grand Prix (F,D)

Custom Sport Steering Wheel (Code 462—UPC N34). Features shallow-dish, three-spoke design with new, soft, simulated leather outer steering rim and center horn button. Available for all models except Firebird, Esprit, Formula and Trans Am. (F)

Rally II Wheels (Code 474—UPC N98). 14-inch or 15-inch wheel size, featuring sporty magnesium wheel appearance, stainless steel capped wheel nuts. Available all other models except Safari and Grand Safari Station Wagons. (D,F)

Formula Steering Wheel (Code 464—UPC NK3). With power steering only and available on Firebird, Esprit, Formula, T-37, LeMans, LeMans Sport, GTO and Grand Prix. Standard on Trans Am. 14-inch diameter with soft, molded, urethome foam rim that gives the look and feel of padded leather. (F)

Honeycomb Wheels with Trim Rings (Code 478—UPC P05). 14-inch wheel size, newly styled and featuring a rugged cast-metal wheel appearance. 15-inch (with 60 series tires) standard on Trans Am without trim rings and available on Formula with Handling Package. Available on Firebird, Esprit, Formula, T-37, LeMans, LeMans Sport, GTO and Grand Prix. (F,D)

Consoles

Console for LeMans Sport or GTO (Code 431—UPC D55). 3- or 4-speed manual transmission. Features soft, padded vinyl exterior covering, color-keyed to match interior. (F)

Console for LeMans Sport or GTO (Code 431—UPC D55). When Turbo Hydra-matic is ordered, console features dark walnut wood grain appearance insert and padded top panel. Color-keyed to interior. On GTO includes "Rally Sport" speed shift unit that permits fully automatic or manual shifting. (F)

APPEARANCE ACCESSORIES

Custom Seat Belts and Front Shoulder Belts (Code 451—UPC AK1). Available in six colors to match every basic interior trim. Features press-to-release pushbutton buckle, locking, self-adjusting front outboard retractors (except Firebird models) and matching shoulder belts. Available all models. Also available are Custom Seat Belts with Front and Rear Shoulder Belts (Code 452—UPC AK2). (F)

(NOTE: Standard Seat and Shoulder Belts available in Black only.)

Body Vinyl Accent Stripes (Code 614—UPC D98). Available T-37, LeMans Coupes and Hardtop Coupes; LeMans Sport and GTO in Black, Red or Yellow. (F,D)

(F) Factory-installed. (D) Can be installed by dealer.
(F, D) Can be either factory- or dealer-installed.

License Plate Frame. Available for both front and rear. Stainless steel to enhance and protect license plate. Clips on easily. Rear frame has finger-pull for ready access to fuel filter cap. (D)

Body-colored Outside Mirrors (Code 434—UPC D35). A pair of aerodynamically styled outside mirrors with left-hand mirror affording remote-control adjustments and exterior housing color-keyed to body. Available for Firebird, LeMans Hardtop Coupe, LeMans Sport, GTO and Grand Prix models. Standard on Esprit, Formula and Trans Am. (F)

CONVENIENCE ACCESSORIES

Instrument Panel Courtesy Lamp (Code 664—UPC U29). Lights when front door is opened. Also, manually operated by switch. Available T-37, LeMans, LeMans Sport and GTO. Standard on Convertibles.

Litter Basket clings to transmission tunnel. Weighted to prevent tipping. Easy to empty. Available in red, black, blue and fawn. (D)

Litter Basket/Tissue Dispenser pins fast to transmission tunnel carpeting. Holds junior-size box of tissues, has removable plastic tray for litter. Black only. (D)

Right-hand Manual Outside Mirror. (Standard on Safari and Grand Safari Station Wagons—available all other models). Matches standard left-hand outside mirror. (D)

Visor Vanity Mirror. Mounts on back of visor. Out of sight when not being used. Available for right (Code 441—UPC D34) and/or left visors (Code 442—UPC D85)—all models except Firebird, Esprit, Formula and Trans Am. (F,D)

Tilt Steering Wheel (Code 504—UPC N33). Adjusts to seven different positions for your personal driving comfort. Makes exit and entrance easier. Provides more lap room. Available all models with variable-ratio power steering. Not available with manual column-shift transmission. (F)

Luggage Compartment Lamp (Code 662—UPC U25). Lights automatically when trunk lid is lifted. Available T-37, LeMans, LeMans Sport, GTO, Catalina, Catalina Brougham and Grand Prix models (except station wagons). (F,D)

Dome Reading Lamp (Code 661—UPC C89). Consists of center lamp and two side lamps. Center lamp functions as a conventional dome lamp, lights from door jamb switches and headlamp switch knob. Side lamps operate from separate switches on lamp housing and shine over the shoulder of front-seat occupants. Available on all models except Firebird, Esprit, Formula, Trans Am and convertible models.

Remote-control Outside LH Mirror (Code 444—UPC D33). Easily adjusted by convenient inside door panel control on left-hand door. Available on all models. (F,D)

Electric Clock (Code 722—UPC U35). It has sweep second hand and built-in, automatic, self-regulator. Dial is illuminated for easy night reading. Available on Firebird, Esprit, Formula, Trans Am, T-37, LeMans, LeMans Sport, GTO and Catalina models. Standard on all others. Included with Rally Gauge Cluster/Clock and Tachometer (Code 714—UPC U30) or Rally Gauge Cluster/Clock (Code 718—UPC W63). (F,D)

Maintenance Products. The following items are GM-approved and bear the GM name. Glass Cleaner (23-oz. pressure can), Windshield Washer Solvent (pint), Vinyl Protector & Cleaner (9½-oz. pressure can), Wax-treated Polishing Cloth, Permanent Type Anti-freeze/Coolant (quart), Touch-up Paint (in either pressure spray can or tube with built-in brush) for all body colors. Available from your Pontiac dealer. (D)

Underhood Lamp (Code 671—UPC U26). Fixed type. Lights automatically when hood is raised. Available on Firebird, Esprit, Formula and Trans Am models, as part of Convenience Lamp Group (Code 664—UPC Y92) only. (FD) Also available on T-37, LeMans, LeMans Sport and GTO models. (F,D)

Soft-Ray Glass (Code 531—UPC AO1). Fully tinted for all windows, (except convertible rear window). Recommended with air conditioning. Upper area of windshield is shaded to reduce glare. Also available for windshield only (Code 531—UPC AO2). (F)

Floor Mats, Front (Code 521—UPC B32); Rear (Code 522—UPC B33). Available all series and include mats for both sides of car. Keep car looking new and clean. Easily removed for washing. Available in Black Ivory, Dark Beige, Dark Saddle, Dark Sienna, Dark Jade and Dark Blue to harmonize with interiors. (F,D)

Full-width Floor Mat (Front only). Durable, long-wearing. Easily removed for cleaning. Available in Black, Ivory, Dark Beige, Dark Saddle, Dark Sienna, Dark Jade and Dark Blue. Not available for Firebird, Esprit, Formula, Trans Am or Grand Prix with bucket seats. (D)

Luggage Compartment Floor Mat. Heavy-duty, rugged, solid Gray vinyl floor mat gives extra protection for trunk compartment as well as cargo. Not available station wagon models. (D)

(F) Factory-installed. (D) Can be installed by dealer.
(F, D) Can be either factory- or dealer-installed.

PASSENGER SAFETY AND CAR BODY PROTECTION

Infant Safety Carrier. This special rear-facing seat is held snugly in place by front or rear seat belt. Built-in chest strap further safeguards baby. Upright section provides support for head and back. Doubles as a handy, sturdy carrier for use outside car. (D)

Deluxe Child Safety Seat. Provides extra protection for a small child. Utilizes standard seat belt. Sturdily constructed with special chest retainer strap to restrict forward movement during quick stops. Ivory color only. Available all models. (D)

Inside Release Hood Lock—a real theft deterrent. A pull-handle, cable-controlled release lets you unlock hood from inside the car only. Standard on Catalina, Safari, Catalina Brougham, Bonneville, Grand Safari and Grand Ville models. Available all other models. (D)

Spare Tire Cover (Code 424—UPC P17). Protects trunk contents. Easily slipped on/off. Dresses up luggage compartment. Available all models except station wagons. Standard on Grand Ville Convertible. Not available with "Space-Saver Spare" Tire. (F,D)

Vinyl Body Side Molding (Code 494 —UPC B84). Helps prevent nicks and scratches to exterior finish. Endura insert molding is mounted in stainless steel. Black only. (See Molding pages 6 and 7.) Available on all models. (F,D)

Door-edge Guards (Code 492—UPC B93). Bright, stainless steel strips that help protect door edges from nicks and scratches. (See Molding pages 6 and 7.) Available all models. (F,D)

Rear-door Child Guard Door Locks (4-door models only). Prevents children from unlocking and opening rear doors. When buttons are down and lock guards are pushed in, rear door can't be opened without inserting key into lock button. 1. Unlock position. 2. Regular locked position. 3. Lock Guard Position. Any regular key may be used to release lock guards. (D)

Fire Extinguisher. Handy 2¾-lb., dry-chemical fire extinguisher for all kinds of fires, including grease, oil, gasoline and electrical. Rechargeable. (D)

POWER ACCESSORIES

Variable-ratio Power Steering (Code 501—UPC N41). Permits fast steering response. Requires fewer turns in slow-speed maneuvering, such as parking. Available all models. Standard on Trans Am, Bonneville, Grand Safari, Grand Ville and Grand Prix. (F)

Electric Door Locks (Code 552—UPC AU5, 2-doors; Code 552—UPC AU3, 4-doors). A great time-saver. Promotes regular locking of doors. Master control located on front door panels on driver's side and passenger's side. (Control on instrument panel on Firebird models.) On 2-door models (except Firebird, Esprit, Formula and Trans Am), electric seat-back locks are included. Front seat backs automatically unlock when doors are opened and automatically lock again when doors are closed. Manual unlocking device still present. Available all models. (F)

Power Disc Brakes, Front (Code 502—UPC JL2). Combined with drum brakes at rear. Single-piston, floating-caliper design provides powerful braking and is easy to apply in emergencies. Provides automatic self-adjustment throughout life of linings. Available all models. Standard on Trans Am, LeMans Station Wagons, Catalina, Catalina Brougham, Safari, Bonneville, Grand Safari, Grand Ville and Grand Prix. (F)

Power Windows (Code 551—UPC A31). The action of all side door windows controlled from single panel on driver's door panel. (Controls on console for Firebird models.) Each window also has its individual control switch. Inoperative with ignition off. Available all models. (F)

4-way Power Bench Seat (Code 561—UPC A42). The seat will move forward, backward, tilt up, down. Available on T-37, LeMans, LeMans Sport, GTO and Grand Prix models with full-width bench front seats. (F)

Power Front Seat, Left-hand Bucket only (Code 564—UPC A46). Moves left-hand bucket seat forward, backward, tilt up or down to any position for your driving comfort. Available all models with bucket front seats except Firebird, Esprit, Formula or Trans Am. (F)

Cruise Control (Code 711—UPC K30). Attain your desired speed, lightly touch button in end of turn-signal indicator and you are all set. To disengage, simply touch the brake pedal. Wonderful for long-distance expressway driving. Available all models with V-8 engines and automatic transmission except Firebird, Esprit, Formula or Trans Am. (F,D)

Rear-window Defogger (Code 541—UPC C50). Electric blower under rear package shelf directs air through directional grille to entire area to help clear away steam. Available all models except convertibles and Grand Prix. (F,D)

Deck-lid Release (Code 421—UPC A90). A real time-saver. No need to get outside car to unlock trunk. Just press button inside glove compartment or console. Trunk can also be locked and unlocked in conventional manner. Available on all models except station wagons. (F,D)

Electrically Heated Rear-window Defroster (Code 534—UPC C49). Rows of small electrical conductors on inside glass surface carry electric current to heat the rear window. Helps keep entire window clear of fog, snow and ice. Includes Soft-Ray glass in rear window. Available all models except LeMans Station Wagons and Convertibles. (F)

RADIOS AND TAPE PLAYERS

Cassette Tape Player (Code 414—UPC U55). Pontiac brings you the sound of cassette. The handy, small cassette cartridge stores in a third the space, carries a complete album of stereo music. Features amazingly fast forward or rewind, built-in amplifier with balance control to vary volume between front and rear speakers. The number of speakers vary—see chart. Tunnel-mounted player comes in black only. Available all models with any Pontiac radio. (F,D)

Stereo Tape Player (Code 412—UPC U57) Affords amazing, lifelike sound. Equipped with built-in amplifiers plus volume and tone control. Plays 8-track stereo tape cartridges. Available with radio only. For player unit location and speakers, see chart. Available all models except Catalina, Safari, Catalina Brougham, Bonneville, Grand Safari and Grand Ville models. (F,D)

(F) Factory-installed. (D) Can be installed by dealer.
(F, D) Can be either factory- or dealer-installed.

Pushbutton AM/FM Stereo Radio (Code 405—UPC U58). Enjoy dual listening pleasure. Tune in on either AM or FM stations and enjoy true stereophonic sound when program is being broadcast in stereo. The number of speakers vary—see chart. Available all models. (F,D)

Pushbutton AM/FM Radio (Code 403—UPC U69). Pushbuttons can be set for either AM or FM stations to let you double your listening pleasure. Completely transistorized with excellent quality and fidelity. Available all Pontiac models. (F,D)

Pushbutton AM Radio (Code 401—UPC U63). Completely transistorized. Fine tone and fidelity. Wide dial provides space for precise tuning. Included in Basic Group. Available all models. (F,D)

Rear Speaker (Code 411—UPC U80). Available all Pontiac models except radios and tape players with stereo systems. Control is escutcheon behind radio station selector knob. You can have sound from back seat only, front only or turn both speakers on for enveloping effect. (F,D)

PERFORMANCE ACCESSORIES

"The Judge" Option (Code 332—UPC WT1). Available GTO only. Includes such items as: 445-cu-in. 4-bbl., H.O. V-8 engine, functional air-intake hood scoops, 3-speed, heavy-duty, floor-mounted, Hurst Tee-handle shifter, de-chromed Rally II wheels, black texture in grille, full-width rear deck body-color painted airfoil (optional black with white car), "Judge" stripes and decals, "Ram Air" decal on hood scoops and "The Judge" emblem on glove box. (F)

Rally Gauge Cluster with Instrument Panel Tachometer (Code 714—UPC U30). Integrates oil, water, fuel gauges with alternator telltale plus wood grain trim and clock where not already standard. Available on T-37, LeMans, LeMans Sport, GTO and Grand Prix.

Heavy-duty Springs and Shocks (Code 621—UPC Y96). For a better feel of the road—excellent cornering and handling. Extra-firm front and rear springs and shocks plus heavier stabilizer bar. Available on all models except Firebird, Esprit, Formula, Trans Am and LeMans Station Wagons. (F)

Heavy-duty Battery (Code 692—UPC UA1). 62-amp-hr., 3250-watt battery for longer life, better cranking ability, more power for accessories. Included with heavy-duty, self-regulating alternator. Available on all models, except with 455-cu.-in. V-8. A 76-amp-hr., 3700-watt battery is provided with 455-cu.-in. V-8 when heavy-duty battery is ordered. (F)

Dual-stage, Heavy-Duty Air Cleaner (Code 422—UPC K45). Dual-filter design consists of wetted paper in filter, surrounded by polyglycol-wetted, polyurethane-foam outer. Fine filtration, extended surface. Standard on Trans Am. Available all other models. (F)

Safe-T-Track Differential (Code 361—UPC G80). Transfers torque to rear wheel that has best traction. Keeps you going with sure handling when your car hits a stretch of slippery road, snow, ice, water, mud, sand, ruts or chuckholes. Available all models. (F)

Safeguard Speedometer (Code 712—UPC U15). You set speed limit you desire with control knob. Buzzer signals if car exceeds this predetermined speed. Not available with Rally Gauge Clusters. Available T-37, LeMans, LeMans Sport, GTO and Grand Prix models. (F)

Ram Air Hood Inlet (Code 601—UPC WU3). Available on Formula and GTO with 455 H.O. 4-bbl. High-output V-8 engine only. Provides direct air intake to carburetor for better engine performance.

Endura Styling Option (Code 602—UPC T41). Available on LeMans Sport series. Affords you the GTO look and the added front-end protection of Endura. Includes GTO front bumper, hood and headlamp assembly. Retains LeMans Sport grille and fender louvers. (F)

Hood-mounted Tachometer (Code 721—UPC UB5). Right out in front of the windshield for easy, instant readout by driver. Available on T-37, LeMans Sport with V-8 engines and GTO. (F,D)

(F) Factory-installed. (D) Can be installed by dealer.
(F, D) Can be either factory- or dealer-installed.

Rear Deck Airfoil (Code 604—UPC WT7). A real "spoiler" that helps keep downward pressure on rear of car. Flat back. Included in "The Judge" option. Available on T-37 and LeMans Hardtop Coupes, LeMans Sport and GTO. (D)

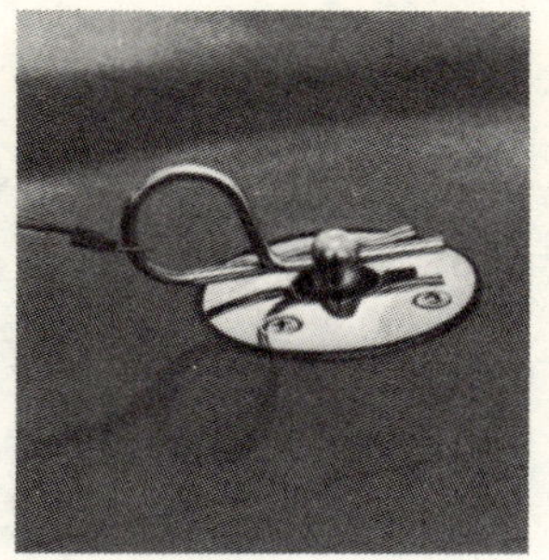

Hood Retainers. Affords double-locking hood protection at all time. Handy plastic covered hold-down cables guard against pin loss. Available all models except Grand Prix. Included in GT-37 option. (D)

VACATION AND TRAVEL ACCESSORIES

Removable Ski Rack Quickly fastens to roof drip moldings. Features adjustable rubber-padded metal tapes to protect car finish, rubber-padded cross members to protect skis, pushbutton release arms. Everything locks securely to guard against theft. As many as eight pairs of skis can be accommodated at one time. (D)

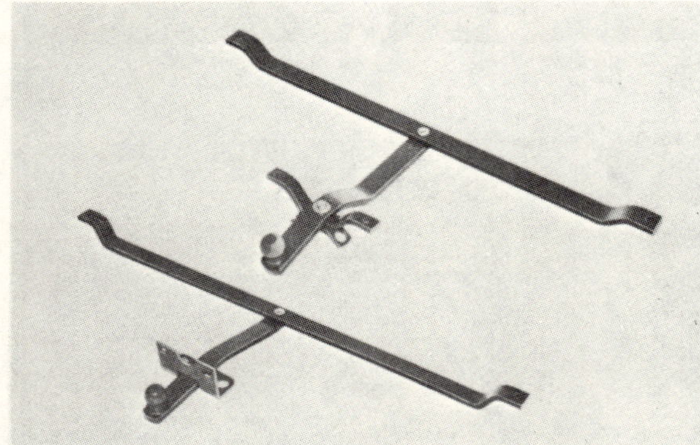

Trailer Hitch (Class I—Light Trailers from 1000 to 2000 lbs. loaded—tongue load up to 200 lbs.) Custom designed for Pontiac vehicles. Chrome plated draw bar and ball. Permanently bolted to structural members of the car. Recommended for boat, snowmobile, tent-type and small utility trailers. Available for all Pontiac models except Firebird. For very light trailers up to 1000 lbs. gross load (100 lbs. tongue load), Firebird Hitch available. (D)

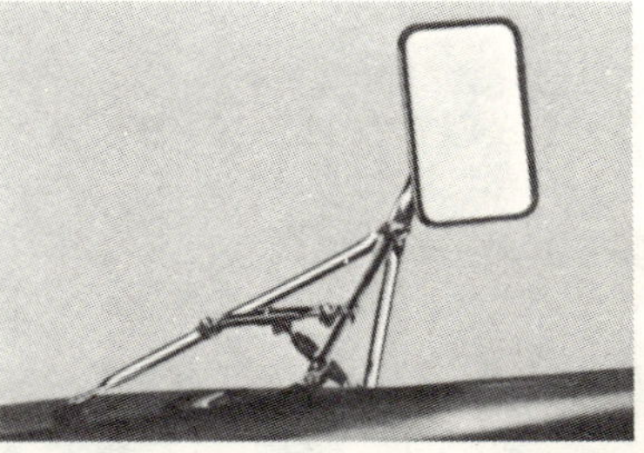

Trailer Towing Mirrors A pair—both right-hand and left-hand. These mirrors are specially designed to fit any Pontiac model. Easy to attach and remove when not in use. Turnbuckle-type fender mounts attach to front wheel opening and held firmly in place when hood is locked. Large 5½" x 8" size. Stainless steel construction. (D)

Gas-cap Lock. Helps prevent fuel theft. Separate key. Available all models. (D)

Trailer Wire Harness—a complete 4-way electrical wiring harness to extend stop lights, tail lights, clearance lights and directional signal. No special attachment wiring required. No splicing. A harness available for every Pontiac model. (D)

Deck-lid Luggage Carrier—available Firebird only. Carries up to 100 lbs. Luggage is securely tied down to handy side rails. Made of bright chrome and stainless steel. Permanently installed on deck lid. (D)

"Space-Saver Spare" Tire (Code 684—UPC N65) Adds approximately 3 cubic feet of usable luggage capacity. Easily inflated with handy pressure can and provides many miles of spare tire driving. (F) **"Space-Saver Spare" Tire Inflators** Replacements available from dealer. (D) See "Instant-Aire" Pump—this page.

"Instant-Aire" Pump—handy emergency air pump that operates off engine vacuum—ideal for inflating tires, camping or sport equipment. Provides maximum pressure of 32 pounds before shutting off. Operates regardless of altitude or temperature. Available for all models. (D)

Highway Emergency Kit—includes antenna emergency flag, fire extinguisher, tire inflater, extra fuses and warning flares. (D)

Car Compass—easy-to-read, suspended dial rotates as car changes direction. Special compensator assures correct directional indications. Pushbutton operates penlight to illuminate dial for easy night reading. (D)

(F) Factory-installed. (D) Can be installed by dealer.
(F, D) Can be either factory- or dealer-installed.

ACCENT WITH VINYL STRIPES

GTO. Vinyl tape body stripe. Available separately. Also available on LeMans with Endura front end. Not part of the GTO package.

BASIC GROUP

LeMans Basic Group
- Turbo Hydra-matic Transmission
- Pushbutton AM Radio
- Deluxe Wheel Covers
- Power Steering
- Whitewall Tires

DECOR GROUP

LE MANS DECOR GROUP
(Code 721–UPC Y80) includes:
- Custom Cushion Steering Wheel
- Deluxe Wheel Covers
- Hood Rear-edge Moldings
- Pedal Trim Plates
- Wheel Opening Moldings

DECOR AND PROTECTION MOLDINGS

A. Hood Rear-edge Molding (Code 651–UPC TJ1)

B. Roof Drip Molding (Code 481–UPC B80)

C. Side Window Reveal Molding (Code 482–UPC B90)

E. Wheel Opening Molding (Code 491–UPC B96)

F. Rocker Panel Molding (Code 484–UPC B83)

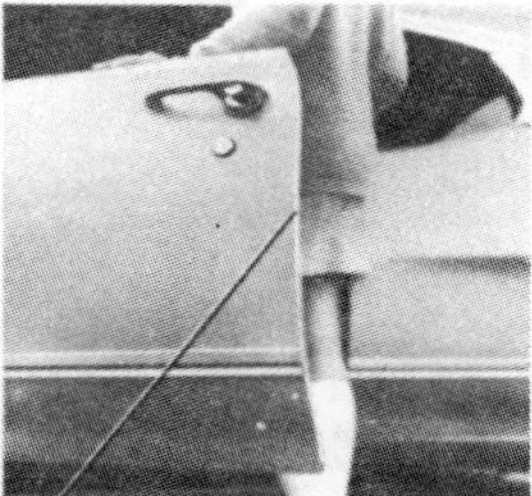

G. Door-edge Guards (Code 492–UPC B93)

H. Body Side Molding (Code 494–UPC B84)

Notes:
1. If a molding is not indicated, either as standard or available with a model, it is not available on that model.
2. Roof Drip Moldings are included with the Cordova Top.
3. The Roof Drip Molding also serves as a roof gutter on the Firebird, Formula and Trans Am—also on Safari and the Catalina 4-door Sedan. If Roof Drip Moldings are not obtained (either separately or with a Cordova Top), these cars will not have roof gutters.
4. Body Side Moldings are available in black only. They are not available with vinyl body side stripes on Firebird, Esprit, Formula or Trans Am, or with Wood Grain Safari Option or with GT Option. Ventura II Body Side Molding does not include Vinyl insert.

MODEL	STANDARD	AVAILABLE
GTO		
Hardtop Coupe	B,F	A,E,G,H
Coupe	F	A,B,C,E,G,H

WHEEL COVERS AND WHEELS

Wheel Trim Rings (Code 471–UPC P06). Shown with standard hubcap. Standard with Rally II Wheels except with GT Option. Has bright, stainless steel surface with hidden holding flanges. Standard on Ventura II with Sprint Option, Esprit and Trans Am. Available on Firebird, Formula, LeMans and Ventura II with standard hubcaps. (F,D)

Honeycomb Wheels (Code 478–UPC P05). A Pontiac exclusive. This is the look of rugged, cast-metal, designed to highlight the angles and sides of the deep-set lug nuts and give the wheel its honeycomb appearance. The honeycomb "face" of the wheel is made of Goodyear Neothane® bonded to a steel disc which has been welded to the wheel. Neothane is highly resistant to nicking and scratching and is unaffected by salt, road tar and other chemicals which normally attack most metal wheels. Available on Firebird, Esprit, Formula, Trans Am, LeMans (except station wagon) and Grand Prix. Chrome Trim Rings are not included with Trans Am or Firebird Handling Package. (F)

Deluxe Wheel Covers (Code 476–UPC P01). Available on LeMans. Same as Firebird Deluxe Wheel Covers except "Pontiac Motor" Identification in Center. (F,D)

Wire Wheel Covers (Code 473–UPC N95). Bright, chrome spokes give a realistic wire wheel appearance as they radiate out to a brushed stainless steel ring. Available on LeMans, Luxury LeMans and Grand Prix. (F,D)

Rally II Wheels (Code 474–UPC N98). The sporty magnesium wheel appearance with stainless steel capped wheel nuts. Standard on Trans Am and GT Option Package. Available on all other models except Safari and Grand Safari. Wheel Trim Rings included except with GT Option. (F)

CONSOLES

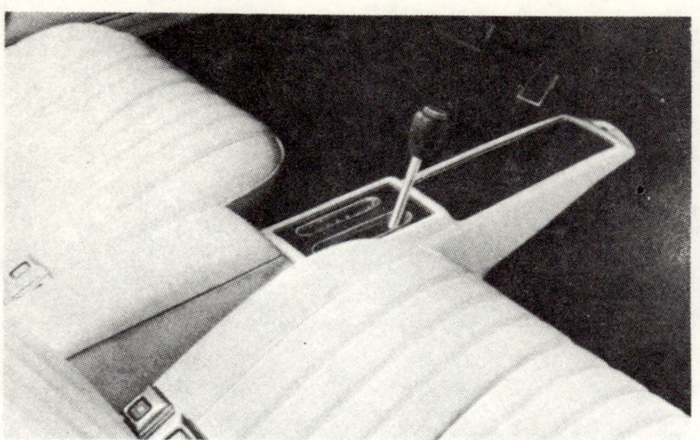

Console for LeMans and Luxury LeMans (Code 431—UPC D55). Available with Turbo Hydra-matic and bucket seats on LeMans and on the Luxury LeMans with bucket seats. Console features dark walnut wood grain appearance insert and padded top panel. Color-keyed to interior with glove box and side latch. (F)

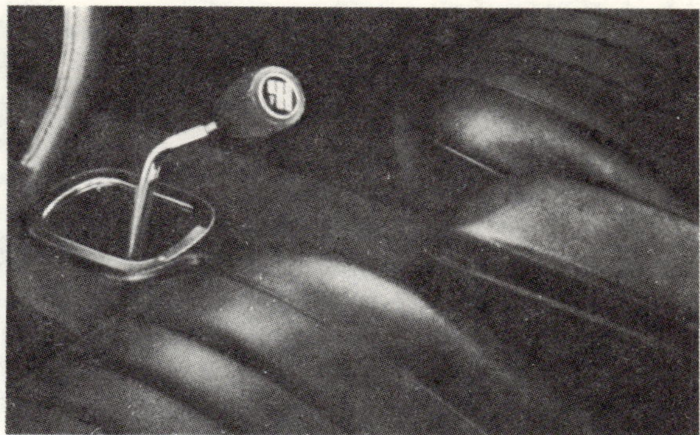

Console for LeMans and Luxury LeMans (Code 431—UPC D55). Available with 3- or 4-speed manual transmission with bucket seats on LeMans with Sport, GT, or GTO Options and on the Luxury LeMans Hardtop Coupe with bucket seats. Console features a soft, padded-vinyl exterior covering, color-keyed to match interior. (F)

STEERING WHEELS

Custom Cushion Steering Wheel (Code 461—UPC N30). Shallow-dish design with cushioned vinyl-covered rim, wood grain appearance inserts and horn buttons in each spoke. Available on Ventura II, Firebird, LeMans, Catalina and Safari. Not available on Trans Am. Standard on all other models. (F)

Custom Sport Steering Wheel (Code 462—UPC N31). Shallow-dish, three-spoke design with soft, simulated leather outer rim. Spokes are brushed stainless steel. Available on LeMans, Luxury LeMans, Grand Prix. Standard on Ventura II with Sprint Option. (F)

Formula Steering Wheel (Code 464—UPC NK3). With Power Steering only. Features 14-inch diameter, Formula spokes, molded urethane foam rim that looks and feels like padded leather. Available on Firebird, Esprit, Formula, LeMans and Luxury LeMans. Standard on Trans Am. (F)

APPEARANCE ACCESSORIES

Custom Seat Belts and Front Shoulder Belts (Code 451—UPC AK1). Available in colors to match every basic interior trim. Features press-to-release pushbutton buckle, locking, self-adjusting outboard front seat retractors (except Firebird models) and matching shoulder belts. Available all models. Custom Seat Belts (Code 454—UPC A39) for convertible models only (F). Rear shoulder belts separately are dealer installed only.

(Note: Standard seat belts and shoulder belts available in Black only.)

Concealed Windshield Wipers (Code 432—UPC C24). Dual-speed, completely concealed, parallel action with articulating left wiper for better visibility. Available on Firebird, Formula and LeMans Coupe. Not available on Ventura II. Standard on all other models. (F)

Body-colored Outside Mirrors (Code 434—UPC D35). A pair of aerodynamically styled outside mirrors color-keyed to match body paint. Left-hand mirror can be adjusted with a remote-control switch inside the car. Available on all models except Ventura II 4-door Sedan, LeMans Coupe, LeMans 4-door Sedan, LeMans Station Wagons, Luxury LeMans Hardtop Coupe, Catalina, Catalina Brougham, Bonneville, Grand Ville, Safari and Grand Safari. Standard on Esprit, Formula and Trans Am. Included with Sprint Option on Ventura II, or GT and WW5 Option and "SJ" Option on Grand Prix. (F,D)

Endura Styling Option (Code 602—UPC T41). A special hood, with long, twin air scoops, the Endura front bumper, valance panel, parking lamps, air extractors on front fenders and separate fiberglass headlamp-mounting panels make your car truly distinctive. Available on all LeMans Series with V-8 engines. Not available with GT Option or LeMans Station Wagons with wood grain side panels. Standard with GTO Option. (F)

ADDITIONAL APPEARANCE ACCESSORIES

License Plate Frame. Available for both front and rear. Stainless steel to enhance and protect license plate. Clips on easily. Rear frame has finger-pull for ready access to fuel filter cap. (D)

Custom Pedal Trim Plates (Code 514—UPC JL1). Bright stainless steel trim dresses up brake and accelerator pedals. Available on all LeMans models with automatic transmission and on Catalina, Safari and Catalina Brougham. Standard on Luxury LeMans, Bonneville, Grand Safari, Grand Ville and Grand Prix. (F)

AIR CONDITIONING

Custom Air Conditioning (Code 582—UPC C60). Available on Ventura II, Firebird, Esprit, Formula, Trans Am, LeMans, Luxury LeMans and Grand Prix. (Not available with 6-cylinder engines on Ventura II and Firebird. Not available with 6-cylinder engines and 2-speed automatic on LeMans. Not available with any 6-cylinder engine in California.) A sliding lever permits selection of OFF, INSIDE, A/C, B/L (BI-LEVEL), HEAT and DEFROST. BI-LEVEL combines upper level cooling with lower level heating when outside temperatures are not warm enough for A/C and not cold enough for HEAT. (F)

SPECIAL EQUIPMENT WITH AIR CONDITIONING

When you order air conditioning on your new Pontiac, this special equipment is included in the price.

- Radiator, Alternator and Battery designed to meet the requirements of the air conditioning unit.
- Special Suspension
- Thermostatically Controlled, 7-blade Fan
- Oversized Tires on LeMans, Luxury LeMans, Catalina and Catalina Brougham

TAPE PLAYERS AND RADIOS

Stereo Cassette Tape Player (Code 414—UPC U55). Available with any Pontiac radio except on Ventura II. Play all of your cassette tapes in the car. Listen to music, lectures, voice letters—whatever you have. Great for students who record notes and lectures. Has earphone jack that lets driver or passenger listen privately. Tunnel-mounted player comes in Black only. (F,D)

Picture shows front floor mounting on Catalina. When ordered with bucket seats and console, however, cassette is located on tunnel behind console.

Rear Speaker (Code 411—UPC U80). Shown on Station Wagon. Available all Pontiac models except with radios and tape players with stereo systems. Control is escutcheon behind radio station selector knob. You can have sound from front only, back only or turn on both speakers for an enveloping effect. Concealed speaker under parcel shelf on all other models. (F,D)

Stereo 8-track Tape Player (Code 412—UPC U57). Amazing, lifelike sound. Equipped with built-in amplifiers plus volume and tone control. Available with radio only. Available on all models except Ventura II, Catalina, Safari, Catalina Brougham, Bonneville, Grand Safari and Grand Ville. (F,D)

AM/FM Stereo Radio (Code 405—UPC U58). Tune in FM stations and enjoy true stereophonic sound when program is being broadcast in stereo. Factory-installed on on all models, except dealer-installed on Ventura II.

AM Radio (Code 401—UPC U63). Included in basic group. Available on all models. Completely transistorized. Five pushbuttons and tone control. (F,D)

AM/FM Radio (Code 402—UPC U69). Completely transistorized with excellent quality and fidelity. Enjoy the dual listening pleasure of AM and FM broadcasting. Available on all models. (F,D)

POWER ASSISTS

Cruise Control (Code 711—UPC K30). Attain your desired speed, lightly touch button in end of turn signal indicator and you are all set. To disengage, simply touch the brake pedal. Wonderful for long-distance expressway driving. Available on all models with V-8 engines and Turbo Hydra-matic transmission except Ventura II, Firebird, Esprit, Formula and Trans Am. (F,D)

Rear-window Defogger (Code 541—UPC C50). Electric blower under rear package shelf directs air through directional grille to entire area to help clear window. Factory-installed on all models except convertibles and Grand Prix. (F,D) Can be dealer-installed on Grand Prix and all other models except convertibles.

Deck-lid Release (Code 421—UPC A90). A real time-saver. No need to get out of the car to unlock the trunk. Just press button inside glove box or console. Trunk can be locked and unlocked in conventional manner. Available on all models except station wagons, Ventura II, Firebird, Esprit, Formula and Trans Am. (F,D)

Electrically Heated Rear-window Defroster (Code 534—UPC C49). Row of small electrical conductors on inside glass surface carry electric current to heat the rear window. Helps keep entire window clear of fog, snow and ice. Includes Soft-Ray glass in rear window. Available on all models except with 6-cylinder engines, Ventura II, LeMans Station Wagons and all convertible models. (F)

Electric Door Locks without seat back locks for 2 and 4 door models (Code 554—UPC AU3). Available except for Ventura II models. Switch is on instrument panel on Firebirds.

Electric Door Locks with Seat Back Locks (Code 552—UPC AU5, 2-doors). Promotes regular locking of doors and it's a great time-saver. The master control is located on the front door panels on the driver's side and passenger's side. Front seat backs automatically lock when doors are closed and unlock when doors are opened. Manual unlocking device still is present. Available all 2-door models except Firebird, Esprit, Formula, Trans Am and Ventura II. (F)

Power Windows (Code 551—UPC A31). The action of all side door windows controlled from single panel on driver's door panel. On the Catalina Brougham, Bonneville, Grand Prix or Grand Safari the switches are located on a new pod at the end of the door armrest as shown in picture. On the LeMans, Luxury LeMans, Catalina and Safari controls are on the driver's door panel. Controls are on the console on the Firebird models. Each window also has its individual control switch. Windows will not operate when ignition is off. Available all models except Ventura II. (F)

Variable-ratio Power Steering (Code 501—UPC N41). Permits fast steering response. Requires fewer turns in slow-speed maneuvering such as parking. Available all models. Standard on Trans Am, Catalina, Catalina Brougham, Bonneville, Grand Safari, Grand Ville and Grand Prix. (F,D)

Power Drum Brakes (Code 511—UPC J50). Just a light touch of the brakes provides excellent braking pressure. Available on Ventura II, LeMans (except station wagons) and Luxury LeMans. (F,D) (Can be dealer-installed on LeMans models.)

Power Front Disc Brakes (Code 502—UPC JL2). Combined with drum brakes at rear. Single-piston, floating-caliper design provides powerful braking and is easy to apply in emergencies. Automatic self-adjustment throughout life of linings. Available all models. Standard on Trans Am, LeMans Station Wagons, Catalina, Safari, Catalina Brougham, Bonneville, Grand Safari, Grand Ville and Grand Prix. (F)

Power Front Seat, Left-hand Bucket only (Code 564—UPC A46). Moves left-hand bucket seat forward, backward, tilts up or down to any position for your driving comfort. Available on all models with bucket seats except Ventura II, Firebird, Esprit, Formula and Trans Am. (F)

4-way Power Bench Seat (Code 561—UPC A41). The seat will move forward, backward, tilt up, down. Available on all LeMans models, Luxury LeMans and Grand Prix. (F)

CONVENIENCE ACCESSORIES

Tilt Steering Wheel (Code 504–UPC N33). Adjusts to seven different positions for your personal driving comfort. Makes exit and entrance easier. Provides more lap room. Available all models with variable-ratio power steering except Ventura II. Not available with manual, column-shift transmission. Not available with standard steering wheel on LeMans or Catalina. Console must be ordered on Firebird with any automatic transmission. (F)

Remote-controlled Outside Left-hand Mirror (Code 444–UPC D33). Easily adjusted by convenient control on inside, driver door panel. Available on all models. Dealer-installed in body color or chrome–chrome pictured. (F,D)

Visor Vanity Mirror. Mounts on back of visor. Out of sight when not being used. Available for right (Code 441–UPC D34) and/or left visors (Code 442–UPC DH5) all models. (F,D) Left-hand mirror not available on Firebird or Ventura II. (F)

Underhood Lamp (Code 671–UPC U26). Fixed-type. Lights automatically when hood is raised. Available on Ventura II, Firebird, Esprit, Formula and Trans Am as part of lamp group only. Also available on LeMans and Luxury LeMans. (F,D)

Right-hand Manual Outside Mirror. Matches standard left-hand outside mirror. Available all models. Body color or chrome-chrome pictured. Standard on Safari and Grand Safari. (D)

Luggage Compartment Lamp (Code 662–UPC U25). Lights automatically when trunk lid is lifted. Available only as part of lamp group on Ventura II, Firebird, Esprit, Formula and Trans Am. Also available on LeMans, Luxury LeMans, Catalina and Catalina Brougham. Standard on Bonneville, Grand Ville and Grand Prix. (F,D)

Instrument Panel Courtesy Lamp (Code 664–UPC U29). Lights when front door is opened. Also manually operated by switch. Available on LeMans and Luxury LeMans. Standard on convertibles. (F,D)

Maintenance Products. The following items are GM approved and carry the GM name. Glass Cleaner (pressure can), Windshield Washer Solvent, Vinyl Protector Cleaner (pressure can), Wax-treated Polishing Cloth, Permanent-type Antifreeze/Coolant, Touch-up Paint for all body colors (pressure can or tube with built-in brush). Available from your Pontiac dealer. (D)

Ashtray Lamp (Code 672–UPC U28). Lights automatically when headlamps or parking lights are turned on. Available on all LeMans models. Lamp is available also for right hand ashtray (pictured) for Catalina, Catalina Brougham, Safari, Bonneville and Grand Safari. Lamp is standard on Firebird. Included in Convenience Lamp Group on Ventura II. (F,D)

Glove Compartment Lamp (Code 674–UPC U27). Available on all Firebird and LeMans. Included in Convenience Lamp Group on Firebird, Ventura II. Standard on all other series. (F,D)

Dome Reading Lamp Group (Code 661 – UPC C89). Consists of center lamp and two side lamps. Center lamp functions as a conventional dome lamp, lights from door jamb switches and headlamp switch knob. Side lamps operate from separate switches on lamp housing and shine over the shoulders of front seat occupants. Available on all models except Ventura II, Firebird, Esprit, Formula, Trans Am and convertibles. (F)

ADDITIONAL CONVENIENCE ACCESSORIES

Electric Clock (Code 722 – UPC U35). It has a sweep second hand and built-in, automatic, self regulator. Dial is illuminated for easy night reading. Available on Ventura II, Firebird, Esprit, Formula, LeMans, Luxury LeMans and Catalina. Standard on all others. Included with Rally Gauge Cluster/Clock and Tachometer on Firebird, Esprit and Formula (Code 714–UPC U30) or Rally Gauge Cluster/Clock (Code 718–UPC W63). (F,D)

Thick Foam Front-seat Padding (Code 571–UPC B50). Available only on LeMans models.

Soft-Ray Glass (Code 531–UPC A01). Fully tinted for all windows, (except convertible rear window). Recommended with air conditioning. Upper area of windshield is shaded to reduce glare. Also available for windshield only (Code 531 –UPC A02). (F)

Litter Basket clings to transmission tunnel. Weighted to prevent tipping. Easy to empty. Available in Red, Black, Blue and Fawn. (D)

Litter Basket / Tissue Dispenser pins fast to transmission tunnel carpeting. Holds junior size box of tissues. Has removable plastic tray for litter. Black only. (D)

SAFETY AND PROTECTION

Rear Bumper Guards (Code 732–UPC V32). Available all models except Ventura II and Grand Prix. Front and Rear Bumper Guards (Code 731–UPC V30). Available Ventura II. Excellent protection from minor bumps. Help prevent chipping and scratching. Help reduce damage in minor collisions. (LeMans pictured) (F,D)

Vinyl Body Side Molding (Code 494–UPC B84). Helps prevent nicks and scratches to exterior finish. Vinyl insert molding is mounted in stainless steel, black only. (See moldings on page 4.) Available all models except LeMans with GT Option and station wagons with Wood Grain options. Not available with LeMans Rally stripes. Ventura II Body Side Molding does not include vinyl insert. Not available on Trans Am or Firebird with vinyl side stripes. (F,D)

Inside Hood Release. A pull-handle, cable-controlled release lets you unlock hood from inside the car only. Offers protection from theft of engine components. Available on Firebird, Esprit, Formula, Trans Am, LeMans, Luxury LeMans and Grand Prix. Standard on all other models execpt Ventura II. (D)

Infant Safety Carrier. This special, rear-facing seat is held snugly in place by front or back seat belt. Built-in chest strap further safeguards baby. Upright section provides support for head and back. Included contour fitting pad for greater comfort. Doubles as a handy, sturdy carrier for use outside car. (D)

Floor Mats, Front (Code 521–UPC B32; Rear Code 522–UPC B33). Available for all series. Includes rubber mats for both sides of your car. Easily removed for washing. Available in Black, Ivory, Dark Beige, Dark Saddle, Dark Sienna, Dark Jade and Dark Blue to harmonize with interiors. (F,D) Pictured is indoor-outdoor type carpet floor mat in Blue, Black, Brown and Green. Dealer installed only.

ADDITIONAL SAFETY AND PROTECTION ACCESSORIES

Fire Extinguisher. Handy 2¾-lb., dry-chemical fire extinguisher for all kinds of fires, including grease, oil, gasoline and electrical. Rechargeable. (D)

Door-edge Guards (Code 492 – UPC B93). Bright, stainless steel strips that help protect door edges from nicks and scratches. Available all models. (F,D)

Spare Tire Cover (Code 424–UPC P17). Protects trunk contents. Slips easily on and off. Available all models except Ventura II, Firebird and station wagons. Not available with "Space-Saver Spare" Tire. (F,D)

Gas Cap Lock. Helps prevent fuel theft. Separate key. Available all models. (D)

PERFORMANCE ACCESSORIES

Hood-mounted Tachometer. Right out in front of the windshield for easy, instant readout by driver. Available on V-8 engines on Firebird, Esprit, Formula, Trans Am (Trans Am Standard Equipment includes instrument panel tachometer), LeMans, Luxury LeMans and Grand Prix. (D)

Rally Gauge Cluster with Instrument Panel Tachometer (Code 714—UPC U30). Integrates oil, water and fuel gauges with alternator telltale. Includes wood grain trim. Available on LeMans and Luxury LeMans. (F)

Rally Gauge Cluster with Clock (Code 718—UPC W63). This option groups oil, water, fuel and voltmeter together and includes a clock where not already standard. Available on LeMans, Luxury LeMans, Firebird, Esprit, Formula and Grand Prix. Standard on Grand Prix SJ option.

Rear Air Spoiler (Code 611—UPC D80). Available on Formula and LeMans. Adds sporty Trans Am look. Spoiler is a 3-piece, rear deck attachment.

Safe-T-Track Differential (Code 361 — UPC G80). Transfers torque to rear wheel that has best traction. Keeps you going with sure handling when your car hits a stretch of slippery road, snow, ice, mud, sand, ruts, water or chuckholes. Available on all models. Standard on Trans Am. (F)

GROUP OPTIONS

GTO Option (Code 334—UPC W62). The one—the only—the most famous sport car option! Available on LeMans Coupe and LeMans Hardtop Coupe.

- Heavy-duty, 3-speed, Floor-shift, Manual Transmission
- 400 cu. in., V8, 4 bbl. Engine
- G70—14 Black Tires
- Dual Exhausts with Side Splitters
- Endura Front Bumper
- GTO Hood with Twin Air Scoops
- Front Fender Air Extractors
- Firm Shocks
- Front and Rear Stabilizer Bars
- GTO Decal Identification
- Swirl-finished Aluminum Trim Plate

WW5 Option (Code 704—UPC WW5). Available with GTO Option only. Designed to transform the GTO into a Trans Am-type car.

- 455 cu. in., V8, 4 bbl, H.O. Engine
- Turbo Hydra-matic or 4-speed, Floor-shift, Manual Transmission
- Safe-T-Track Rear Axle
- Body-colored, Left- and Right-hand Outside Mirrors (Hardtop Coupe only)
- Formula Steering Wheel
- Roof Drip Moldings (standard on hardtop coupe)
- Carpeting (standard on hardtop coupe)
- Power Front Disc Brakes
- Rally Gauge Cluster with Instrument Panel Tachometer
- GTO/H.O. Identification
- LeMans Handling Package
- Unitized Ignition System
- Hood Ram Air

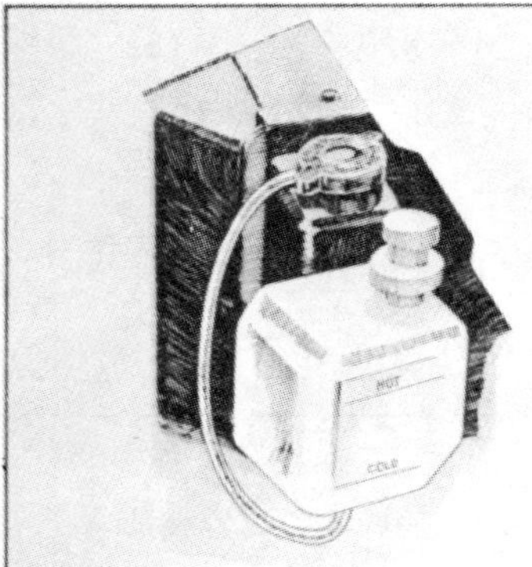

Coolant Recovery System. Helps prevent engine overheating due to excessive loads, high temperatures or hilly terrain. As pressure builds up in a hard-working engine, the coolant expands, but the system prevents it from spilling out through the overflow tube. Instead, the coolant passes into a reservoir tank. Later, as the engine cools, the overflowed coolant is pulled back into the system. Because no air is allowed in the system, cooling efficiency is maintained and overheating is prevented, prolonging radiator hose and water pump life. (D)

Hood Retainers. Afford double locking hood protection at all times. Handy, plastic-covered, hold-down cables guard against pin loss. Available on Ventura II, Firebird, Esprit, Formula, Trans Am, LeMans and Luxury LeMans. (D)

ADDITIONAL ACCESSORIES

Dual Horns (Code 681 — UPC U05). Emit a loud, commanding sound. Available on Firebird and LeMans. Standard on all others except Ventura II. (F)

Heavy-duty Battery (Code 692—UPC UA1). Available for all models when more electrical power is needed. (F)

Heavy-duty Radiator (Code 701—UPC V01). Great cooling capacity, standard with air conditioning. Available all models. (F)

Dual-stage, Heavy-duty Air Cleaner (Code 422—UPC K45). Dual-filter design consists of wetted paper inner filter, surrounded by polyglycol-wetted, polyurethane-foam outer filter. Fine filtration. Extended surface. Available all models except Ventura II and with 455 cu. in., V8, H.O. 4 bbl. engine. (F)

APPEARANCE ACCESSORIES

Cordova Top (UPC C08. White, Code 1. Black, Code 2. Beige, Code 3. Chamois, Code 4. Green, Code 5. Dark Burgundy, Code 6. Blue, Code 7.) An outstanding appearance accessory, in pebble-grain texture, for a rich look. Available on all models except LeMans Safari, Trans Am and Grand Ville Convertible. Roof drip moldings included, if not already standard on model. (F)

Body-colored Outside Mirrors (Code 434—UPC D35). A pair of aerodynamically-styled outside mirrors color-keyed to match body paint. Left-hand mirror can be adjusted with a remote control lever inside the car. Available on all models. Standard on Esprit, Formula and Trans Am. Included with Sprint Option on Ventura and Ventura Custom and "SJ" Option on Grand Prix. (F,D)

Metal Sliding Sunroofs (Code 572—UPC C03 for Manual, Code 571—UPC CA1 for Power Operated). Get that open-air feeling without being windblown, with these all-new and great metal sliding sunroofs. Open, the sunroof slides away out of sight; closed, it fits flush with the remainder of the roof. Choose either manual or power operated. Exterior color and interior trim match those of car ordered. Available on the LeMans, Luxury LeMans, and Grand Am Two-door Colonnade Hardtops, LeMans Sport Coupe, and Grand Prix. (F)

Custom Pedal Trim Plates (Code 511—UPC JL1). Bright stainless steel trim dresses up brake and accelerator pedals. Available on all LeMans models and on Catalina and Safari. Standard on Ventura Custom, Luxury LeMans, Grand Am, Bonneville, Grand Safari, Grand Ville and Grand Prix. (F)

License Plate Frame. Available for both front and rear. Stainless steel to enhance and protect license plate. Easily installed. (D)

Custom Seat Belts and Front Shoulder Belts (Code 451—UPC AK1). Available in colors to match every basic interior trim (Black belts with White interiors). Outboard front seat and shoulder belts feature the new (standard) three-point attachment, with a single buckle for seat and shoulder belt. (F) (NOTE: Standard seat belts and shoulder belts available in Black only.)

CUSTOM INTERIORS AND CONSOLES

Console for LeMans Sport Coupe and Luxury LeMans with Manual Transmission (Code 431—UPC D55). Available with three- or four-speed manual transmission with bucket seats on LeMans Sport Coupe, and on the Luxury LeMans with bucket seats. Console features a soft, padded-vinyl exterior covering, color-keyed to match interior. (F)

Console for LeMans Sport Coupe and Luxury LeMans with Automatic Transmission (Code 431—UPC D55). Available with Turbo Hydra-matic and bucket seats on LeMans Sport Coupe, and on the Luxury LeMans with bucket seats. Console features American walnut wood-grain appearance insert and padded side panel. Color-keyed to interior, with glove box and side latch. (F)

SERIES	MODEL	DECOR AND PROTECTION MOLDINGS						
		A—Bright Metal Roof Drip Molding	B—Side-window Reveal Molding	C—Windowsill Molding	D—Door Edge Guards	E—Rocker Panel Molding	F—Wheel Opening Molding	G—Body SideMolding
LeMANS	2- & 4-Door Colonnade Ht.	Std	NA	A*	A	Std	A*	A
LeMANS SPORT COUPE	2-Door Colonnade Ht.	Std	NA	A*	A	Std	A*	A

1973 DECOR AND PROTECTION MOLDINGS

A. Bright Metal Roof Drip Molding (Code 481—UPC B80)

C. Windowsill Molding (Code 484—UPC B85)

D. Door Edge Guards (Code 492—UPC B93)

E. Rocker Panel Molding (Code 484—UPC B83)

F. Wheel Opening Molding (Code 491—UPC B96)

G. Body Side Molding (Code 494—UPC B84)

*These moldings are included with the decor group on these models. (See decor groups, Page 21. Also check basic groups and protection groups for moldings which are included with these groups.)

A—Available NA—Not Available Std—Standard

WHEELS, WHEEL COVERS AND STEERING WHEELS

Honeycomb Wheels (Code 478—UPC P05). A Pontiac exclusive, the deep-set "honeycomb" design gives the look of rugged cast metal. The honeycomb face is made of Goodyear Neothane®, bonded to a steel disc that is welded to the wheel rim. Neothane is highly resistant to nicking and scratching and is unaffected by salt, road tar and other chemicals which normally attack most metal wheels. Includes trim rings. Available on Firebird, Esprit, Formula, Trans Am, LeMans, LeMans Safari, LeMans Sport Coupe, Grand Am and Grand Prix. (F)*

Rally II Wheels (Code 474—UPC N98). This stylish wheel has a sporty magnesium wheel appearance, with stainless steel capped wheel nuts. Wheel trim rings included. Standard on Trans Am. Available on all others, including all series Safaris. (F)*

Custom Cushion Steering Wheel (Code 461—UPC N30). Shallow-dish design with cushioned vinyl-covered rim, wood-grain appearance or Black insert, and horn buttons in each spoke. *In colors with new simulated American walnut insert:* Standard on Luxury LeMans, Bonneville, Grand Ville and Grand Safari. Available on LeMans, LeMans Safari, LeMans Sport Coupe, Catalina and Safari. *In colors with new Black insert:* Standard on Ventura Custom, Sprint Option, Esprit and Formula. Available on Ventura and Firebird. *In Black with new Black insert:* Standard on Grand Prix. (F)

Wheel Trim Rings (Code 471—UPC P06). These rings have a bright, brushed stainless steel surface and bright edge, with hidden holding flanges. Standard on the Trans Am and with Rally II Wheels. Available on the Ventura, Firebird, Formula, LeMans, LeMans Safari and LeMans Sport Coupe with standard hubcaps. (F,D)

Custom Sport Steering Wheel (Code 462—UPC N31). Three-spoke shallow-dish design, with soft, simulated leather outer rim and center. Spokes are brushed stainless steel. Black only. Available on Ventura, Ventura Custom, LeMans, LeMans Safari, LeMans Sport Coupe and Luxury LeMans. (F)

Deluxe Wheel Covers—14" (Code 476—UPC P01). An all-new design. Standard on the Ventura Custom, Esprit and Luxury LeMans. Available on the Ventura, Firebird, Formula, LeMans, LeMans Safari and LeMans Sport Coupe. (F,D)

Custom Finned Wheel Covers (Code 472—UPC P02). Deep-set Black matte fins on a brushed stainless steel disc, surrounded by a brushed-finish trim ring. The fins heighten the appearance of functional cooling. Standard on Grand Am and Grand Prix Model SJ. Available on Firebird, Esprit, Formula, LeMans (but not LeMans Safari), LeMans Sport Coupe, Catalina, Bonneville, Grand Ville, Safari, Grand Safari and Grand Prix. (F,D)

VINYL ACCENT STRIPES—IN A VARIETY OF COLORS

Vinyl Accent Stripes (Code 631—UPC D98). An inexpensive, yet very distinctive, way to personalize your new Pontiac is to highlight its stylish lines with vinyl accent stripes, in your choice of colors. (F)

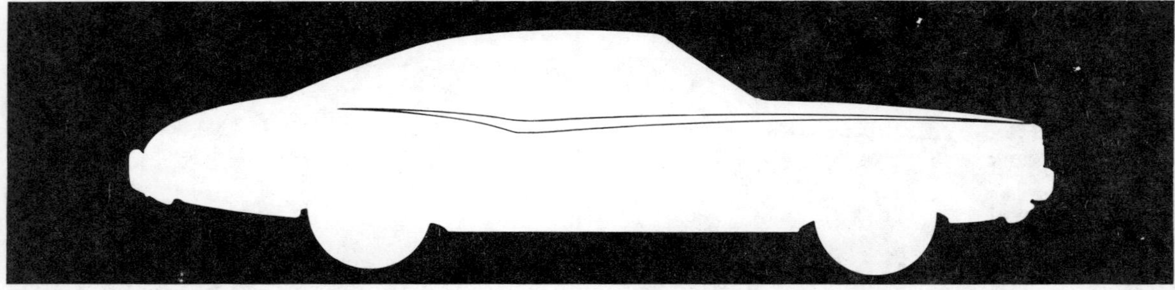

LeMans and LeMans Sport Coupe Series. (2-door models only)

RECOMMENDED STRIPE COLOR USAGE CHART

Body Colors	LeMans LeMans Sport Coupe	GTO Decal
C—Cameo White	(1)* (2)* (3)* (4)*	Red
D—Porcelain Blue	Lt. Blue/Black/Bright Blue	Black
E—Admiralty Blue	Lt. Blue/Black/Bright Blue	White
F—Regatta Blue	Lt. Blue/Black/Bright Blue	White
H—Desert Sand	Cream/Dark Brown/Orange	White
J—Golden Olive	Yellow/Black/Lime Green	White
K—Verdant Green	Yellow/Black/Lime Green	White
L—Slate Green	Yellow/Black/Lime Green	Black
M—Brewster Green	Yellow/Black/Lime Green	White
S—Florentine Red	Black/Red	White
V—Ascot Silver	Black/Red	Black
Y—Valencia Gold	Cream/Dark Brown/Orange	White
Z—Burma Brown	Cream/Dark Brown/Orange	White
A—Starlight Black	(2)* (3)* (4)*	Red
G—Mesa Tan	Cream/Dark Brown/Orange	White
W—Burnished Umber	Cream/Dark Brown/Orange	White

PONTIAC AIR CONDITIONING

Custom Air Conditioning (Code 582—UPC C60). Available on Ventura, Ventura Custom, Firebird, Esprit, Formula, Trans Am, LeMans, LeMans Safari, LeMans Sport Coupe, Luxury LeMans and Grand Am. (Not available with any six-cylinder engine.) Simple sliding lever control provides full temperature and performance range. (F)

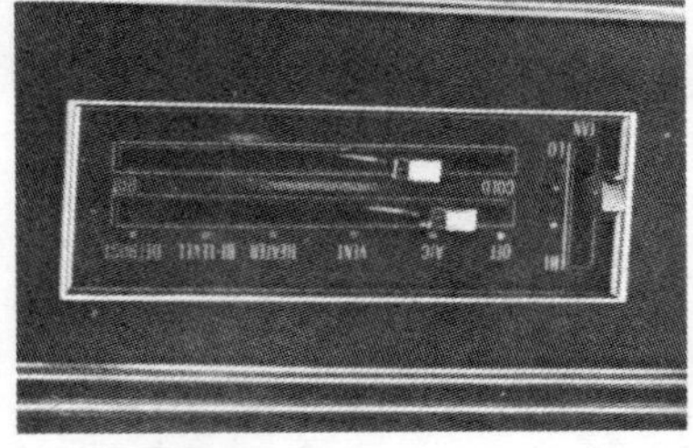

Shown on LeMans.

TAPE PLAYERS AND RADIOS

Stereo AM/FM Radio/Tape Player (Code 419—UPC UM2). Plays popular eight-track, stereo tape cartridges. Radio and tape player combine into a single unit with radio dial face functioning as the tape player door. (System has multiple speakers.) FM radio plays in full stereophonic sound with stereo broadcasting. Another version is available with AM Radio only (Code 417—UPC UM1). Available all models except Ventura and Ventura Custom, Firebird, Esprit, Formula and Trans Am. (F,D)

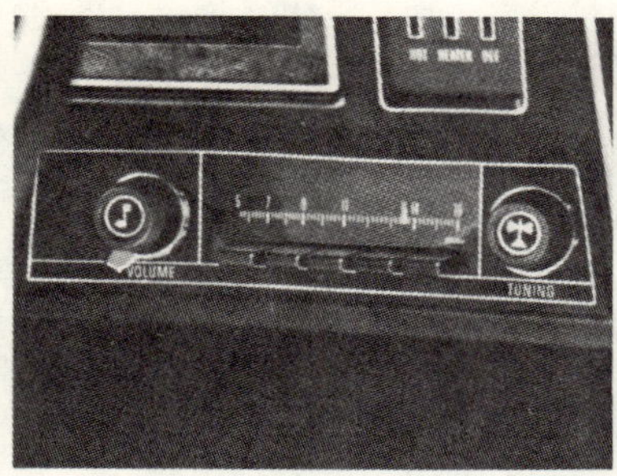

AM Radio (Code 411—UPC U63). Included in basic group. Available on all models. Completely transistorized. Five pushbuttons and tone control. (F,D)

AM/FM Radio (Code 413—UPC U69). Enjoy the dual listening pleasure of AM and FM broadcasting. Completely transistorized, with excellent quality and fidelity. (Five pushbuttons can be set to 10 stations—five AM, five FM—on all full-sized Pontiacs.) Available on all models. (F,D)

AM/FM Stereo Radio (Code 415—UPC U58). Tune in FM stations and enjoy true stereophonic sound when program is being broadcast in stereo. Factory-installed on all models, except dealer-installed on Ventura and Ventura Custom. (F)

Rear Speaker (Code 421—UPC U80). With the addition of this rear speaker, you can have sound from the front only, back only, or turn on both speakers for an enveloping effect. Control is in escutcheon behind radio station selector knob. Available on all models except with stereo radios and tape players, which use other speakers. (F,D)

POWER ASSISTS

Cruise Control (Code 562—UPC K30). Ideal for long-distance freeway driving. Simply attain your desired speed, lightly touch the button in the end of turn signal indicator, momentarily release accelerator pedal, and the car will maintain that speed. To disengage, simply touch the brake pedal. Car can be accelerated beyond speed setting and will drop back to setting with release of accelerator. Available on all models with V-8 engines and Turbo Hydra-matic transmission except Ventura, Ventura Custom, Firebird, Esprit, Formula and Trans Am. (F,D)

Power Front Disc Brakes (Code 502—UPC JL2). Combined with power drum brakes at rear. Single-piston, floating-caliper design provides powerful braking and is easy to apply in emergencies. Automatic self-adjustment throughout life of pads. Available all models. Standard on Trans Am, LeMans Safari, Grand Am, Catalina, Bonneville, Grand Ville, Safari, Grand Safari and Grand Prix. (F)

Electric Door Locks without Seat-back Locks for Two- and Four-door models (Code 554—UPC AU3). Convenient for any driver, particularly desirable for families with small children. Available on all models except Ventura and Ventura Custom. (F)

Variable-ratio Power Steering (Code 501—UPC N41). Permits fast and easy steering response. Requires far fewer turns in slow-speed maneuvering such as parking. Available all models. Standard on Trans Am, Grand Am, Catalina, Bonneville, Grand Ville, Safari, Grand Safari and Grand Prix. (F,D)

Six-way Power Bench Seat (Code 561—UPC A42). Just move a lever and you can raise, lower, tilt forward or backward, or move forward or backward, the entire front seat. Helps lessen fatigue on long trips, provides a more precise driving position, affords greater comfort and convenience for drivers of different stature. Available on all models except Ventura and Ventura Custom, Firebird, Esprit, Formula and Trans Am. When 60/40 seat is ordered (available on Grand Ville and Grand Safari), driver's side is powered, passenger's side is manually adjusted. (F)

Electric Door Locks with Seat-back Locks for Two-door models (Code 552—UPC AU5). Promotes the regular locking of doors, saves time and is a boon to rear-seat passengers. Control switches are located on the door panels of the driver's side and passenger's side. Front-seat backs automatically lock when doors are closed and unlock when doors are opened. Manual unlocking devices still are present. Available all Two-door models except Ventura and Ventura Custom, Firebird, Esprit, Formula and Trans Am. Not available with bucket-seat models, including Grand Am and Grand Prix. (F)

Power Front Seat, Left-hand Bucket only (Code 561—UPC AC3). Same six-way power feature, but on left-hand bucket seat only. Available with bucket seats on LeMans Sport Coupe, Luxury LeMans 2-door, Grand AM and Grand Prix. (F)

Deck-lid Release (Code 564—UPC A90). A top choice for convenience and time saving. No need to get out of your car to unlock the trunk. Just press the Deck-lid Release button inside glove box or console. Trunk also can be closed and opened in the conventional manner. Available on all models except station wagons, Ventura and Ventura Custom. Dealer installed only on Firebird, Esprit, Formula and Trans Am. (F,D)

Power Windows (Code 551—UPC A31). Passengers can raise or lower windows by using individual switches, or driver can control all windows from a central panel on driver's door (console on Firebird, Esprit, Formula and Trans Am). Windows will not operate when ignition is off. Available all models except Ventura and Ventura Custom. Available on Firebird, Esprit, Formula and Trans Am with console only. (F)

Rear Window Defogger (Code 541—UPC C50). Electric blower under rear window shelf directs air through directional grille to help keep the window clear. Factory- or dealer-installed on all models except Grand Am, Grand Ville Convertible, Grand Prix, GTO Option or with the LeMans Handling Package. (F,D)

Electrically-heated Rear Window Defroster (Code 534—UPC C49). Small electrical conductors on inside glass surface carry electric current to heat the rear window. Helps keep the entire window clear of fog, snow and ice. Includes Soft-Ray glass in rear window. Available on all models except Ventura, Ventura Custom, LeMans Safari, Grand Ville Convertible and models with six-cylinder engines. (F)

CONVENIENCE ACCESSORIES

Tilt Steering Wheel (Code 504—UPC N33). Adjusts to seven different positions for your personal driving comfort. Makes exit and entrance easier. Provides more lap room when required. Available all models. Not available with manual, column-shift transmission. Not available with standard steering wheel on LeMans, LeMans Safari, LeMans Sport Coupe, Catalina and Safari. Console must be ordered on Firebird, Esprit, Formula or Trans Am with any automatic transmission. (F)

Visor Vanity Mirror. Mounts on back of visor, out of sight when not being used. Available for **right visor (Code 441—UPC D34)** or **left visor (Code 422—UPC DH5)**, on all models. Left-hand mirror not available on Ventura and Ventura Custom, Firebird, Esprit, Formula and Trans Am. (F) Left- and right-hand mirrors available dealer-installed on all models. (D)

Remote Controlled, Outside Left-hand Mirror (Code 444—UPC D33). Easily adjusted by convenient lever control on driver's door panel. Available on all models. Factory- or dealer-installed in chrome. (F,D)

Right-hand Manual Outside Mirror. Matches standard left-hand outside mirror. Standard on Safari and Grand Safari. Available all models. Chrome finish. (D)

Electric Clock (Code 711—UPC U35). Has a sweep second hand and built-in, automatic, self-regulator. Dial is illuminated for easy night reading. Available on Ventura, Ventura Custom, Firebird, Esprit, Formula, LeMans, LeMans Safari, Luxury LeMans, Catalina and Safari. Standard on all others. Included with **Rally Gauge Cluster/Clock and Tachometer (Code 714—UPC WW8)**, or **Rally Gauge Cluster/Clock (Code 712—UPC W63)**. (F,D)

Litter Basket/Tissue Dispenser clings to transmission tunnel carpeting. Holds junior size box of tissues. Available in Black, Dark Blue, Dark Green and Chamois. (D)

Soft-Ray Glass (Code 531—UPC A01). Fully tinted for all windows (except convertible rear window). Recommended with air conditioning. Upper area of windshield is shaded to reduce glare. Available all models. Also available for windshield only (Code 532—UPC A02). (F)

LAMPS AND LAMP GROUPS

Select from a desirable offering of lamps and lamp groups to "upgrade" your new Pontiac with greater style, comfort, convenience, safety and resale value. In most cases, you'll add lamps to your new Pontiac by selecting the **lamp group** for your model—the order code and UPC code are the same in every case. **(Code 344—UPC Y92).** (F) This makes it easier to order and save money, too. Because of this simplification, some lamps are available on some models *only* as part of the group. Other lamps (described) are available individually. *You'll find the lamp groups described in the "Groups" section on Pages 20-21, which outlines availability according to the groups.*

Ash Tray Lamp. Lights automatically when headlights or parking lights are turned on. Standard on Firebird, Esprit, Formula, Trans Am, Luxury LeMans, Grand Am, Catalina, Bonneville, Grand Ville, Safari, Grand Safari and Grand Prix. Available as part of the lamp group on the Ventura, Ventura Custom, LeMans, LeMans Safari and LeMans Sport Coupe. **Right-hand Ash Tray Lamp.** Standard on Grand Ville and Grand Safari. Available as part of the lamp group on the Catalina, Bonneville and Safari. **Ash Tray Lamps** also may be **dealer-installed** on Ventura, Ventura Custom, LeMans, LeMans Safari, LeMans Sport Coupe, Catalina, Bonneville and Safari. (D)

Instrument Panel Courtesy Lamp. Lights when front door is opened. Also can be manually operated by switch. Standard on Grand Am, Bonneville, Grand Ville, Grand Safari and Grand Prix. Available as part of the lamp group on the Ventura, Ventura Custom, Firebird, Esprit, Formula, Trans Am, LeMans, LeMans Safari, LeMans Sport Coupe, Luxury LeMans, Catalina and Safari. Instrument Panel Courtesy Lamp also may be dealer-installed on the LeMans, LeMans Safari and LeMans Sport Coupe. (D)

Glove Compartment Lamp. Lights when compartment door is opened. Standard on all models except Ventura, Firebird, Esprit, Formula, Trans Am, LeMans, LeMans Safari and LeMans Sport Coupe. Available on these models as part of the lamp group.

Luggage Compartment Lamp. Provides light in luggage compartment area. Operates when trunk lid is opened. Standard on Bonneville, Grand Ville and Grand Prix. Available as part of the lamp group on Ventura (but not Ventura Hatchback Coupe), Ventura Custom, Firebird, Esprit, Formula, Trans Am, LeMans, LeMans Sport Coupe, Luxury LeMans, Grand Am and Catalina. **Luggage Compartment Lamp** also may be **dealer-installed** on all models except Ventura and Ventura Custom Hatchback Coupes, Safaris and the Grand Prix. (D)

Dome and Reading Lamp. Consists of center lamp and two side lamps. Center lamp functions as a conventional dome lamp; operates from doorjamb switches and headlight switch knob. Side lamps operate from separate switches on lamp housing and shine over the shoulders of front-seat occupants. Not available on Ventura, Ventura Custom, Firebird, Esprit, Formula, Trans Am and Grand Ville Convertible. **Available individually** on LeMans, LeMans Safari, LeMans Sport Coupe, Luxury LeMans, Grand Am, Catalina, Bonneville, Grand Ville, Safari, Grand Safari and Grand Prix. **(Code 661—UPC C95)** (F). Available as part of the lamp group on the Grand Am, Bonneville, Grand Ville and Grand Prix.

PROTECTION ACCESSORIES

Front Bumper Guards (Code 731—UPC V31). Provide added protection from minor bumps, help prevent marring of chrome. Available on all models except Firebird, Esprit, Formula, Trans Am and Grand Am. Available only in combination with Protective Rubber Bumper Strips. (F,D)

Rear Bumper Guards (Code 732—UPC V32). To additionally guard against marring, damage from minor impact. Standard on Safari and Grand Safari. Available all other models except Ventura and Ventura Custom. (F,D)

Protective Bumper Strips (Code 734—UPC VE5). Rubber strips that run horizontally along front and rear bumpers to protect them from minor dings and scratches. Standard on Grand Am. Available on front bumper only of Safari and Grand Safari. Available all other models except Firebird, Esprit, Formula and Trans Am. When ordered on the Ventura and Ventura Custom, front bumper guards must be ordered, too. (F)

Infant Safety Carrier. This special, rear-facing seat is held snugly in place by front or back seat belt. A built-in chest strap further safeguards baby, and an upright section provides support for head and back. Includes contoured pad for greater comfort. Doubles as a handy, sturdy carrier for use outside car. (D)

Fender Splash Guards. Stylish guards give wheel openings a sporty look, help protect rocker panels from dirt and stone nicks. Available all models—front and/or rear. (D)

Floor Mats, Front (Code 621—UPC B32), Rear (Code 622—UPC B33). Includes individual rubber mats for both sides of your car. Available for all models in a full range of colors to harmonize with interiors. (F,D) Check with your Pontiac salesman for additional styles that are available as dealer-installed accessories.

Spare Tire Cover (Code 454—UPC P17). Helps protect trunk contents. Slips easily on and off. Not available with station wagons, Ventura, Ventura Custom, Firebird, Esprit, Formula, Trans Am or with "Space-saver Spare Tire." Includes trunk sideboards on LeMans, LeMans Sport Coupe, Luxury LeMans, Grand Am and Catalina. (F) The Spare Tire Cover only may also be dealer-installed. Available all models except the Ventura Hatchback Coupe, Ventura Custom, Safaris or with the Space-saver Spare Tire.

Fire Extinguisher. Handy, 2¾-lb. dry-chemical extinguisher for car or home. Puts out all kinds of fires including grease, oil, gasoline and electrical. Rechargeable. (D)

PERFORMANCE ACCESSORIES AND OPTIONS

Safe-T-Track Differential (Code 371—UPC G80). Transfers torque to rear wheel that has the better traction. Helps keep you going through snow, ice, mud, sand, ruts, water or chuckholes. Available on all models. Standard on Trans Am. (F)

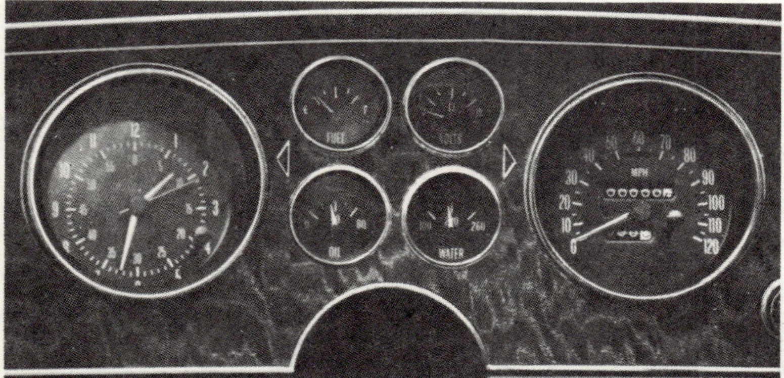

Rally Gauge Cluster with instrument panel clock shown on Grand Prix.

Rally Gauge Cluster with Clock (Code 712—UPC W63). Groups oil, water, fuel and voltmeter together and includes a clock where not already standard. Available on Firebird, Esprit, Formula, LeMans, LeMans Safari, LeMans Sport Coupe, Luxury LeMans and Grand Prix. Standard on Grand Am and Grand Prix SJ Option. Does not include voltmeter on LeMans, LeMans Safari, LeMans Sport Coupe or Luxury LeMans. (F)

Rally Gauge Cluster with Instrument Panel Tachometer (Code 714—UPC WW8). Integrates tachometer and speedometer with oil, water and fuel gauges and alternator telltale. Includes wood-grain trim. Available on LeMans, LeMans Sport Coupe, Luxury LeMans and Grand Am. (F) A similar gauge cluster, which includes a clock and voltmeter, is available on Firebird, Esprit and Formula. The tachometer and clock are combined as a single unit. Standard on Trans Am. (F)

Automatic Level Control (Code 651—UPC G67). Air-adjustable rear shock absorbers help maintain a level ride, even with heavy trunk or trailer tongue loads. Vacuum-operated air compressor in engine compartment automatically keeps rear of car level when fully loaded. Available on LeMans, LeMans Safari, LeMans Sport Coupe, Luxury LeMans, Grand Am, Catalina, Bonneville, Grand Ville, Safari, Grand Safari and Grand Prix. (F,D)

Superlift Shock Absorbers (Code 652—UPC G66). With tire-type, air-filler valve. Similar benefits of Automatic Level Control. Available on LeMans, LeMans Safari, LeMans Sport Coupe, Luxury LeMans, Grand Am, Catalina, Bonneville, Grand Ville, Safari and Grand Safari. (F,D)

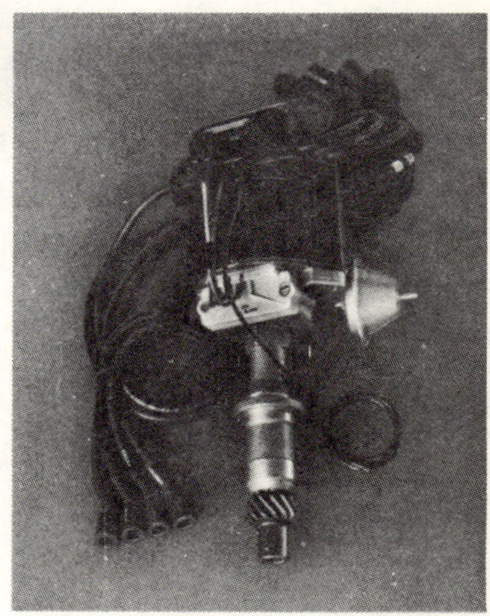

Unitized Ignition System (Code 694—UPC K65). A solid-state ignition system with a magnetic pulse unit which replaces breaker points, and a miniature ignition coil built into the distributor cap. It thus eliminates the need for the usual periodic replacements of points and condenser. You'll notice greatly increased spark plug life, improved cold and wet-weather starting. The system gives higher voltages and faster voltage rise time to maintain proper voltage throughout entire rpm range, including high speeds. Permanently water-proofed. Available on 400 4-bbl. V-8 (except with 3-speed manual) and 455 4-bbl. V-8. Not available with S.D. 455 4-bbl. V-8. (F)

Delco Maintenance-Free Battery (Code 691—UPC TP1). This highly efficient power source is designed so that (with proper installation and operation) it will continue to deliver full starting power without the addition of water or the periodic servicing and cleaning that are normally required with conventional batteries. Standard on the Grand Prix Model SJ. Available on all other models except the Ventura and Ventura Custom. (F)

Heavy-duty Battery (Code 692—UPC UA1). Available for all models when more electrical power is needed. (F,D)

Heavy-duty Radiator (Code 701—UPC V01). Increased cooling capacity to handle greater engine loads. Standard with air conditioning. Available all models. (F)

Dual-stage, Heavy-duty Air Cleaner (Code 542—UPC K45). Dual-filter design consists of wetted paper inner filter, surrounded by polyglycol-wetted, polyurethane-foam outer filter. Fine filtration. Recommended for driving in extremely dusty conditions. Available all models. (F)

Dual Horns (Code 681—UPC U05). Twin horns emit a loud, commanding sound, with a more pleasing tone than a single horn. Available on Ventura, Ventura Custom, Firebird, LeMans, LeMans Safari and LeMans Sport Coupe. Standard on all others. (F)

LeMans, LeMans Safari, LeMans Sport Coupe, Luxury LeMans and Grand Am

Handling Package, LeMans and LeMans Sport Coupe (Code 342—UPC Y99). Offers sports-car handling at an attractive price. Available on Two- and Four-door LeMans and LeMans Sport Coupe.

- Fast Variable-ratio Power Steering
- G60—15 Black Tires
- Firm Shocks
- Front and Rear Stabilizer Bars
- 15x7" Wheels

GTO Option, LeMans and LeMans Sport Coupe (Code 341—UPC W62). The original and most famous LeMans option! Available on Two-door LeMans and LeMans Sport Coupe.

- Blacked-out Grille
- Dual Air Hood Scoops (N.A.S.A. type)
- Firm Shock Absorbers
- GTO Identification
- G60—15 Black Tires
- Heavy-duty, Extra-large Front and Rear Stabilizer Bars
- Moon Hubcaps
- Performance Dual Exhausts with Chrome Extensions
- 400 4-bbl. V-8
- 3-speed, Heavy-duty, Manual Transmission with Floor Shifter
- 15x7" Wheels

Basic Group (Code 331—UPC Y88).

- Turbo Hydra-matic Transmission (standard on Grand Am)
- Whitewall Tires (White-letter Tires with GTO and Handling Package)
- AM Radio
- Deluxe Wheel Covers (LeMans Safari and LeMans Sport Coupe)
- Power Steering (standard on Grand Am)
- Electric Clock (Luxury LeMans)
- Protective Rubber Bumper Strips (standard on Grand Am)
- Power Disc Brakes (standard on LeMans Safari, Grand Am)
- Dual Horns (LeMans, LeMans Safari, LeMans Sport Coupe)

Decor Group, LeMans, LeMans Safari and LeMans Sport Coupe (Code 332—UPC Y80).

- Windowsill Moldings, including Hood Rear-edge Moldings
- Custom Cushion Steering Wheel
- Custom Pedal Trim Plates
- Deluxe Wheel Covers
- Wheel Opening Moldings

Protection Group (Code 334—UPC Y95).

- Vinyl Body Side Moldings
- Protective Rubber Bumper Strips (std. Grand Am)
- Door Edge Guards

Lamp Group (Code 344—UPC Y92).

- Luggage Compartment Lamp (except LeMans Safari)
- Glove Box Lamp (LeMans, LeMans Safari, LeMans Sport Coupe)
- Ash Tray Lamp (LeMans, LeMans Safari and LeMans Sport Coupe)
- Instrument Panel Courtesy Lamp (standard Grand Am)
- Dome and Reading Lamp (Grand Am)
- Rear Compartment Courtesy Lamp (LeMans Safari)

Removable Ski Rack, for snow skis or water skis. Installs quickly on all Pontiac models with a threaded mechanism. Plastic-coated hooks securely fasten the rack, even without drip moldings. Rubber feet adjust to the roof contour, helping prevent damage to the car finish. The anodized aluminum construction results in light weight and excellent corrosion resistance. Highly compressible plastic inserts in the arms protect skis and permit them to be carried in pairs. A unique and exclusive over-center latch makes closing the rack easy, even with six pairs of skis. Locks are provided at all four corners to prevent theft of skis and rack. (D)

Car Compass. Easy-to-read, suspended dial rotates as car changes direction. Special compensator assures correct directional indications. Pushbutton operated penlight to illuminate dial for night reading. (D)

Trailer Hitch (Code 671—UPC UR2). A Class I hitch to be used in towing light trailers (up to 2,000 pounds loaded) with light tongue loads (up to 200 pounds). Chrome-plated draw bar and 1⅞" diameter ball. Permanently bolts to structural members of the car. Available in custom designs for every Pontiac model except Ventura and Ventura Custom, Firebird, Esprit, Formula and Trans Am. (F,D) Another hitch is available for these models, to be used in towing very light trailers (up to 1,000 pounds gross weight and 100 pounds tongue load). (D)

Trailer Wire Harness. Five-wire (Code 672—UPC U86), Seven-wire (Code 674—UPC U94). A complete, four-way electrical wiring harness for stop lights, taillights, clearance lights and directional signal. No special attachment wiring required. No splicing. A harness available for every Pontiac model. Five-wire is available factory-installed on all models of intermediate and full-size Pontiacs and the Grand Prix; and dealer-installed on all models. Seven-wire is available, with trailer groups only, factory-installed on all models of intermediate and full-size Pontiacs and the Grand Prix.

Trailer-towing Mirrors. Specially designed to fit any Pontiac model. Turnbuckle-type fender mounts attach to front wheel openings and are held firmly in place when hood is closed. Large 5½" x 8" mirrors. Stainless steel construction. Designed to fit both left-hand and right-hand fenders. (D)

TOWING A TRAILER? If you plan to tow other than a light trailer, a factory-installed trailer-towing group is either necessary or highly recommended. Ask your Pontiac salesman for a copy of the 1973 Trailer-towing Guide, or write to: Sales Promotion Department, Pontiac Motor Division, Pontiac, Michigan 48053, for your free copy.

1974

1974 PONTIAC APPEARANCE ACCESSORIES

Cordova Top (Code 29: 1-white, 2-black, 3-beige, 4-russet, 5-green, 6-burgundy, 7-blue, 8-brown, 9-saddle, 0-taupe UPC—C08). Available on all models except LeMans Safari and Luxury LeMans Safari. Beige, russet and taupe not available on Catalina, Bonneville and Grand Prix 2-door hardtop models. (F)

Custom Pedal Trim Plates (Code 511—UPC JL1). Standard on Ventura Custom, Firebird Esprit, Luxury LeMans, Grand Am, Bonneville, Grand Ville, Grand Safari and Grand Prix. Available on all other models. (F)

Stainless Steel License Plate Frames. Available for front and rear of all models. (D)

Custom Seat Belts and Front Shoulder Belts (Code 691—UPC AK1). In colors to match every basic interior trim (with black belts in white interiors). Available with all models. (Note: Standard seat belts and shoulder belts are available in black only.) (F)

Ventura and Ventura Custom Bucket Seats, available in the Coupe and Hatchback Coupe, are available in Oxen and Madrid Morrokides in white, saddle, green and red; green or red interiors with white seats; or with white interior with red or green appointments. (Black seats are available in 4-dr. Sedan.) (F)

NOTE: You'll notice an F or D, or both, at the end of each accessory description. When there is only an F, that particular accessory can be bought and installed only through the factory, at the time you order your car. When only a D is shown, that accessory can be obtained only from your dealer. When both F and D are listed, you can get that accessory from either the factory or the dealer.

1974 PONTIAC DECOR AND PROTECTION MOLDINGS

SERIES	MODEL	PONTIAC DECOR AND PROTECTION MOLDINGS						
		A—Roof Drip Moldings	B—Side Window Reveal Moldings	C—Windowsill Moldings	D—Body Side Moldings	E—Door Edge Guards	F—Wheel Opening Moldings	G—Rocker Panel Moldings
VENTURA	Hatchback Coupe, Coupe and 4-door Sedan	A	A	NA	A	A	A	A
VENTURA CUSTOM	Hatchback Coupe, Coupe and 4-door Sedan	Std	A	NA	A	A	A	Std

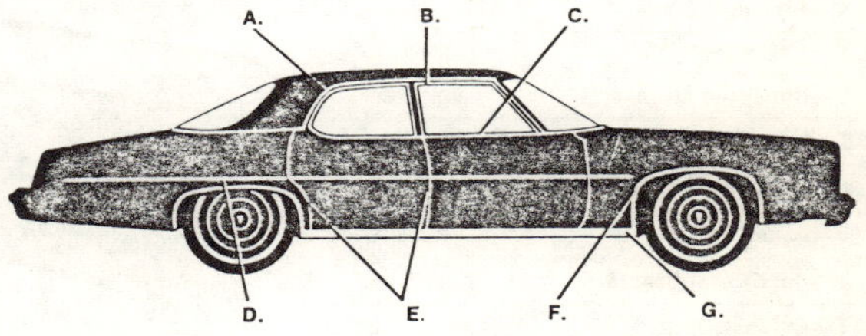

A. Roof Drip Moldings (Code 481—UPC B80) (F)

B. Side Window Reveal Moldings (Code 482—UPC B90) (F)

D. Vinyl Body Side Moldings (Code 494—UPC B84) (F,D)

E. Door Edge Guards (Code 492—UPC B93) (F,D)

F. Wheel Opening Moldings (Code 491—UPC B96) (F)

G. Rocker Panel Moldings (Code 484—UPC B83) (F)

1974 PONTIAC WHEELS, WHEEL COVERS, STEERING WHEELS

Wire Wheel Covers. Available for all models. (D)

Custom Cushion Steering Wheel. Order Code 461—UPC N30. New colors with black insert. Standard on Firebird Esprit, Firebird Formula, Ventura Custom and Ventura Sprint Package. Available on Firebird and Ventura. Carryover design in colors with matching insert. Standard on Grand Prix. (F)

Custom Sport Steering Wheel. Order Code 462—UPC N31. Carryover design in black. Standard on Grand Am, available on Pontiac Grand Prix. Now also available on Luxury LeMans, LeMans Sport Coupe, LeMans, Luxury LeMans Safari, LeMans Safari, Ventura Custom, Ventura. (F)

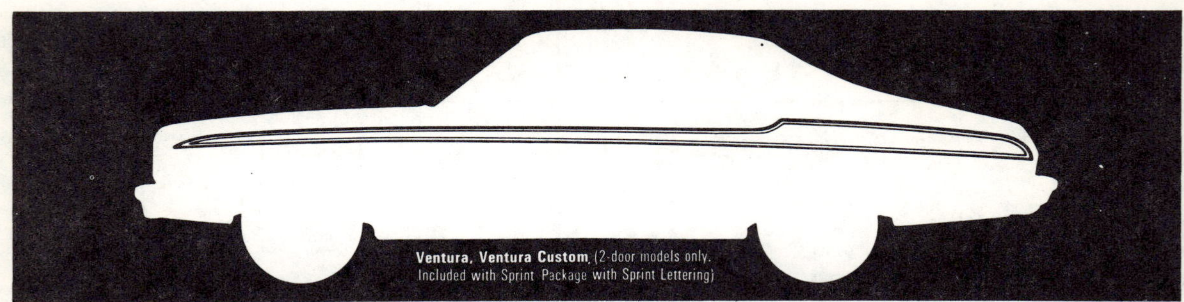

RECOMMENDED STRIPE COLOR USAGE CHART

Body Colors	Ventura Ventura Custom
A—Starlight Black	
C—Cameo White	Black
D—Porcelain Blue	
E—Admiralty Blue	Brt. Blue/Lt. Blue
F—Regatta Blue	Brt. Blue/Lt. Blue
G—Carmel Beige	Orange/Cream
H—Denver Gold	Orange/Cream
J—Limefire Green	Green/Yellow
K—Gulfmist Aqua	Black
L—Lakemist Green	
M—Fernmist Green	Green/Yellow
N—Pinemist Green	Green/Yellow
R—Buccaneer Red	Black
S—Honduras Maroon	Orange/Cream
T—Sunstorm Yellow	Black
U—Shadowmist Brown	
V—Ascot Silver	Black
W—Fire Coral Bronze	Orange/Cream
Y—Colonial Gold	Orange/Cream
Z—Crestwood Brown	Orange/Cream

Shown on Ventura.

Custom Air Conditioning (Code 582—UPC C60). Available on all models (not with six-cylinder engine). (F)

AM/FM Radio (Code 413—UPC U69). Completely transistorized. Available on all models. (F,D)

Manual Radio Antenna. Dealer installed on the Ventura and Ventura Custom when radio is dealer installed. A concealed windshield antenna is standard on all other models (with or without a radio) and is included on the Ventura and Ventura Custom when radio is factory installed. (D)

Rear Speaker (Code 421—UPC U80). Available on all models except those with stereo radios and tape players, which use other speakers. (F,D)

AM/FM Stereo Radio (Code 415—UPC U58). tran- Available on all models. (F,D)

AM Radio (Code 411—UPC U63). Completely transistorized. Available on all models. (F,D)

1974 PONTIAC CONVENIENCE ACCESSORIES

Electric Clock (Code 711—UPC U35). Illuminated dial, sweep second hand and automatic regulator. Standard on Grand Am, Bonneville, Grand Ville, Grand Safari and Grand Prix. Available on all other models. (F,D)

Visor Vanity Mirror (Right Visor Code 441—UPC D34; Left Visor Code 442—UPC DH5). Both available on all models dealer installed (D). Right-hand available factory installed (F) on all models; left-hand available factory installed (F) on all models except those in the Firebird and Ventura models.

Nonglare Rearview Mirror (Code 442—UPC D31). Available on Ventura and Ventura Custom; standard on all other models. (F)

Tilt Steering Wheel (Code 504—UPC N33). Adjusts to seven different positions. Available on all models; not available with manual column-shift transmissions. (F,D)

Cigar Lighter (Code 652—UPC U37). Also serves as an accessory plug. Available on Ventura and Ventura Custom; standard on all other models. (F)

Left-hand Remote Controlled Chrome Mirror only (Code 444—UPC D33). Available on all except Firebird models. (F,D)

Right-hand Manual Chrome Mirror. Matches standard left-hand mirror. Standard on all Pontiac station wagons; available on all other models. (D)

Left-hand Remote, Right-hand Fixed Sports Mirrors (Code 434—UPC D35). Body-colored. Available on all models. (F,D)

Litter Container/Tissue Dispenser. Fits over transmission hump. Fits all models. (D)

Space-saver Tire (Code 684—UPC N65). Available on Ventura, Ventura Custom, Grand Am, Grand Prix and the Firebird models; standard on Ventura Hatchback and Ventura Custom Hatchback. (F)

Instant Air. Connects with manifold to provide compressed air for filling tires, mattresses, beach toys, etc. Ideal for family camping. (D)

Soft-Ray Glass (Code 571—UPC A01). Fully tinted for all windows (except convertible rear). Recommended with air conditioning. Available all models; available for **Windshield only (Code 572—UPC A02).** (F)

Rear Window Defogger (Code 594—UPC C50). Electric blower under rear window shelf directs air through directional grille to help keep the window clear. Factory or dealer installed on all models except LeMans Safari, Luxury LeMans Safari, Grand Am, Grand Ville Convertible and Grand Prix. (F,D)

1974 PONTIAC PROTECTION ACCESSORIES

Front Bumper Guards (Code 731—UPC V31). Chrome with rubber facing strip. Available on Ventura, Ventura Custom, LeMans, LeMans Sport Coupe, Luxury LeMans, Catalina, Catalina Safari, Bonneville, Grand Ville, Grand Safari and Grand Prix. (F,D)

Rear Bumper Guards (Code 732—UPC V32). Rubber coated steel. Available on Ventura and Ventura Custom only. (F)

Protective Bumper Strips (Code 734—UPC VE5). Available on Ventura, Ventura Custom, LeMans, LeMans Sport Coupe, Luxury LeMans, LeMans Safari, Luxury LeMans Safari, Catalina, and Catalina Safari. Standard all others. (F)

Wheel Tire Gauge. Attaches to tire valve to register accurate tire pressure at all times. (D)

Fender Splash Guards. Protect rocker panels from dirt and stone nicks; adds sporty look. Available all models, front and/or rear. (D)

Floor Mats (Front Code 622—UPC B32; Rear Code 624—UPC B33). Individual mats for both sides. Available for all models in full range of colors. (F,D)

Infant Safety Carrier. Rear-facing with built-in chest strap. Can be used outside the car. (D)

Child Safety Seat. Comfortably holds child up to 40 lbs. in weight or 40″ in height. (D)

Trailer Hitch (Code 701—UPC VR2). A Class I hitch to be used in towing light trailers (up to 2,000 pounds loaded) with light tongue loads (up to 200 pounds). Chrome-plated draw bar and 1⅞″ diameter ball. Permanently bolts to structural members of the car. Available in custom designs for every Pontiac model except Ventura and Ventura Custom, Firebird, Firebird Esprit, Firebird Formula and Firebird Trans Am (F,D). Another hitch is available for these models to be used in towing very light trailers (up to 1,000 pounds gross weight and 100 pounds tongue load. (D)

Trailer-towing Mirrors. Specially designed to fit any Pontiac model. Turnbuckle-type fender mounts attach to front wheel openings and are held firmly in place when hood is closed. Large 5½″ x 8″ mirrors. Stainless steel construction. Designed to fit both left-hand and right-hand fenders. (D)

Car Compass. Easy-to-read, suspended dial rotates as car changes direction. Special compensator assures correct directional indications. Pushbutton operated penlight to illuminate dial for night reading. (D)

Trailer Wire Harness. Five-wire (Code 702—UPC U89). Seven-wire (Code 704—UPC U94). A complete, four-way electrical wiring harness for stop lights, taillights, clearance lights and directional signal. No special attachment wiring required. No splicing. A harness available for every Pontiac model. Five-wire is available factory installed on all models of intermediate and full-size Pontiacs and the Grand Prix; and dealer installed on all models. Seven-wire is available, with trailer groups only, factory installed on all models of intermediate and full-sized Pontiacs and the Grand Prix.

Towing a Trailer? If you plan to tow other than a light trailer, a factory installed trailer-towing group is either necessary or highly recommended. Ask your Pontiac salesman for a copy of the 1974 Trailer-towing Guide, or write to: Sales Promotion Department, Pontiac Motor Division, Pontiac, Michigan 48053, for your free copy.

Ventura Hatchback Camper. Turn a Ventura Hatchback or Ventura Custom Hatchback into a camper with this unique option. Easily put up and taken down. (D)

1974 PONTIAC POWER ASSISTS

Variable-ratio Power Steering (Code 501—UPC N41). Fast and easy steering response. Requires far fewer turns in slow-speed maneuvering such as parking. Available all models. Standard on Firebird models, Grand Am, Catalina, Bonneville, Grand Ville, Catalina Safari, Grand Safari and Grand Prix. (F,D)

Power Front Disc Brakes (Code 502—UPC JL2). Combined with power drum brakes at rear. Automatic self-adjustment throughout life of pads. Available all models. Standard on Firebird Trans Am, LeMans Safari, Luxury LeMans Safari, Grand Am, Catalina, Bonneville, Grand Ville, Catalina Safari, Grand Safari and Grand Prix. (F,D)

Rear Window Defogger (Code 594—UPC C50). Electric blower under rear window shelf directs air through directional grille to help keep the window clear. Factory or dealer installed on all models except LeMans Safari, Luxury LeMans Safari, Grand Am, Grand Ville Convertible and Grand Prix. (F,D)

Power Drum Brakes (Code 512—UPC J50). Just a light touch of the brakes provides excellent braking pressure. Available on Ventura and Ventura Custom. (F,D)

1974 PONTIAC LAMPS AND LAMP GROUPS

Select from a desirable offering of lamps and lamp packages to "upgrade" your new Pontiac with greater style, comfort, convenience, safety and resale value. In most cases, you'll add lamps to your new Pontiac by selecting the **Lamp Package** for your model—the order code and UPC code are the same in every case **(Code 654—UPC Y92)** (F). Because of this simplification, some lamps are available on some models only as part of the group. Other lamps (described) are available individually.

Instrument Panel Courtesy Lamp. Lights when front door is opened. Also can be manually operated by switch. Standard on Grand Am, Bonneville, Grand Ville, Grand Safari and Grand Prix. Available as part of the lamp package on the Ventura, Ventura Custom, Firebird, Firebird Esprit, Firebird Formula, Firebird Trans Am, LeMans, LeMans Safari, LeMans Sport Coupe, Luxury LeMans, Luxury LeMans Safari, Catalina and Catalina Safari. (F)

Ash Tray Lamp. Lights automatically when headlights or parking lights are turned on. Standard on Firebird, Firebird Esprit, Firebird Formula, Firebird Trans Am, Luxury LeMans, Grand Am, Catalina, Bonneville, Grand Ville, Luxury LeMans Safari, Catalina Safari, Grand Safari and Grand Prix. Available as part of the lamp package on the Ventura Custom, LeMans, LeMans Safari and LeMans Sport Coupe. **Right-hand Ash Tray Lamp.** Standard on Grand Ville and Grand Safari. Available as part of the lamp package on the Catalina, Bonneville and Catalina Safari. Ash Tray lamps also may be dealer installed on Ventura, Ventura Custom, LeMans, LeMans Safari, LeMans Sport Coupe, Catalina, Bonneville and Catalina Safari. (D)

Luggage Compartment Lamp. Provides light in luggage compartment area. Operates when trunk lid is opened. Standard on Bonneville, Grand Ville and Grand Prix. Available as part of the lamp package on Ventura, Ventura Custom (but not Hatchback Coupe), Firebird, Firebird Esprit, Firebird Formula, Firebird Trans Am, LeMans, LeMans Sport Coupe, Luxury LeMans, Grand Am and Catalina. Luggage Compartment Lamp also may be dealer installed on all models except Ventura and Ventura Custom Hatchback Coupes, Safaris and Grand Prix. (D) Available individually (Code 662—UPC U25) on LeMans, LeMans Sport Coupe, Luxury LeMans, Grand Am and Catalina. (F)

Glove Compartment Lamp. Lights when compartment door is opened. Standard on all models except Ventura, Firebird, Firebird Esprit, Firebird Formula, Firebird Trans Am, LeMans, LeMans Safari and LeMans Sport Coupe. Available on these models as part of the lamp package. (F)

1974 PONTIAC PERFORMANCE ACCESSORIES AND OPTIONS

Safe-T-Track Differential (Code 371—UPC G80). Transfers torque to the rear wheel that has best traction in snow, mud, sand, ruts, water, chuckholes or ice. Available on all models. Standard on Firebird Trans Am. (F)

Dual Horns (Code 681—UPC U05). Twin horns emit a loud, commanding sound with a more pleasing tone than a single horn. Available on Ventura, Ventura Custom, Firebird, LeMans, LeMans Safari and LeMans Sport Coupe. Standard on all others. (F)

Heavy-duty Battery (Code 591—UPC UA1). Available for all models when more electrical power is needed. (F)

Rally Gauge Cluster and Tachometer (Code 714—UPC U17). Ventura and Ventura Custom with bucket seats and console. (F)

Dual-stage, Heavy-duty Air Cleaner (Code 604—UPC K45). Dual filter design consists of wetted paper inner filter, surrounded by polyglycol-wetted polyurethane-foam outer filter. Fine filtration. Recommended for driving in extremely dusty conditions. Available all models. (F)

Heavy-duty Radiator (Code 701—UPC V01). Increased cooling capacity to handle greater engine loads. Standard with air conditioning. Available all models. (F)

ADDITIONAL PONTIAC OPTIONS AND ACCESSORIES

Pontiac Ventura and Ventura Custom

GTO Package
Order Code 342—UPC WW3
(2-dr. Coupes and Hatchbacks)
- Distinctive Grille w/Parking Lights
- Rally II Wheels w/o Trim Rings
- 350-cu.-in., V-8, 4-bbl. Engine
- Dual Exhausts with Chrome Extensions
- Specific Shocks and Springs w/Front and Rear Stabilizer Bars
- E70—14 Black Tires
- Outside Sport Mirrors—L.H. Remote Control
- GTO Identification on Deck Lid, Front Fender and Grille Panel
- Functional Shaker Hood Scoop
- 3-Speed Floor Shift

Steel-belted Radial Tires w/RTS
UPC WY5
- FR78—14 WSW or White Letter Steel-belted Radial Tires
- Radial Tuned Suspension including Springs, Shocks, Front and Rear Stabilizer Bars

Lamp Package
Order Code 654—UPC Y92
- Luggage Compartment Lamp
- Glove Compartment Lamp (std. Ventura Custom)
- Ash Tray Lamp
- Instrument Panel Courtesy Lamp
- Rear Door Dome Lamp Switches (4-dr. models)